WHAT WE DON'T TALK ABOUT WHEN WE TALK ABOUT FAT

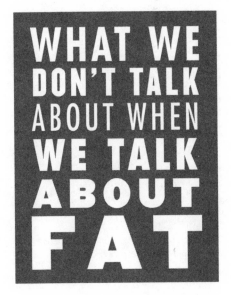

AUBREY GORDON

BEACON PRESS ✦ BOSTON

BEACON PRESS
Boston, Massachusetts
www.beacon.org

Beacon Press books
are published under the auspices of
the Unitarian Universalist Association of Congregations.

23 22 21 20   8 7 6 5 4 3 2

This book is printed on acid-free paper that meets the uncoated paper
ANSI/NISO specifications for permanence as revised in 1992.

Text design and composition by Kim Arney

Library of Congress Cataloging-in-Publication Data

Names: Gordon, Aubrey, author.
Title: What we don't talk about when we talk about fat / Aubrey Gordon.
Description: Boston : Beacon Press, [2020] | Includes bibliographical
   references.
Identifiers: LCCN 2020015803 (print) | LCCN 2020015804 (ebook) |
   ISBN 9780807041307 (hardcover) | ISBN 9780807041321 (ebook)
Subjects: LCSH: Obesity—Social aspects—United States. | Overweight
   persons—United States—Social conditions. | Discrimination against
   overweight persons—United States.
Classification: LCC RC628 .G674 2020 (print) | LCC RC628 (ebook) |
   DDC 616.3/98—dc23
LC record available at https://lccn.loc.gov/2020015803
LC ebook record available at https://lccn.loc.gov/2020015804

For Grandpa Gordon

CONTENTS

INTRODUCTION

I have always been fat.

Not *chubby* or *fluffy* or *husky* or *curvy*—fat. As I write this, I weigh 342 pounds and wear a women's size 26. My body mass index (BMI) describes my body as "super morbidly obese" or "extremely obese." Although my body is not the fattest in existence, it is the fattest the BMI can fathom. Three years ago, I weighed just over 400 pounds and wore a size 30 or 32, depending on the cut of the clothing. At my high school graduation, I wore a red wrap top in the highest size I could find at the time—a women's 24.

For me, the size of my body is a simple fact. I do not struggle with self-esteem or negative body image. I do not lay awake at night, longing for a thinner body or some life that lies a hundred pounds out of reach. For me, my body isn't good or bad, it just *is*. But for the rest of the world, it seems, my body presents major problems.

Friends, family, strangers, and coworkers alike offer unsolicited diet advice and recommend bariatric surgeons. Other shoppers pick over my cart at the grocery store, freely removing items they don't think I should eat. Doctors refuse to treat me, and some offices set weight limits on the patients they'll see—weight limits that my body reliably exceeds. I pray that I do not need an MRI or a CAT scan, not because of the complex and frightening health troubles those tests may illuminate but because I likely will not fit into the equipment's narrow tunnels and fixed walls. Strangers tell me, both online and in person, that my body is a death sentence and that every bite I take is a step toward a slow suicide. When I drive, disembodied shouts often echo from passing cars: *GET OUT AND TRY WALKING FOR A CHANGE.* These days, I mostly leave my windows rolled up.

Bodies like mine are seen by others as an open invitation to express disgust, fear, and insidious *concern*. They are seen as an invitation to laugh, a prop for hackneyed would-be comics to recite the same punchlines over and over again. They are fodder not just for cruel teenagers or overgrown adult bullies, but for *everyone*. Loved ones tut-tut when they see me reach for a second helping of anything, anxious that I may think myself deserving of as much food as them. The bulk of the anti-fat attitudes I have faced have come at the hands of thin people who deeply believed they were doing right and doing good, emboldened by a culture that wholeheartedly agreed with them.

In books, political cartoons, films, and TV shows, fat bodies make up the failings of America, capitalism, beauty standards, excess, and consumerism. Fat bodies represent at once the poorest of the poor and the pinnacle of unchecked power, consumption, and decay. Our bodies have borne the blame for so much. Whole artistic worlds are built on the premise that bodies like mine are monstrous, repulsive, and—worst of all—contagious. From individuals to institutions, academia to the evening news, fat people are made bogeymen. And that spills into daily experiences of abuse, driven by intentions both good and ill, but always with the same outcome: an intense shame for simply daring to exist in the bodies many of us have always had.

There is a minefield of abuse reserved for the very fat. I have come to view the world through the prism of that abuse, negotiating my days around reducing it. *Who will shout at me? Which doctors will refuse to see me? Which dates will mock my body? Which strangers will photograph me, make a meme of my skin?* I avoid eye contact with strangers, knowing that our locking eyes are too often misconstrued as an invitation to shout or detail their judgments of my body. I deploy a charm offensive, calming agitated aggressors before they get the chance to unleash their fury. I have learned how to keep abusers at bay alone, knowing that no one else will intervene to support or defend me. I have developed this sad and necessary skill set because, in my soft and certain marrow, I know that the abuse faced by fat people is not understood to warrant a reckoning.

But the most difficult part of anti-fat attitudes isn't bullying, harassment, fear, or violence. I have come to expect epithets and aggression, have come to weather their heat and pressure. But I have never become accustomed to the complete lack of empathy from so many around me. As a white, queer woman, describing the challenges I may face from misogyny and homophobia may be difficult, but it's increasingly met with some measure of sympathy. But when I disclose the abuse I have faced as a fat person, I am frequently met with a steely refusal to believe it. *Did you do something to aggravate them?*

Maybe they thought they were helping. They were probably just concerned for your health. When anti-fatness turns institutional, as with staggeringly prevalent employment discrimination or punitive airline policies, others' responses curdle, turning from indifference to outright defense. Suddenly, people who otherwise relish complaining about delayed flights and cramped legroom become airlines' staunchest defenders.

People who don't wear plus sizes may struggle to hear the severity and irrationality of anti-fat abuse and bias. It may be difficult to believe, even unfathomable, that there's a world so different from their own. But anti-fat bias has always been there, as noxious and ubiquitous as polluted air. Still, thinner people aren't forced to reckon with it. As ubiquitous as it may be, for many thinner people, anti-fatness doesn't present a barrier to healthcare, employment, transportation, or meeting other basic needs. Life in a thinner body means that the world is redacted, presented only in part.

The depth and breadth of anti-fatness can be difficult to believe, too, because anti-fat attitudes, comments, policies, and practices are ubiquitous. We cannot see the air we've been breathing for years, cannot touch the shifting ground beneath our feet. Anti-fatness has become invisible, a natural law. To many people who don't wear plus sizes, objecting to fat hate is as irrational as debating gravity. Why waste outrage on a simple fact of the world we live in? The thin Greek chorus in my life, when faced with the ubiquitous sharp edges of fat hate, have too readily insisted that *you can't change the world, you can only change yourself*, by which they have meant me.

For the most part, our woefully limited cultural conversation about fat people backs them up. Fatness is reliably demonized, discussed only in the context of how not to be fat (weight loss) or how fat will kill us immediately (the "obesity epidemic"). Fat experiences are only shared to contrast a more real story from a thin person or as a pitiable and wretched reality to conjure thin gratitude. Fat people are frequently spoken about or at, but we're rarely heard. Instead, bodies and experiences like mine become caricatured and symbolic, either as a kind of effigy or as a pornography of suffering. Bodies and experiences like mine are rarely allowed to just be *ours*.

In recent years, a growing number of fat memoirs have joined the fold, but this book isn't that. It isn't a memoir of fat pain that will offer thin people comfort or relief that they're *not that fat*. It isn't another entry in the canon of books about the perils of being fat or the frightening specter of the "obesity epidemic." It isn't a weight loss book. You won't read about my longing for a thinner body or the lengths I'll go to in order to lose weight. This book will not reassure you that *at least she's trying to lose weight*. It is not rooted in the near-ubiquitous cultural dogma that fat people are duty-bound to become thin before asking to be treated with respect and dignity.

This book diverges from the well-trod path when it comes to fatness and fat people. In it, you'll find a mix of memoir, research, and cultural criticism all focused on unearthing our social and cultural attitudes toward fat people, along with the impacts those attitudes can have on fat people, ourselves. Where our cultural conversation focuses relentlessly on personal responsibility and the perceived failures of fat people, this book seeks to zoom out, offering personal stories while simultaneously identifying the macro-level social, institutional, and political forces that powerfully shape the way each of us thinks of fat people, both in general and in particular.

In recent years, the long-standing body positivity movement has taken center stage, focused on in talk shows and sitcoms, utilized by the magazines and advertisers that for so long weaponized the images of very thin bodies against so many of us. This may seem like a potent force for fat justice and liberation. It is not.

While the modern body positivity movement has deep roots in the fat acceptance and fat liberation movements, its most recent wave of popularity owes its success to two women who don't wear plus sizes. Connie Sobczak, an author, and Elizabeth Scott, a licensed clinical social worker, founded an organization called the Body Positive in 1996.[1] Sobczak had personally struggled with an eating disorder, and Scott specialized in treating them. The organization's mission is simple: "The Body Positive teaches people how to reconnect to their innate body wisdom so they can have more balanced, joyful self-care, and a relationship with their whole selves that is guided by love, forgiveness, and humor."[2] The Body Positive trains its members to build five core competencies:

1. Reclaim Health
2. Practice Intuitive Self-Care
3. Cultivate Self-Love
4. Declare Your Own Authentic Beauty
5. Build Community[3]

Given the founders' background in eating disorder recovery work, The Body Positive's stated goals and framework make a lot of sense. Many eating disorder survivors, fat and thin, struggle with low self-esteem, insufficient self-love, and reckoning with their body image enough to "declare [their] own authentic beauty." The broader body positivity movement has run with that framework, too, focusing its work on building self-esteem and positive body image. Its rise has certainly been a net gain for many. Opening up spaces to talk about our relationships with our bodies and the insecurities we may grapple with is a significant step forward. For survivors of eating disorders and body dysmorphic disorder, body positivity has been a true lifeline for their mental health and recovery.

Like thin people, fat people can struggle with our body image and self-esteem. But unlike thinner people, that's only the start of our body-related challenges. As you will read in the pages ahead, fat people face overwhelming discrimination in employment, healthcare, transit, the treatment of eating disorders, and more. While body image is certainly a piece of the puzzle for fat people, it is a relatively small one. While the body positivity movement's aims are laudable, they're simply a solution for a very small part of the much larger looming problems faced by fat people—especially fat people at the larger end of the plus-size spectrum.

By the numbers, while body positivity may be increasing individual self-esteem, it doesn't seem to have made a dent in the prevalence of anti-fat attitudes and behaviors. Harvard University analyzed results from its famed implicit bias tests, looking at data from those who took its tests between 2007 and 2016—during the precipitous rise of the body positivity movement. They found that implicit bias was on the decline in nearly every category. According to Harvard's lead researcher on the study, anti-fat bias has changed the most slowly of all *explicit* stated attitudes. And when it comes to *implicit* bias—that is, the bias we unconsciously act on—anti-fatness is getting significantly worse. "It is the only attitude out of the six that we looked at that showed any hint of getting *more* biased over time."[4] While body positivity seems to be everywhere, it doesn't appear to be changing our deeply held, deeply harmful beliefs about fatness and fat people.

The rise of body positivity has also led to extremely challenging dynamics within the movement. Because body positivity is so deeply focused on internal, individual change, conversations about power, privilege, and oppression often don't come naturally to self-proclaimed body positive people.

When people in more marginalized bodies—particularly fat people, disabled people, transgender and nonbinary people, and people of color—request conversations that grapple with the thornier realities of our lives, which are formed more by other people's behaviors than our own internal self-image, those requests are often roundly rejected by many body positive activists. When fat people open up about our experiences, thinner body positive activists often rewrite those accounts of institutional discrimination and interpersonal abuse as "insecurities," whitewashing the vast differences between our diverging experiences. Fat people who tag photos with #BodyPositive are regularly met with accusations of "glorifying obesity" or "promoting an unhealthy lifestyle." Mainstream social media accounts still post before and after weight loss photos, claiming body positivity while celebrating bodies for looking less fat. The most recognized faces of body positivity, frequently models and actors, are disproportionately white or light-skinned, able-bodied, and either straight size (that is, not plus size) or at the smallest end of plus size. While it may not be an intentional one, for many fat activists, the message is clear: body positivity isn't for us.

As a result, fat activists use a variety of terms to describe our work and distinguish it from the body positivity movement's largely interior focus on self-esteem. Some fat activists strive for *body neutrality*, a viewpoint that holds that bodies should be prized for their function, not their appearance, and that simply feeling impartial about our bodies would represent a significant step forward for those of us whose bodies are most marginalized.[5] Others fight for *fat acceptance*, which seeks to counter anti-fat bias with a tolerance-based model of simply accepting the existence of fat people and ceasing our constant attempts to make fat bodies into thin ones. Some urge us toward *body sovereignty*, "the concept that each person has the full right to control their own body."[6] Fat activists' frameworks are as varied as fat people ourselves.

While these approaches work for many, I describe mine as work for *fat justice*. Body positivity has shown me that our work for liberation must explicitly name fatness as its battleground—because when we don't, each of us are likely to fall back on our deep-seated, faulty cultural beliefs about fatness and fat people, claiming to stand for "all bodies" while we implicitly and explicitly exclude the fattest among us. I yearn for more than *neutrality*, *acceptance*, and *tolerance*—all of which strike me as meek pleas to simply stop harming us, rather than asking for help in healing that harm or requesting that each of us unearth and examine our existing biases against fat people. Acceptance is a step forward, but it's a far cry from centering fat people's humanity in our cruel and ceaseless conversations about fat bodies.

A conversation about fat justice, though, will require so much of each of us. People who don't wear plus sizes will need to hear and believe fat people's experiences—experiences that may differ from their own so dramatically as to strain credulity. They will hear stories of strangers mooing from a passing car or passersby throwing trash at fat people walking down a city street. They will hear stories of doctors telling their patients to *stop shoving food in your face long enough to pay attention.* Remarks like these are so deeply unkind that it's hard to imagine why someone would think they're acceptable to say out loud. But by the simple virtue of living in our bodies, fat people are seeing things straight-size people can't yet—things that only happen in the presence of bodies like ours. Straight-size people will need to resist the urge to reject fat experiences out of hand because of a lack of context. Instead, they'll need to find the context. They'll need to look harder, to sharpen their vision. They'll need to learn to see anti-fatness everywhere, because it is. Anti-fatness may not make sense to straight-size people. It doesn't make sense to me, either. But straight-size people's tasks will be threefold: not to buckle under the weight of their own discomfort, to stay in the conversation long enough to learn, and to take proactive action to counter anti-fat bias and help defend fat people.

Advancing fat justice will require a lot of fat people too. It will require us to take the risks we've taken so many fruitless times before—the risks of sharing our most challenging experiences of anti-fat bias, of opening our bodies and lives up to even more public conversation and debate. Ours will be the work of courageous and frightening vulnerability, of holding a standard of humanity, dignity, and respect that so many tell us we simply do not deserve. And it will be the work of building a bold vision for a more liberated world—for fat people, and for people of all sizes.

Regardless of our size, working toward fat justice will call upon our most honest, compassionate selves. It will require deep vulnerability, candor, and empathy. Together, we can create a tectonic shift in the way we see, talk about, and treat our bodies, fat and thin alike. We can find more peace in the skin we live in, declaring a truce with the bodies that only try to care for us. But more than that, we can build a more just and equitable world that doesn't determine our access to resources and respect based on how we look.

We can build a world that doesn't assume fat people are failed thin people, or that thin people are categorically healthy and virtuous. We can build a world that conspires against eating disorders and body dysmorphia, working toward more safety for eating disorder survivors of all sizes. We can build a world in which fat bodies are valued and supported just as much as thin ones.

A FAT JUSTICE GLOSSARY

Throughout this book, you will read a number of terms that may not be familiar to you, or whose use you may struggle to embrace. Different fat activists may each offer their own definitions for these commonly used terms, so these definitions are far from universal. Here's how I define and use them in the pages that follow.

Fat

A neutral descriptor for predominantly plus-size people. While *fat* is frequently used to insult people of all sizes, many fat activists—those of us who are undeniably, indubitably fat by any measure—reclaim the term as an objective adjective to describe our bodies, like tall or short. It is used accordingly in a matter-of-fact way throughout the pages ahead. Fat stands in contrast to an endless parade of euphemisms—*fluffy, curvy, big guy, big girl, zaftig, big boned, husky, voluptuous, thick, heavy set, pleasantly plump, chubby, cuddly, more to love, overweight, obese*—all of which just serve as a reminder of how terrified so many thin people are to see our bodies, name them, have them.

Fat hasn't become a bad word because fatness is somehow inherently undesirable or bad—it has fallen out of public favor because of what we attach to it. We take *fat* to mean unlovable, unwanted, unattractive, unintelligent, unhealthy. But fatness itself is simply one aspect of our bodies—and a very small part of who each of us is. It deserves to be described as a simple and unimportant fact.

Body size, like so many aspects of human experience and identity, exists on a spectrum, so there are no hard and fast rules for who qualifies as "fat enough to be fat." When I look for my fat people—the community I call home—I look for people who are united by experiences of widespread exclusion. I don't just look for people who've been called fat, as all of us have, but folks who are shut out of meeting their basic needs because of the simple fact of their size. Not just people who struggle to find clothing they like, but people who struggle to find clothing *at all*. Not just people who feel un-comfortable on buses or airplanes, but people who are publicly ridiculed for daring to board public transit at all. For my fat people, our size isn't just an internal worry, it's an inescapable external reality. We aren't held captive by our own perceptions but by others' beliefs that we are immoral, unlovable, irredeemable. All of us have felt the sting of the rejection of our bodies—either at our own hand, or another's. But not all of us have been repeatedly, materially harmed by the universality of that rejection. That's an experience shared by those of us who are unquestionably, undeniably fat. But that's one of many, many approaches to defining fatness. There are nearly as many definitions of fat as there are people in the world.

Smaller Fat People and Very Fat People

Different levels of fatness invite different experiences. People who wear smaller plus sizes (say, a size 14 or 16 in the US) regularly hear comments about how they've got *such a pretty face—you'd be a knockout if you just lost twenty pounds*. But people who wear extended plus sizes (a size 34, for example) face open street harassment, hearing slurs, and jeers from passing cars. Ash, the host of *The Fat Lip* podcast, has established a framework for understanding and pinpointing these important gradations, based on US women's clothing sizes:

> *Small fat:* 1X–2X, sizes 18 and lower, Torrid 00 to 1. Find clothes that fit at mainstream brands and can shop in many stores.

> *Mid-fat:* 2X–3X, sizes 20 to 24, Torrid 2 to 3. Shop at some mainstream brands, but mostly dedicated plus brands and online.

> *Superfat:* 4X–5X, sizes 26-32, Torrid 4 to 6. Wear the highest sizes at plus brands. Can often only shop online.

> *Infinifat:* 6X and higher, sizes 34 and higher, some Torrid 6. Very difficult to find anything that fits, even online. Often require custom sizing.[7]

These gradations are frequently used within fat spaces to help pinpoint the privileges we experience by virtue of our relative proximity to thinness. Because they can be a lot to remember, throughout this book I use "smaller fat people" to refer to small and mid-fats and "very fat people" or "larger fat people" to refer to superfats and infinifats.

Anti-Fatness and Anti-Fat Bias

Anti-fatness and anti-fat bias are umbrella terms that describe the attitudes, behaviors, and social systems that specifically marginalize, exclude, underserve, and oppress fat bodies. They refer both to individual bigotry as well as institutional policies designed to marginalize fat people. Anti-fatness and anti-fat bias are also sometimes referred to as fatphobia, fatmisia, sizeism, weight stigma, or fattism. The *Macmillan Dictionary* defines fatphobia as an "irrational fear of, aversion to, or discrimination against obesity or people with obesity."[8]

Healthism

Closely linked to both anti-fatness and ableism, healthism posits that health is both a virtue and a moral imperative. The term, coined by Robert Crawford in 1980, was originally defined in the *International Journal of Health Services* as a "preoccupation with personal health as a primary—often the primary—focus for the definition and achievement of well-being. [. . .] By elevating health to a super value, a metaphor for all that is good in life, healthism reinforces the privatization of the struggle for generalized well-being."[9] That is, healthism as a framework often disregards the influence of social determinants of health, institutional policies, and oppression on individual health. Fall Ferguson, attorney and former president of the Association of Size Diversity and Health, later added that healthism "emerges as the assumption that people *should* pursue health. It's the contempt in the nonsmoker's attitude toward smokers; it's the ubiquitous sneer against couch potatoes. Healthism includes the idea that anyone who isn't healthy just isn't trying hard enough or has some moral failing or sin to account for."[10]

Many who shame fat people for our bodies, our food, and our movement rely on a logic of healthism that implies that we are duty-bound to appear healthy—that is, thin. Healthism is a pervasive system of social thinking that has harmful implications for disabled people, chronically ill people, mentally ill people, fat people, and others. As "wellness" replaces "dieting" as a way of talking about weight loss, understanding healthism is key to pulling apart the ways in which size and health are used to write-off people who don't or can't perform health. Even in body positive spaces, healthism persists as a way to marginalize fat people through the frequent refrain *I'm body positive as long as you're healthy.*

Plus-Size Clothing

Clothing that cannot be reliably purchased in department stores and from mainstream clothing retailers and must be purchased from either a limited plus-size section or from specialty plus-size retailers, such as Torrid or Lane Bryant. In the US, this generally refers to women's sizes 16 to 28. As of 2018, people who wear plus sizes have just 2.3 percent of the clothing options that thinner people have.[11]

Extended Plus-Size Clothing

Clothing that cannot be purchased from mainstream retailers *or* from most plus-size retailers. In the US, women's extended plus sizes are usually size 30 and up. Even basic essentials, such as jeans and blazers, are often unavailable in extended plus sizes. When extended plus-size clothing is available, it is almost exclusively available for purchase at exorbitant prices and only online. In some cases, extended plus-size clothing requires custom sizing or construction.

Straight-Size Clothing

A term from the fashion industry, straight size refers to clothing that can be purchased from nearly any clothing retailer. US straight sizes are usually sizes 00 to 14 and are available at almost every store in a given shopping mall. Straight size is a way of referring to people with relative size privilege, instead of using value-laden terms such as "normal" or "regular" or inaccurate terms like "average" (in the US, the average size is plus size[12]). If you don't know whether you wear straight or plus sizes, you're probably straight size. Those of us who wear plus sizes and extended plus sizes rarely have the relative luxury of forgetting.

Obese and Overweight

Weight classification determined by the BMI as being fat enough to present health risks. The term "obese" is derived from the Latin *obesus*, meaning "having eaten oneself fat," inherently blaming fat people for their bodies.[13] The term "overweight" implies that there is an objectively correct weight for every body. A growing number of fat activists consider obese to be a slur. Both terms are derived from a medical model that considers fat bodies as deviations that must be corrected, so both are used sparingly throughout this book.

Diet Culture

Diet culture is a system of beliefs and practices that elevates thin bodies above all others, often interpreting thinness as a sign of both health and virtue. It mandates weight loss as a way of increasing social status, strengthening character, and accessing social privilege. Christy Harrison, a registered dietitian and MPH, adds that diet culture "demonizes certain ways of eating while elevating others, which means you're forced to be hypervigilant about your eating, ashamed of making certain food choices, and distracted from your pleasure, your purpose, and your power."[14] Diet culture disproportionately benefits people whose bodies are naturally predisposed to be thin and people with the wealth and privilege to pay the high prices of customized diet foods, personal trainers, weight-loss surgery, and more. Even as "wellness" gains popularity as a way to talk about weight loss, it bears a striking resemblance to diet culture.

INTO THIN AIR

It happened on the tarmac at the Long Beach airport.

In the terminal, quarters were tight, and flights were delayed. Passengers were irritated by closeness, strangers' skin too near their own. Their faces twisted, then calcified with aggravation.

Our flight was oversold, and I was reassigned at the last minute to a middle seat. When the ticket agent handed me my new boarding pass, I looked at her pleadingly, feeling the full width of my size 28 body. *I know,* she said. *I'm sorry.*

I retreated from the agent's desk, defeated. I remember looking for warm faces, desperate to find softness in the frustrated passengers that would flank me. *Who could I trust to tolerate the breadth of me? Whose face bore the marks of mercy?*

I planned carefully, working diligently to avoid taking any more space or time than I needed. I couldn't afford to give my fellow passengers more reasons to take aim at my body. I lined up early, checked my suitcase at the gate, and took my seat quickly. I watched the passengers file down the cabin's aisle, again searching their faces for something forgiving. Then my seatmate arrived.

When he sat down, he didn't meet my eyes. He adjusted the arm rest, assertively claiming it as his own. He needn't have—I had long since learned that any free space belonged to the thin. My arms were already crossed tight over my chest, thighs squeezed together, ankles overlapped beneath my seat. My body was knotted, doing everything it could not to touch him, not to impose its soft skin. I folded in on myself, muscles aching with contraction.

Suddenly, he stood up, fighting against the stream of passengers in the narrow aisle to speak with a flight attendant, then returned to his seat, looking thwarted. Moments later, he got up again. I couldn't hear what he was saying, but there was an urgency in his face. I wondered what their summit had been about. He returned to his seat again, his mouth straight and muscles tense. I considered asking if he was alright, but his agitation threw me. I was a young woman and he an older, upset man, the two of us in an enclosed space for hours to come. I had spent a lifetime learning not to put my hand on the hot stove of men's agitation.

He got up a third time. That's when I heard him say, *Unbelievable*, his voice sharp with irritation. The fourth time, I heard *paying customer*, angrily over-enunciated, all convex consonants.

He returned to his seat and let out the sharp, belabored sigh of a wronged customer. He crossed his legs away from me, leaning into the aisle, chin in hand, glowering. He checked over his shoulder repeatedly, constantly scanning the cabin. I moved gingerly, not yet knowing the blast that was coming for me.

At long last, a flight attendant approached him and crouched in the aisle, whispering something in his ear. My seatmate rose silently, gathered his things, and moved up one row. Before he sat down, he looked at me for the first time.

"This is so you'll have more room," he said. His voice was cold.

The flight attendant looked at him, puzzled. "This won't be a vacant seat," she corrected. "Someone will still be sitting here." My former seat mate looked away, then took his seat.

That was when I realized what had happened: he had asked to be re-seated. The nearness of my body was too much for him to bear. All that agitation, all that desperate lobbying—all to avoid two hours next to me. I'd never feared it before. I didn't think I needed to.

The next thought came quickly, urgently: *Don't cry. You can't cry.*

But it was too late. Hot tears stung my eyes, then spilled onto my cheeks. I stared at my lap, my eyes fixed on the width of my thighs. I glanced up and saw a woman's face, blank as a canvass, eyes wide and empty. Her neck was craned so she could see me. She was watching me like television.

I stayed like that, with my body knotted up into its most compact shape and eyes locked low for the rest of our trip. Flight attendants visited my row frequently, offering free wine, beer, and snacks to the passengers sitting on either side of me—apologetic offerings for having to tolerate a body like mine. The flight attendants didn't speak to me. My seatmates didn't look at me. I had been erased.

As we began our descent, I planned my route from the gate to the bathroom, where I could cry until the humiliation had drained me. I just had to get there. When passengers filtered into the aisle to retrieve their bags, my former seatmate looked at me for the second time.

"You know, I wouldn't do this to a person with a walker," he said.

"What?" I struggled to find my words. I hadn't expected to talk to him. I hadn't expected to talk to anyone.

"I wouldn't do this to a person with a walker, or a pregnant woman," he repeated.

"I know," I said, stunned. "That's what makes this terrible."

There it was. A stranger telling me, in no uncertain terms, that my body entitled him to treat me however he saw fit. He could complain openly, scoff at the fact of my body, publicly decry it to anyone who'd listen, and he would only be met with sympathy. He would never treat me with basic dignity. He would never be expected to.

I watched him as he disappeared onto the jetway. When he was finally gone, my eyes settled back to the aisle, where they met the woman's. She watched me again, silent and blank-faced.

Since then, I have thought often of what I could have done differently. Whether unprompted kindness would have interrupted the momentum of his anger. Whether I should have confronted him more directly or if I could have made another plea to the ticket agent. Whether I should have skipped the flight altogether. Whether I should ever fly again.

In the years since, I have found ways to minimize the likelihood of humiliation. I check my bag and save up for first-class tickets, which means I don't fly often. I see my family less often than I would like and I find reasons not to take work trips. Despite my best efforts, when I do fly, the experience remains punishing at every turn. Still, couples stare at me while I wait to board at the gate, openly discussing my body and trying to sneak a picture. Still, passengers issue full-throated complaints about sharing space with my body. Still, they complain to flight attendants, loudly, while I sit silently beside them, my body a knot of tension, forever tightening, while I will it to shrink.

The world around me rejects my body as if it were an organ transplant.

The physical world isn't built for bodies like mine, even as our numbers are growing. As of 2016, according to the Centers for Disease Control and Prevention (CDC), 39.8 percent of adults in the United States have BMIs that are considered obese, compared to 34.3 percent a decade earlier.[1] Yet still, our physical environments cater to thinner bodies, seemingly in aspiration, while the realities of our bodies are intently ignored. Too much furniture is flimsy, leaving me uncertain about what will bear me and what will leave me chagrined on a pile of splintered wood, so I often stand instead. Portable seating, like folding chairs and low-slung beach seating, often holds less than two hundred pounds and is categorically out of the question. Theater seating, with its rigid backs and metal arms, digs into my sides, leaving bruises in my soft flesh. Healthcare equipment—exam tables, MRIs, scales—often come with weight limits, leaving me routinely afraid that I will be unable to address the healthcare problems that bring me to a doctor's office. Until some recent unexpected weight loss, I was unable to buy clothing in *any* brick and mortar store and was relegated exclusively to the online world of terrible fit and prices triple (or quadruple) that which straight-size people pay.

Wherever I go, the message is clear: my body is too much for this world to bear. And it's reinforced by the people around me. Like the man on the plane, strangers take it upon themselves to tell me what I already know: that I won't fit and that I'm not welcome. Many openly roll their eyes when I step onto public transit, often glaring at me or placing their bags and jackets on the seat next to them. When I walk into department stores, the staff greets me immediately and tells me that Lane Bryant is four doors down. Strangers sometimes feel moved to shout at bodies like mine, simply proclaiming my shameful fatness or issuing directives about what to eat, how to move, or how my fatness will hasten my death.

In all these places, my body is a catalyst for panic and resentment, but in airplanes my skin becomes the target of unbridled anger. The sight of my body at an airport gate or in the aisle of a 737 leaves otherwise kind people filled not just with irritation, but with deep resentment, and sometimes with all-out rage. Thinner people who would never dream of shouting slurs at me on the street will readily text friends about the indignation of being forced to be near a body like mine, or they will complain to a flight attendant, who may then escort me from the flight, leaving me stranded in another city without recompense or recourse. A violent kind of disgust that otherwise lies dormant reveals itself in airplanes, lashing out at any fat person that dares to travel. While I work so fearfully to retain my seat, often paying double and rarely receiving additional space, thin people are easily pushed too far by the simple fact of proximity to a body like mine.

I understand why my fellow passengers are on edge. Airplanes are designed for profit, aimed at fitting as many human bodies as they can, with limited regard for passengers' comfort. I have yet to meet anyone who raves about the cushy seating in the coach section of a commercial airliner. Flying is expensive, cramped, trying, and taxing. Luggage gets cumbersome. We miss connections. Our relationships get strained. And at the height of all that stress—boarding—my wide, soft body becomes their target. Rather than being a compatriot stuck in the same cramped, uncomfortable position as everyone else, I become a scapegoat for all their frustration. In moments like those, it's hard to get angry with a corporation, its executives, and industrial designers; it's much easier to get angry with the fat person who dared to fly.

But airline seat sizes have a surprisingly checkered past—and one that has been explicitly guided by airlines' resistance to regulation and pursuit of unchecked profit at every turn. In the last decade alone, the average seat width has narrowed from 18½ inches to just 17 inches—a nearly 10 percent reduction in ten years.[2] The average seat pitch—a standard industry measurement of legroom—has also shrunk, from an average of 35 inches to just 31.[3] Airline bathrooms are getting smaller too. A *Wall Street Journal* reporter measured bathrooms on an old aircraft, which were 33 to 34 inches wide, while bathrooms on newer Boeing 737s were roughly 20 percent narrower—a scant 26 inches wide.[4]

And that's just in the last decade. Notably, in 1978, the United States opted to deregulate the airline industry, opening the floodgates to more cramped space in the air.[5] The Airline Deregulation Act of 1978 was "the first total dismantling of a federal regulatory regime since the 1930s,"[6] and its architect, Cornell University economist Alfred Kahn, also served as a significant force in energy deregulation in the US,[7] contributing to a now-catastrophic global climate crisis.[8] Airline deregulation ended federal subsidies to provide service to smaller towns and more rural locations, leaving the service of the nation's newest transportation industry to be determined solely by profits, leading to rising fares (previously regulated by the now-defunct

Civil Aeronautics Board), decreasing wages for airline workers, and a 1981 pilots' strike that grounded 35 percent of commercial flights in the US.[9] Functionally, deregulation allowed airlines to escape government account-ability for prices and accommodations alike. Following September 11, 2001, security protocols changed and, simultaneously, airlines began to charge for services that were previously included for every traveler. Meals were now only available for a fee. Pillows and blankets, previously stocked for nearly every passenger, were now only available in limited quantities. Even passing through simplified security checkpoints—as they all had been prior to the turn of the millennium—came with a TSA precheck price tag.

A national security incident paved the way for a new set of practices de-signed to increase profit margins by charging for what little creature comforts had previously been provided for free—and no creature comfort was more sought after than a larger seat or more legroom. Smaller seats, too, allowed for more ticket sales and an increased profit margin for airlines. Accordingly, commercial airlines made $14.7 billion in profits in 2017—up 7.4 percent from 2016.[10] And this trend of ever-shrinking space shows no signs of slow-ing. Every few months, new rumors of even more cramped space emerge, with proposals of partially standing seats, and smaller and smaller bathrooms.[11]

There have been some attempts to regulate seat size in recent years. In 2017 the US Court of Appeals for the District of Columbia Circuit ordered the Federal Aviation Administration (FAA) to address continually shrinking seat sizes.[12] The FAA responded with an internal ruling stating that they would not regulate seat size.[13] That same year, the United States Congress stepped in,[14] introducing the Seat Egress in Air Travel Act (SEAT Act), seek-ing to force the FAA to establish a minimum width, length, and pitch of airline seats, but failing to codify what those sizes ought to be.[15] As I write this, even the relatively toothless SEAT Act has yet to pass.

As airplane seats shrink and Americans grow, airlines' so-called "pas-senger of size" policies become more and more unpredictable for fat pas-sengers to navigate. Nearly all major airlines publish policies on how they will engage with fat passengers who may not fit in their ever-shrinking seats. In some cases, these policies are clear and direct, as in the case of Southwest Airlines, which provides fat passengers with a second seat, automatically re-funding the extra cost upon landing or providing the second seat altogether free of charge.[16] Others are oddly byzantine, like Alaska Airlines', which requires passengers to book a second seat by phone and will only refund that seat if all of the traveler's flights "depart with an open seat available," and the passenger calls the airline again to request that refund.[17] Spirit Airlines requires the purchase of a second seat and offers no refund.[18] Still others, like Virgin America, fail to publish their policy altogether. (As a very fat person, I have read the policies of these airlines and other transportation options, committing them to memory. My travel depends on it.)

Regardless of those policies' content, they are wildly unevenly applied, leaving fat passengers to wonder: When will we be allowed to remain on our flight, narrowly escaping detection? When will we be asked suddenly and without warning to pay the day-of price for an additional seat, even if one isn't available? When will we be escorted from the plane, to be watched by hundreds of our fellow passengers' prying eyes?

Sadly, those fears aren't unfounded—for many fat people, they're borne out in our lived experience. In 2017 Natalie Hage, a plus-size model and influencer, caught an American Airlines flight from Dallas to Los Angeles. Hage unexpectedly found herself in a middle seat on her nearly three-hour flight. Within seconds, her seatmate appeared to be surreptitiously photographing her. When Hage looked down at his phone, she saw a text exchange between her seatmate and a friend.

> FRIEND: Hopefully she didn't have any Mexican food.
> SEATMATE: I think she ate a Mexican.
>   If the news reports a DFW Airbus A321 leaving the runway
>   without rotating, that would be my flight.

Hage waited until the end of the flight to confront the man about his behavior. He denied it until she produced photographs of his text exchange. Finally, the man apologized—but only after an extended, video-taped confrontation.[19]

Sometimes, the exclusion fat people face on airplanes is a result of other passengers' actions, but all too often it's a matter of enforcing airlines' formalized policies. In 2016 passenger Errol Narvaez was traveling home after a weekend in Las Vegas when his seat disappeared. United Airlines had moved his reserved aisle seat to a center seat—less than ideal for a fat person. When his seatmate complained, Errol was escorted off the plane, past thirty-six rows of watchful faces. "You don't know what it's like, having to walk up the whole plane—Row 36, 35, 34," he told reporters.[20]

United, like nearly all major airlines, has a policy in place that allows them to eject fat passengers from their flights. Flight attendants enforced that policy when the rest of the passengers were seated, an audience in a theater, watching a fat person try, and fail, simply to get home unnoticed. The ticket agent rebooked Narvaez's flight for a 2:00 a.m. arrival, attempting to charge the beleaguered passenger a $117 ticket change fee for a six-hour delay, a sleepless night, and the privilege of public humiliation. With all of that—on the plane, at the ticket counter, in the airport—not one person spoke up in his defense. Hundreds of travelers watched him endure public humiliation—as he put it, a "walk of shame" past each one of them—and not one person spoke up. Like so many passengers before him, Errol Narvaez was more cargo than passenger: inanimate, cumbersome, and in the way. His humanity was disregarded, and he became more object than human.

Vilma Soltesz paid an even higher price. Vilma and her husband, Janos, had flown from their home in the Bronx to Hungary in 2012 without any challenges, having bought Vilma two seats for their flights. But Vilma faced some significant health complications while she was abroad, and her doctor ordered her back to New York as soon as possible. Vilma and Janos purchased new tickets home (two for Vilma, one for Janos). Upon boarding their return flight on KLM, they found that their assigned seats had physically broken beforehand. The couple were escorted off the flight and left to wait in the airport for five hours before being told to find a car, drive five more hours to Prague in the Czech Republic, and board a Delta flight home. When the couple boarded the second flight, a nation away, they were once again removed, allegedly due to Vilma's size and use of a wheelchair. Finally, they returned to Hungary once more for a Lufthansa flight. For a third time, they were denied the seats they paid for. Even in the midst of a health crisis, not one airline accommodated Vilma and Janos. While they waited and waited, tried and tried, Vilma's health continued to deteriorate. Within a matter of weeks, she was dead, half a world away from her home and her doctor.[21]

Errol Narvaez weighed 385 pounds when he was removed from his flight. Vilma Soltesz was 407 pounds when she passed away. When I read their stories, I weighed 400 pounds. The message from stories like these was clear: no one will protect bodies like ours. As long as we're fat, we might as well be dead.

In 2015 Nicole Arbour briefly became a household name. The comedian made a video called "Dear Fat People" whose shock value led it to quick viral success. In it, Arbour lets loose a frustrated rant about fat people, all triggered by her alleged encounter with a fat family at an airport.

> As I get to the front of the line, a family comes to the front and gets to butt me. Fattest, most obese—I'm talking TLC special fat. . . . They got to go to the front of the line because they were complaining that their knees hurt too much to stand in it. "Oh, I just came an hour early, like I was supposed to. But you overeat, let me help you." And they complain, and they smell like sausages, and I don't even think they ate sausages, that's just their aroma. They're so fat that they're that standing sweat fat. Crisco was coming out of their pores like a fucking play-doh fun factory. . . .
>
> I'm sitting in the aisle, and then a stewardess walks up to me. "Hi ma'am, I hate to ask, but we've got a disabled passenger. Would you mind switching seats?" And of course, because I'm not an asshole, I'm like "oh my god, of course, yes." Oh look, it's fat family. And Jabba the son sits right beside me. I just lost my shit. His fat was on my lap. I took the handle, I squished it down, and I said "MY SEAT, YOUR SEAT." I actually took his fat and I pushed it into his seat and I held it. He was fine. He was just fat. Make better choices.

Arbour's video, with its blunt approach and crass language sparked a nationwide conversation about what is and isn't okay to say to and about fat people. Notably, however, the conversation stopped short of considering the impact of Arbour's video on actual fat people.

In a tense appearance on *The View*, Arbour defended the video as comedy designed to provoke. "That video was made to offend people, just like I do with all my other videos. It's just satire, I'm just being silly, I'm just having a bit of fun, and that's what we did. And that topic was actually voted in by fans, some of them who are fat [sic]."[22] *The View* cohost Joy Behar, herself a comic, called out Arbour's defense. "You sort of hide behind this 'it's not healthy' thing and that's bull and you know it. [. . .] I'd be interested to see you do that live and see how many laughs you get."[23]

Arbour was roundly rejected for her video, but it still received over twenty-seven million views and became a touchstone in conversations about fatness and fat people. While "Dear Fat People" was an especially outrageous example, it didn't stand alone in its views on fatness and fat people—especially fat people on airplanes.

Six years before Arbour's viral video, The Young Turks (TYT) held a conversation about fat people on planes. Despite its role as a widely viewed left-wing news and opinion show on YouTube, The Young Turks' take was strikingly similar to Arbour's. Co-hosts Cenk Uygur and Ana Kasparian discussed the issue with a discomfort that quickly turned to honest disgust. Kasparian described a photograph taken by an American Airlines flight attendant of a fat passenger in a cramped airline seat that didn't fit his body.

"I love how Ana's trying to be polite about it," said Uygur. "He *seems* to be taking up a lot of room? Does he *seem* that way?"

Kasparian relented, laughing. "What do you want me to say? There's a fat motherfucker on the plane."

As the conversation proceeded, Uygur initially acknowledged that the passenger was "trying his best not to get in [the] way" and was "probably super uncomfortable, sitting halfway on the seat"—even acknowledging that the airline's policy may be discriminatory. But the two co-hosts quickly agreed that the passenger should have to buy two seats.

"I mean, look," Kasparian added, "I think it's discrimination when it's something that the person can't help, right? [. . .] We're facing a huge obesity epidemic, right? Okay, so we've got a bunch of fatties in the United States, and if they want to travel, too bad, we're gonna give them two seats and they just have to pay for one? That just doesn't make any sense to me. I don't think that's fair.[24]

It was surreal to watch it all unfold, this litigation of my body, a voiceless inconvenience, an inanimate obstacle. Like Nicole Arbour, the Young Turks insulted fat people. Like Arbour, they acknowledge, then write off, the idea that someone might be fat for reasons beyond their control. And like Arbour, they focus exclusively on the comfort and safety of thin people sitting nearby, easily bypassing any consideration for the fat person in question. The similarities are striking. But Nicole Arbour's video received 27 million views and faced significant backlash before being taken down by YouTube. The Young Turks' video, as of this writing, has received just under 1.5 million views and remains available online. So why did one incite outrage and the other receive so little attention?

The difference is that Arbour's video offers no counterpoint and comes across to many viewers as crass and crude. The Young Turks, while arguing similar points, do so in what *feels* like a more measured way. But funda-mentally, both videos argue the same points and lay out a road map of core cultural beliefs about fat people—especially fat people in public spaces: Fat people shouldn't be so fat. Fat people inconvenience thin people with our bodies. Fatness is a choice for most. Arbour's crime wasn't that she *believed* fat people were disgusting, it's that she openly *said it.*

That, it seems, is where our conversation about how to treat fat people has stalled. Very few public conversations surface our core beliefs about fat people, hold them up to the light, examine them. Very few engage with the facts. In the case of airplanes, the ever-shrinking seats, the inconsistent poli-cies, and the heartbreaking losses fat people continue to suffer. Very few of those public conversations challenge us, individually, to face our own biases against fatness and fat people. Instead of expressing outrage at the concrete harm we do to fat people, the painful and wrongheaded beliefs we stub-bornly cling to, and the systems set up to exclude and underserve fat people, we opt for the easier conversation. We opt for politeness. We opt for *if you can't say anything nice, don't say anything at all.*

Instead of confronting our own beliefs, we confront the few who give voice to those beliefs. And instead of fixing the problem, we silence it. But anti-fat bias isn't just a problem for public figures, nor is it a simple prob-lem of politeness. A growing body of research in recent decades has taken a closer look at the prevalence of anti-fat bias in the general population. Its findings are increasingly damning.

In 2019 Harvard University released a study based on the results of their immensely popular online implicit bias test. The test asks participants to move through rapidly flashing slides of words and images to measure their uncon-scious biases around race, gender, sexual orientation, disability, weight, and other characteristics. The study, published in *Psychological Science*, reviewed the results of over four million test takers over the course of nine years.

On some fronts, the findings were promising. According to the study's lead author, Tessa Charlesworth, "The most striking finding is that sexual-ity attitudes have changed toward neutrality, toward less bias, by as much as 33 percent on implicit measures," with nearly half of people also self-reporting changes in their own attitudes.[25] Similarly, if less dramatically, test takers' implicit bias on the basis of race also decreased by 17 percent.

While most measures of implicit bias decreased or remained stable, one measure exploded: anti-fat bias. In those nine years, pro-thin, anti-fat bias increased by a full 40 percent. Not only that, but weight-based bias was the slowest changing of all explicit attitudes—that is, the attitudes that test takers self-reported. According to Charlesworth:

> It is the only attitude out of the six that we looked at that showed any hint of getting *more* biased over time. . . . And of course again the question might be: why? What is specific about body-weight attitude?
>
> We can only speculate: Body weight has been the target of much discussion, but discussion in a negative light. We often talk about the "obesity epidemic," or about "the problem" with obese individuals.
>
> Also, we typically think about body weight as something that people can control, and so we are more likely to make the moral judgement of, "Well, you should just change."

The raw numbers are striking too. In 2016 a full 81 percent of test takers showed pro-thin, anti-fat bias. That's four out of five of us.

These implicit bias findings are uncomfortable to read, and they run counter to popular assumptions about how bias works. In public discourse, we often discuss bias and hate as things we *decide* to take on—that our default setting is an unbiased one, and that it's up to us to decide to take up the mantle of hate. In the popular imagination of many white folks, racism is relegated to virulent, organized white supremacists. Misogyny is the work of overt, proud chauvinist men. Homophobia is the domain of Fred Phelps and Pat Robertson, a cruel and outspoken minority. Few of us think of ourselves as biased because we're not like *them*. Few of us think of ourselves as hating any group of people. Still, our implicit biases often belie that self-image and the more comforting stories we tell ourselves.

But acknowledging our biases isn't a matter of making ourselves into villains, all black hearts and gleeful misdeeds. Acknowledging our biases is a matter of recognizing the social contexts that encourage them. Weight-loss ads flood the airwaves despite the fact that no diet has proven to lead to major, sustained weight loss. A Stanford study comparing low fat and low carbohydrate diets found that neither proved particularly effective for long-term weight loss, leading to an average loss of just over one pound per month for study subjects. Some lost more; many lost less.[26] Still, we are constantly confronted with an impossible ideal and snake oil that promises to bring it to fruition. Media messages about *revenge bodies* and *baby weight* and *beach bodies* abound, conditioning our feelings about our own bodies and the ways that we treat those who are fatter than us.

Our biases aren't just encouraged by private media, either. During those pivotal nine years of booming anti-fat bias, Michelle Obama was the First Lady of the United States, and her flagship campaign was aimed at ending obesity. Throughout the Obama years, the US established a series of federal and state programs aimed at asserting the personal responsibility of adults, children, and their parents to become and remain thin. Between the private and public sectors, billions of dollars have been spent seeding body dissatisfaction that would increase profits for weight-loss companies. In the process, both sectors seeded this astronomical rise in anti-fat attitudes, actions, and policies—all targeted at the fatness we learned to fear in ourselves. But those many shots we have learned to take at ourselves have long landed blows at fat people in the process.

Fat people aren't impacted equally, either, in part because we aren't distributed evenly. According to the CDC, women are more likely to be fat than men, and Black and Latinx people are more likely to be fat than white people.[27] Fatness is frequently used as a stand-in for poverty, even intellectual disability. In *The Obesity Myth*, Paul Campos argues that as overt racism, sexism, and classism fell out of favor among white and wealthy Americans, anti-fat bias offered a stand-in: a dog whistle that allowed disdain and bigotry aimed at poor people and people of color to persist, uninterrupted and simply renamed.

We also like to think that unlike Nicole Arbour, though we also have unkind thoughts about fat people, we keep them to ourselves. We believe that they don't influence our actions, and that we are able to remain clear-headed and objective, even when those judgments enter our minds. But again, the data points to something else. In nearly every facet of public life that's been studied, fat people face immense bias and often overt discrimination.

One informal survey of over five hundred hiring managers tested their attitudes toward potential employees based on size. Based solely on photographs, 21 percent described the fattest woman they were shown as "lazy" and "unprofessional" more than any other size. Just 18 percent said she had "leadership potential," and only 15 percent would even consider hiring her.[28] A study from Vanderbilt University found that fat women were more likely to work in more physically active jobs behind the scenes and less likely to work in jobs interacting with customers or representing a company.[29] Another

Wharton study found that "obesity serves as a proxy for low competence. People judge obese people to be less competent even when it's not the case."[30]

Anti-fat bias doesn't just impact our ability to get hired—it also impacts our wages. Scientists at the University of Exeter found that, in England, women who are just one stone (14 pounds) over their BMI-mandated weight earned over 1,500 pounds ($1,867) *less* than a thinner woman.[31] In the United States, the findings are even more troubling. A 2010 study published in the *Journal of Applied Psychology* found staggering salary inequities based on size. "Heavy women earned $9,000 less than their average-weight counterparts; very heavy women earned $19,000 less. Very thin women, on the other hand, earned $22,000 more than those who were merely average."[32] Conversely, men's salaries *increased* with weight gain—until those men became fat.[33]

The aftershocks of our bias aren't just limited to the workplace, either. Fat people feel its effects in the criminal justice system too. A 2013 Yale University study published in the *International Journal of Obesity* found that men were more likely to find a fat woman guilty of the same crime. "Male participants rated the obese female defendant guiltier than the lean female defendant, whereas female respondents judged the two female defendants equally regardless of weight. Among all participants, there were no differences in assessment of guilt between the obese male and lean male defendants."[34] And the bias isn't just limited to jurors. In 2017, a Quebec judge made headlines by saying that a fat seventeen-year-old woman might have been "flattered" by being sexually assaulted, saying the woman "is a bit overweight, but she has a pretty face. [. . .] The court specifies that she is a pretty young girl."[35] While his remarks were publicly decried, he faced no formal censure or consequences.

Anti-fat bias is so ubiquitous and unquestioned that the New York Police Department (NYPD) union used it as a defense against murder. On July 17, 2014, Eric Garner, a Black man, was killed on video. He lay on the ground, an officer's arm wrapped around his neck, while three other officers looked on. Garner repeatedly told officers he couldn't breathe before he was finally choked to death—all for selling loose cigarettes on the street in New York City. Shortly thereafter, the coroner ruled Garner's death a homicide. The case seemed open and shut: Garner's death was taped and widely circulated. In the wave of police killings of unarmed Black men, this one seemed as close to an open-and-shut case as possible. As the case progressed, however, its resolution slipped further and further out of reach. Prosecutors declined to file criminal charges in the case. The officer who killed Garner, Daniel Pantaleo, has kept his job thus far, though he has been relegated to desk duty. In 2019, the NYPD held administrative hearings to determine whether or not Pantaleo would be permitted to keep his job. His defense team argued that Pantaleo should not be held accountable for his actions because Garner was fat. "He died from being morbidly obese," Stuart London, the police union attorney leading the team, said during an administrative hearing. "He was a ticking time bomb that resisted arrest. If he was put in a bear hug, it would have been the same outcome."[36]

By London's logic, a fat person can't be murdered, given the widespread and false belief that being fat is simply a death sentence. While the defense's argument ran in multiple newspapers, just one mainstream headline called attention to its cruel logic. *New York Magazine* ran the story with the headline "NYPD Union Lawyers Argue That Eric Garner Would Have Died Anyway Because He Was Obese."[37]

We create public policy around our bias, ensuring that fat people are not protected from even the most naked abuse. As of 2020, in forty-eight states, it is perfectly legal to fire someone, refuse to hire them, deny them housing, or turn them down for a table at a restaurant or a room in a hotel simply because they're fat. Michigan, Washington State, and San Francisco are the United States' three jurisdictions to ban size-based discrimination.[38] In the rest of the nation, however, those who experience weight stigma in the workplace are left to fend for themselves with little, if any, legal recourse at all. In 2013, twenty-two cocktail waitresses sued Atlantic City's Borgata Hotel Casino & Spa for weight-based discrimination. They were regularly weighed in at work and were suspended if they gained "too much weight." Despite this overt discrimination, the court denied the servers' claim and upheld the hotel's legal right to discriminate.[39]

Whatever we may think of our own beliefs, however hard it may be to stretch beyond our own experience of the world as an unbiased meritocracy, this growing body of research proves that for fat people, it simply isn't. We get fewer jobs and earn significantly less money. In court, we are more likely to be found guilty by jurors and judges alike.

All of this happens because anti-fat bias exists in *all of us*. It exists in all of us because it exists in every corner of our culture: our institutions, media, and public policy. How could we avoid it? Ninety-seven million Americans diet, despite the $66 billion industry's failure rate of up to 98 percent.[40] *The*

Biggest Loser was a smash hit for its twelve years on the air, reaching over seven million viewers at the height of its popularity.[41] Magazines like *Woman's World* reliably feature cover stories like "Lose 13 Lbs Every 5 Days on the World's Hottest Diet" alongside "Ring in 2019 with Munchies!"[42] And the United States has not poured endless federal and state dollars into public education campaigns aimed at regulating corporate food production, subsidizing nutritious foods, or ending poverty and economic instability—top predictors of individual health, according to the US Office of Disease Prevention and Health Promotion.[43] Instead, *fat bodies themselves* are targeted in the "war on obesity" and the "childhood obesity epidemic." Anti-fatness is like air pollution. Some days we may see it; others, we may not. But it always surrounds us, and whether we mean to or not, we are always breathing it in.

But where does all that bias come from? Like so many morality panics before it, it's difficult to identify a single source of our cultural and political commitment to sidelining and scapegoating fat bodies. Its roots are many and varied. As it stands, these forces—often driven by profit and political expediency—are today as strong as they've ever been. The power and profitability of anti-fatness means that most of us have already internalized hurtful, harmful, and inaccurate messages about fat people. Whatever we may want to think about ourselves, we've got to make the shift from thinking of anti-fat bias as *something we decide to do out of animus* to *something that exists within us unless and until we uproot it.* If we are passive, we absorb the bias in the world around us, overwhelmingly suggested to us by people and institutions that stand to gain power and profits by scapegoating fat people. It is up to us to both change those systems and to unlearn these enculturated attitudes. In so doing, we can make the world a little less punishing for the 70 percent of Americans who are fat.[44]

I tell a friend about the man on the plane. The way he looked at me. The way he treated me. His naked revulsion at my body, at having to be near me. "All because I'm fat," I say.

"Oh my God, no!" my friend cuts in. "You're not fat, you're beautiful."

I tell her the rest of the story. She asks why I bought a middle seat. I tell her I didn't. She asks why I provoked him. I tell her I didn't. She tells me she finds it hard to believe. I tell her it's true. Her voice becomes clipped, irritated.

"I guess if you hate it that much, you should just lose weight."

This, then, is my life as a fat person. I am expected to absorb the discomfort and outright bias against my body in a world built for thin people. The responsibility is mine and mine alone. Should my body cost an airline more, it is my responsibility to pay them. Should my body cause discomfort for anyone around me, it is my responsibility to apologize and to comfort them. Should I begin to question why my body is forever a problem, it is my responsibility to keep quiet. And should these problems become untenable for me, it is my responsibility to "just lose weight." The decent thing, after all, is to transform my body for the sake of those around me.

It is no one's responsibility to hear me. It is no one's responsibility to care for my body. It is no one's responsibility to ask about my comfort. At times, someone may do me the service of offering "tough love," berating the body I have always had and the practices they assume created it, but I am never owed consideration, much less an apology. If there is a problem, I caused it with my gluttony and sloth. My body is my original sin. Every road leads back to the penance I must do for the body I have always had.

No matter the problem, no matter the actions of an aggressor, the fault is mine. Regardless of the politics or life experience of the person I am talking to, the answer comes like clockwork. *I guess if you hate it that much, you should just lose weight.*

But despite its ubiquity in conversations about fatness and fat people, that is the logic of abuse. *You made me do this. I wouldn't hurt you if you didn't make me.* Just because we are accustomed to hearing it doesn't make it healthy, productive, humane, or helpful. Its functions are threefold: One, to absolve us of any responsibility to address a widespread social problem. Two, to free us from having to re-examine our own beliefs and biases. And three, to silence and isolate fat people, to show us that any complaint we lodge and any issue we raise will be for naught, and may even cost us relationships, respect, comfort, and safety.

Nearly all of us, fat and thin alike, have spent a lifetime learning to see fat people as problems, pariahs, or scapegoats. But what if, instead of doing what we know how to do—instead of comfortably, distantly blaming fat people—we looked at ourselves? What would happen if we interrogated our own beliefs? What would happen if we acknowledged our own complicity in hurting and harming fat people? What would become of us if we sat quietly with our own misconceptions, examined them, looked at the effects they created? What if, for once, we spoke *with* fat people instead of *about* fat people?

CHAPTER 2

BECOMING AN EPIDEMIC

I was in fourth grade, sitting in a doctor's office, the first time my face flushed with shame. I was, I had just learned, overweight.

"It's probably from eating all that pizza and ice cream. It tastes good, doesn't it? But it makes your body big and fat."

I was confused. Dinners at home were usually fish or chicken, rice, and steamed vegetables; breakfasts were cottage cheese and cantaloupe, or whole wheat toast topped with ricotta cheese and jam. It was 1992, and I was the child of a Weight Watchers mother whose family meals often followed suit. None of that seemed to matter in the doctor's office.

"Just imagine that your body is made out of clay. If you can just stay the same weight, as you grow, you'll stretch out. And once you grow up, you'll be thin and beautiful. Won't that be great?"

I felt my face sear with shame. My skin was neon, hot and bright, noisy and garish. I had learned so much in that one moment: *You're eating too much junk food. You're not beautiful. You're indulging too much. Your body is wrong. You must have done it.* Something was wrong with my body. I'd failed a test I didn't even know I'd taken.

The years ahead in my childhood and adolescence became an exercise in weathering the storm of conversations like these. Well-meaning, supportive adults eagerly pointed out my perceived failings at every turn. Even when I wasn't in the doctor's office, everyone seemed to have recommendations, hypotheses, requirements, edicts. Otherwise compassionate, thoughtful people abruptly shifted into harsh judgments and zero-tolerance attitudes, all bootstraps and personal responsibility. After all, I was responsible for my own body, and my body was an undeniable display of failure.

More and more foods, I was told, were off-limits. It wasn't just that I shouldn't eat them; it was that they were *sinful, bad, tempting.* Foods containing fat were the primary culprits, demons sent to tempt and torment us. My agnostic family was suddenly awash in religious language, building a heaven and a hell with each meal, and it was clear that I was tempted by devil's food. *Get thee behind me, pizza!*

Many of those foods—eggs, nuts, avocados—would later fall back in the good graces of healthy eating, redeemed years later by a ruthless culture. At the time, though, they were collateral damage in a crusade to cut calories at all costs. Fiber, vitamins, minerals, fatty acids, protein—they were all sacrificed at the altar of *calories in, calories out.* The focus was never on enjoying nutritious foods, just on deprivation, will, and lack. Ours was an orthodoxy of hunger, a never-ending fast. It was self-flagellation, a forced performance to display my commitment to changing an unacceptable body.

Food wasn't there to satiate hunger, to fuel activity, or to enjoy. Instead, it became emotionally and morally laden. A slice of cheddar cheese became a referendum on my willpower, work ethic, character. A bite of ice cream was *a moment of weakness.* One scoop was cause for concern; two scoops called for an intervention.

Those interventions started at age nine, and they never stopped. The first intervention was a children's summer program, which included additional group treatment after school for the rest of the year. It wasn't until adulthood that I realized that this children's program was known by most of its alumni by another name: *fat camp.*

Fat camps, known in the early twentieth century as "fat farms" or "reduction clubs," have been around for over a century. Like *The Biggest Loser, Celebrity Fit Camp,* and *Extreme Makeover,* fat camps prioritize extreme workout routines and very low calorie diets (VLCDs) to result in significant, if short lived, weight loss. Unlike their televised counterparts, fat camps disproportionately target children. In 2011, *Dr. Oz* featured footage of the talk show's guests attending Camp Shane, a popular fat camp in Michigan. In the studio, the show's graphics were splashed across the TV screens: *Is it child abuse to have a child who is fat?*[1] In 2017 *Women's Health* featured a list of "the 6 best weight-loss camps for women," touting "expert-approved"

programs that charge up to a thousand dollars a night.[2] Today, camps like
Camp Shane, Wellspring, the Warrior, and Canyon Ranch's "Life Enhance-
ment Center" charge thousands of dollars for their short-term, residential
weight-loss programs.

On my first day, I gripped my mother's hand as we entered a strange
school, emptied of students and unsettlingly quiet. Distant voices echoed
down desolate halls, growing louder as we approached the gym. My eyes lin-
gered in the doorway as we passed. Fat children played joylessly with grimy
dodgeballs while adults shouted directions from the sidelines. *Lift your knees,
Jessica! It's a better workout. Keep that heart rate up! Don't slow down, Tyler!* I loved
dodgeball and handball at school, but here, they were drained of their fun,
spontaneity, and joy. Instead, they became a punishing exercise, a reminder
to these children of their failings, a Sisyphean task that they were doomed to
repeat until their bodies were drained, degraded and, thankfully, *thin.*

But I hadn't graduated to the gym yet. No, my first day would be in a
classroom, sitting in a circle with a dozen other fat children. An adult asked
our names before launching into a lengthy lecture about what kinds of food
we should and shouldn't eat, parsed into two stark columns.

Salad: *should.*

A gallon of ice cream: *should not.*

Pasta: *should.*

Fruit juice: *should.*

Four cheeseburgers: *should not.*

Fast food every night: *should not.*

A baby loaf brick of cheddar cheese: *should not.*

Who had eaten a brick of cheddar cheese? I wondered silently. Like so many
of the *should not* examples, it felt pointed in its exaggerated specificity. I
searched other children's faces, looking carefully for a spark of recognition
or shame. One child looked down. Another blinked back tears. None of
us spoke.

The lecture built a scaffolding for us, a vast and rickety framework to
hold up our failing bodies. I struggled to make sense of it, because so much

of it was designed to solve problems that weren't my own. My parents rarely ordered fast food, primarily cooking whole foods at home. I didn't binge eat, though the lecturer seemed to presume we all did. I didn't like running, but I loved swimming and planned to join my neighborhood swim team later that summer. I raced my neighbor regularly, challenging her to beat me in freestyle laps, then backstroke, then butterfly. I did all of that with a round belly, soft arms, and a fat and rosy face. I didn't know who this instruction was for, but I was increasingly certain it wasn't for me.

Much of the lecture was irrelevant and the rest of it dripped with condescension. Despite our young age, many of us had already begun to count calories, to read nutrition labels, to opt for salads, and to ask for dressing on the side. Our bodies had brought us an unrequested expertise well beyond our years. Still, here stood a thin adult, explaining that a carton of ice cream might taste good, but it didn't make for a healthy dinner.

At night, I paged through the workbook provided to each of us. Illustrations and parables of fat children stared back at me. Cindy was an emotional eater who didn't tell her parents how she really felt, opting instead for chocolate chip cookies from a cookie jar that came to life, tut-tutting back at her. Matt was a fat kid with fat parents, and he avoided dieting because he was afraid his parents would think he was trying to show off. Another fat girl wanted to lose weight so that the other kids would stop making fun of her. This theme—that weight loss is the solution to bullying—was frequently echoed throughout the workbook, as if the bullied were to blame for their own suffering. When one child explained that her classmates called her names, the talking cookie jar affirmed that bullying happens everywhere, and the only way to solve it is to lose weight. This, I learned, was what to expect: that if I was bullied for my size, no one would stand up for me. That, unlike other forms of bullying, fat shaming wouldn't be met with reprimand, but with resignation and sometimes even hope—*maybe it will motivate you to lose some weight*. These little parables crystallized what I was learning every day: that any abuse that came my way was ultimately my fault. That I should be grateful for the "tough love." That I should keep my mouth shut.

Unlike the children in my workbook, I wasn't the only dieter in my family. My mother was a regular at Weight Watchers, and my father prided himself on bragging at 8 p.m. that he hadn't eaten anything all day. I kept a food journal written with a felt-tip Pentel pen, my young handwriting clumsily stretching beyond the confines of my diary's wide ruled paper: *blueberries,*

½ cup; Yoplait fat-free yogurt, lemon burst, 6 ounces. At night, I dreamed of lay-ing my belly on a cold, metal table (a laboratory or a coroner's office?) and slicing it off with a fish knife in one smooth stroke, bloodied but finally free. Sometimes I still do.

Because so many foods were quarantined, any occasion to eat them be-came a rare opportunity to indulge, the way I was told I had always wanted to. Birthday parties at school called for two slices of cake; potato chips required three helpings. Every encounter with forbidden foods became a time to load up on them. As I got older, this meant eating contraband foods in secret and hiding foods to eat when I was alone. Shame taught me to overeat and to fetishize food. The more it was withheld, the more tempting it became.

My strength and activity level deteriorated too. Ultimately, I did join the swim team, winning relay races and swimming the complicated butterfly stroke. I loved volleyball and softball. As I got older, my body precluded me from the sports I loved the most—not because it was incapable, but because it was unsightly. As a swimmer, I'd have to be seen in a swimsuit, exposing the body of which I'd learned to be so deeply ashamed.

Shame diseased my conversations like blight spreading through a crop. I constantly inoculated those around me with an endless string of caveats and excuses for daring to be seen when I wasn't yet thin. Still, I received unso-licited health suggestions, stern lectures, gym recommendations, names of surgeons—an avalanche of advice I was already taking. Talking about diet and exercise, my favorite vegetables and personal bests, were all shorthand to preempt the inevitable. *I know I'm fat, but I'm spending every waking mo-ment to change that. I hope you won't write me off completely.*

Even at such a young age, I had been declared an enemy combatant in the US's war on childhood obesity. Bodies like mine had been declared an epidemic, and we were its virus, personified.

The war on obesity seemed to emerge, fully formed, near the turn of the millennium, but its roots run deeper than that. C. Everett Koop, the sur-geon general under President Reagan, made fatness a priority for his office in the mid-1980s. In 1988, the US Public Health Service (PHS) released "the most comprehensive report on nutrition and health ever prepared by the [US] Government,"[3] which called for an increase in food-related public health programs and legislation. "Of greatest concern," said Koop, "is our excessive intake of dietary fat and its relationship to risk for chronic diseases such as coronary heart disease, some types of cancers, diabetes, high blood pressure, strokes and obesity."[4] Koop estimated that fatness was killing one thousand Americans per day.[5] The report called for an increase in food-related public health programs and legislation, but its recommendations largely took the form of individual mandates:

> Most people should reduce total fat in the diet, but particularly saturated fats, defined as animal or vegetable fats that stay solid at room temperature, such as butter, untrimmed meat and palm oil. They should choose foods relatively low in these fats, including vegetables, beans and peas, fish, poultry with skin removed, lean meats and low-fat dairy products. [. . .] They should eat more whole grain foods, cereals, vegetables and fruits to increase the amount of fiber and complex carbohydrates in the diet.[6]

Notably, the report stopped short of recommendations that would regulate foods, or the subsidies that provided such cheap and plentiful forms of dietary fat, salt, sugars, and high-fructose corn syrup. (The report's only major direction for regulatory public policy came in the form of a directive to fluoridate local water supplies.) Meanwhile, the impossibly complex Farm Bill, whose 2018 renewal ran at over 1,200 pages, subsidized the production of foods that ran directly counter to the PHS recommendations.[7] First passed in 1933, the Farm Bill aimed to standardize and steady food prices during and after the Great Depression by offering financial rewards in the form of subsidies to farmers who grew so-called "commodity crops." Today, those commodity crops include wheat, corn, rice, and soybeans—top ingredients in higher-calorie, lower-nutrient, shelf-stable foods like sugary beverages, chips, and candy bars. Notably, fresh fruits and vegetables are not considered commodity crops, nor are lean proteins, ensuring that healthier foods will remain at a higher price point, reserving the privilege of health for those with the income to support it. While the Farm Bill ostensibly aims to serve consumer interests, the federal government's left hand aggressively deprioritizes the public health interests promoted by its right. Instead, regardless of its initial intent, the Farm Bill functionally lines the pockets of companies like Frito Lay, Coca-Cola, and other corporate food purveyors. The majority of those same corporations rely on low-wage labor, which means that often their workers are also their consumers. As it happens, over the last fifty years, Americans' food intake has continued to drift further from the PHS's nutrition recommendations. While we eat slightly more vegetables and fruit than we used to, we still fall dramatically short of the dietary guidelines in all but two areas: meat, eggs, and nuts, and those "commodity crop" grains.[8]

But more meaningful, precise reforms would have required a well-resourced, savvy lobbying effort. It would've called for an overhaul of a powerful and wealthy industry, and it would've demanded money, social capital, and political will to take on the big businesses that had grown wealthy as a result of the very legislation that needed to be dismantled and reimagined. Instead, the PHS opted for a lexicon of personal responsibility—"most people should." While most people should eat more whole grains, the report didn't suggest significant upstream solutions that would help people with what they should do. But then, root cause analyses have never been the work of the war on obesity. Even this early in its development, its approach was already a patchwork of individualized solutions to systemic problems. It was a series of shoulds, as it would be for years to come.

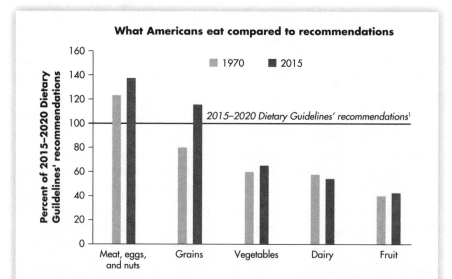

What Americans eat compared to recommendations

1970   2015

2015–2020 Dietary Guidelines' recommendations[1]

Percent of 2015–2020 Dietary Guildelines' recommendations

Meat, eggs, and nuts   Grains   Vegetables   Dairy   Fruit

[1] Based on a 2,000-calorie-per-day diet
Source: USDA, Economic Research Service, Loss-Adjusted Food Availability Data and *2015–2020 Dietary Guidelines.* https://www.ers.usda.gov/data-products/chart-gallery/gallery/chart-detail/?chartId=58334

It wasn't until 2003 that the war on obesity became a top priority across government entities, popularized by a successor of Koop's. Surgeon General Richard Carmona, who later sought the Democratic nomination for US senator representing Arizona, regularly compared the war on obesity to the war on terror. "One of the reporters asked me, 'What is the most pressing issue in health facing the United States today?' [. . .] She thought I was going to say weapons of mass destruction. But I said obesity. She was stunned. I mean, she couldn't say a word for thirty seconds because she didn't expect to hear 'obesity.'"[9] In the wake of a national tragedy, and at the height of its subsequent nationalist panic, Carmona posited that the greatest threat came from within. Suddenly, fat people weren't just neighbors, friends, or family members—we were enemy combatants in some strange new war.

The war on obesity reached its zenith under First Lady Michelle Obama, whose Let's Move! campaign was "dedicated to solving the problem of obesity within a generation, so that children born today will grow up healthier and able to pursue their dreams."[10] As with Weight Watchers, Let's Move! was bolstered by corporate food producers with a stake in maintaining a status quo that bolstered sales of their products. Companies like Coca-Cola, Pepsi, Hershey's, Kraft, and Kellogg's signed on to the First Lady's "healthy weight commitment" as part of the Let's Move! campaign, agreeing to reformulate their foods to become "healthier"—that is, less caloric. Ultimately, many of those changed foods only resulted in minor calorie reductions (ten or twenty calories per portion) and offered corporations a new marketing platform that appeared to give their products the White House's seal of approval.[11]

Let's Move! communications frequently referred to the program as "America's move to raise a healthier generation of kids" through advocating that children lose weight.[12] This subtle but definite shift in language continued to prop up the thinking that conflated weight with health. Thin people "looked healthy"; fat people were met with concern for our health. Weight loss became not about "slimming down" but about "getting healthy." No fat person, it seemed, could be as healthy as any thin person, regardless of our mental health, reproductive health, blood pressure, blood sugar, T-cell count, or any other measure of a vast, multifaceted, and still underexplored bodily system's measure of health. And fat people's health—by which this public health initiative clearly, explicitly meant size—was now an urgent, nationwide priority.

As so many anti-fat initiatives do, Let's Move! talked about fat people (in this case, fat children) without talking to them. This was a campaign against "childhood obesity"—not specific health conditions or the behaviors that may contribute to those health conditions. It wasn't a campaign against corporate campaigns for cheaply produced foods with little nutritional value, nor against the unchecked poverty that called for such low-cost, shelf-stable foods. It was a campaign against a body type—and more than that, a child's body type. Longtime fat activist Lesley Kinzel wrote a response to Let's Move! in *Newsweek*, detailing the harms of growing up as a fat kid "in a world that targets fat people as defective and unacceptable."[13]

> Call it a campaign against childhood couch-sitting. Call it a drive to get kids to go outside and play. Call it a movement to educate children on basic nutrition and how their amazing growing bodies work for them. But don't single out the fat kids.[14]

Michelle Obama's Let's Move! campaign caused some unintended harm at the hands of a beloved First Lady. But more than that, it opened the doors to an even more vicious front in its new war on childhood obesity.

In 2012 Georgia launched its Strong4Life campaign aimed at reducing children's weight and lowering the state's national ranking: second in childhood obesity. Mark Wulkan, surgeon in chief for Children's Healthcare of Atlanta, said the "time for 'warm and fuzzies' [. . .] was over. So instead, his hospital created an aggressive campaign, based in part off a previously successful anti-methamphetamine campaign."[15] But instead of targeting drug addiction in adults, the billboards targeted fatness in children. Somber black-and-white photographs of fat children (which have been blurred) stared unflinchingly at viewers, emblazoned with the word "WARNING" in vibrant red:

> "WARNING: My fat may be funny to you but it's killing me. Stop childhood obesity."

> "WARNING: It's hard to be a little girl if you're not."

> "WARNING: Fat prevention begins at home. And the buffet line."

> "WARNING: Chubby kids may not outlive their parents."

"WARNING: Fat kids become fat adults."

"WARNING: Big bones didn't make me this way. Big meals did."

"WARNING: He has his father's eyes, his laugh and maybe even his diabetes."

The billboards purported to warn parents of the danger of childhood fatness, but to many they read just as readily as public ridicule of fat kids. "My fat may be funny to you, but it's killing me." Strong4Life became one of the nation's highest-profile fat shaming campaigns—and its targets were children. Rather than initiating parent trainings, advocating for increased funding for school nutritional education, changing the contents of school lunches, or alleviating the poverty that relegated so many low-income students to highly processed, low-nutrient foods, Strong4Life opted to rent billboards. And it decided that its most effective strategy would be to blame children and parents for what were clearly the results of predominantly systemic forces.

While these campaigns rang the alarm, declaring an obesity epidemic and a war on childhood obesity, few (if any) of their tactics were based in research. And none sought to evaluate their impacts beyond macrolevel data on the rates of fatness in children. They all doggedly pursued one question, and one question only: How do we get rid of fat kids?

Despite a purported public health crisis, the federal and state programs that comprised the war on obesity were far from data driven. Overwhelmingly, these programs and public messages hinged on shame and fear, a scared-straight approach for fat kids. But a growing body of research shows the paradoxical impacts of that shame, especially on people who are fat. As of 2017, fully half of US states require that schools track students' BMIs.[16] Half of those require so-called "BMI report cards" to be sent home to parents, despite the fact that 53 percent of parents don't actually believe their children's BMI report cards[17] and studies in Arkansas[18] and California[19] have shown that the practice doesn't actually lead to individual weight loss or an overall reduction in students' BMIs. A policy review in Oxford's *Health Education Research* journal cautioned school administrators about "the potential to do harm to the children who are identified as overweight."[20] One eating disorder treatment center called the report cards a "pathway to weight stigma," and one that would likely contribute to development of eating disorders in predisposed students.[21] Like so many health interventions that measure weight above all else, BMI report cards may also shortchange thin students. Strictly size-based health approaches can offer a false sense of security, implying that a lower weight is tantamount to a clean bill of health for those whose behaviors don't contribute to their individual health and largely go unnoticed due to their more socially acceptable size.

A 2005 study in the *Journal of Health and Social Behavior* published research findings that very fat people internalized anti-fat bias, leading to low levels of self-acceptance and self-esteem, purportedly due to their experiences being mistreated due to their size.[22] But the impacts of anti-fat bias didn't end there. A 2012 study in the journal *Obesity* asked fat adults to indicate how often they had experienced weight stigmatizing events, from overt forms of anti-fat bias (employment discrimination, physical attacks, nasty comments) to subtler forms of stigma (others making negative assumptions, inappropriate comments from doctors, being stared at, physical barriers or obstacles, or being avoided, excluded, or ignored). The highest-rated category was "others making negative assumptions," which 74 percent of women and 70 percent of men reported experiencing. But even the lowest-ranked category—being physically attacked—was an experience shared by 10 percent of women and 11 percent of men. Twenty-eight percent of women and 23 percent of men reported overt job discrimination. But whatever the subcategory, the effects of stigma were especially dire for young people, very fat people, and those who started dieting earlier in life.

> Experiencing stigma was positively correlated with BMI [. . .] suggesting that
> as weight increases, more stigma is experienced. [. . .] Individuals who began
> dieting earlier in life reported more stigmatizing situations that people who
> started dieting later. [. . .] Age was negatively associated with stigma, indicat-
> ing that younger individuals reported more stigma than older individuals.[23]

Despite the staggering prevalence of anti-fat stigma, respondents found compelling coping mechanisms, most popularly including heading-off negative remarks, using positive self-talk, and praying. Seventy-nine percent of respondents reported using eating as a coping mechanism, 74 percent isolated themselves, and 41 percent left the situation or avoided it in the future. Rather than motivating fat people to lose weight, weight stigma had led to more isolation, more avoidance, and fewer social and material supports.

Even people who perceive themselves as fat are impacted by anti-fat bias. A 2014 study, "The Ironic Effects of Weight Stigma," studied college women who perceived themselves as fat and those who didn't. Both groups were shown a weight-stigmatizing article and were then sent to a waiting room with candy, chips, and other high-calorie foods. The women who perceived themselves as fat were more likely to partake in the snack foods and to express more concern about being the target of anti-fatness. That is, exposure to anti-fatness increased fat women's likelihood of eating high-calorie foods. Notably, women of all sizes expressed concern about being targeted by anti-fat bias and stigma, though they experienced that fear differently and drew conclusions that directly contradicted the study's findings. "Among those who are not overweight and who have a hard time understanding what it is like to be overweight, stigma feels like it would help strengthen other people's resolve to eat less because it strengthens their own."[24]

But perhaps most tellingly, since the outset of the war on obesity, anti-fat bias has skyrocketed. In her essay "Fat Panic and the New Morality," author and professor Kathleen Lebesco uses sociologist Stanley Cohen's model to argue that the war on obesity has transcended a public health initiative and has transformed into a full moral panic. "Moral panics are marked by concern about an imagined threat; hostility in the form of moral outrage toward individuals and agencies responsible for the problem; consensus that something must be done about the serious threat; disproportionality in reports of harm; and volatility in terms of the eruption of panic."[25] For two decades now, the war on obesity has done just that, spending millions of dollars and spilling gallons of ink looking down its nose at fat people in cold judgment. *Well, you should just change.* And disproportionately, it has targeted its disdain at some of the most vulnerable fat people within its reach—children.

The war on childhood obesity had given up on me, and over time, I learned to give up on myself. At least, that is, until I mustered the willpower to become thin.

I had spent my elementary and middle school years as a member of my neighborhood swim team, eventually rising to the rank of a student coach. I loved everything about swimming: the warm sun and cool water on my skin, and the Lycra racing suit that made me feel like a seal, slick and fast. I loved the strength in what seemed like my body's greatest magic trick: pulling myself through liquid that felt like I was flying. I loved competition too. I was a sometimes-winner, but I loved the bustle and energy of swim meets, the camaraderie of relay races, and the thrilling grace of a quick kick turn. Practices were exhilarating. We'd swim laps for two or three hours at a time and then, when the pool reverted to free swim hours, we'd stay. I'd stay in the water for as long as I could manage, long after my fingerprints became unrecognizable and my blonde hair was tinged green with chlorine. I was certain I was born to be in the water.

My strongest stroke for competition was the most complicated: I swam butterfly. Later, in adulthood, I would find a secret sisterhood of other fat-kid swimmers, all of whom swam the fearsome butterfly. We would reminisce about the feeling of our bodies rising above the surface, then crashing down beneath it, the ache in our arms from half-swimming, half-flying through the water. Our bodies weren't held back by their fat—to the contrary, they were powered by it. The momentum of our fat bodies propelled us forward, harder and faster than other swimmers. Our teammates would comment on our strength and speed. Our fat made us remarkable, though many of us only realized that in adulthood.

As childhood turned into adolescence, all that joy and pride began to slip away. It started slowly, teammates bemoaning the size of their thighs, which were, of course, our power: big thighs allowed us to push off, to dive, to kick, and to win. But as my teammates aged, they learned lessons ahead of me: that only some bodies were suitable to be seen in swimwear, and that those that weren't were obliged to offer explanations and excuses, laments to excuse their unacceptable bodies. Only some bodies were *beach bodies*, and theirs hadn't made the cut. Neither, I learned, had mine.

The locker room became a place for workshopping our bodies, collectively critiquing ourselves and those around us. So, too, did school. Classmates began complaining about any swells in their skin, longing for concave where only convex would appear. Breasts and buttocks were a welcome roundness, within reason, but bellies, thighs, and arms would be openly lamented. In sixth grade, I brimmed with pride as I made the mistake of telling a classmate I belonged to a swim team. She listed a litany of insecurities about her much thinner body and told me all the things she'd heard older girls say about people who are too fat to wear shorts, much less racing suits. *Good for you, I guess*, she told me. *I could never.* That was my last summer on the swim team.

In high school, I found myself in the comfortable darkness of theater class. In years one and two, we focused on acting. Despite auditioning for nearly every production at my tiny high school, I was cast just once: as a maid who says only "yes sir" and "no sir." The fat girl was only fit to serve.

I wondered if I was a bad actor, or if I had been too eager. To this day I do not know. I only know that a thinner girl took it upon herself to explain to me that my auditions weren't longshots—they were impossibilities. Lead roles for women in productions were often love interests, and who could fall for a fat girl? The audience could only extend its imagination so far.

Over time, my interests became defined by the negative space around them. My body wasn't suitable for swimming, so I sang. It wasn't acceptable for acting, so I wrote. Any physical activity in gyms or outdoors was met with outright mockery or pitying, condescending congratulations, so I stayed inside. Even in adulthood, as I moved into political organizing, I insisted on staying out of media, knowing the tidal wave of overt criticism and subtle discrediting that would follow. I refused to be a liability to the movement.

My strengths and passions didn't define my path in life—others' responses to my body did. And over time, those responses built me a cage.

Fat camp wasn't my first foray into weight loss, and it was far from my last. In middle school, my mother brought me to her Weight Watchers meeting. At the tender age of eleven, I had already attended kids' weight-loss programs, kept food diaries, and counted calories. I had honed my skill at eyeballing portions of food, readily spotting the difference between a one-third cup and a one-half cup of blueberries. But despite my best efforts, my stubborn body clung to its fat. And so, I was at Weight Watchers.

I descended the steps of a neighborhood community center, entering a shadowy basement with low ceiling tiles and long fluorescent lights. I stood in line while a "Success Story" weighed each attendee individually, marking our weekly weight in a ledger before ushering us into the meeting room.

I was an outlier—a chubby, pink-cheeked preteen in a room full of fortysomething women. I paid close attention as they spoke, listening not only for their successes and failures but for how adult women talked about their lives. This was a coming-of-age moment. I was being ushered into womanhood through one of its most enduring aspects: the unending, thankless quest to lose weight.

I listened keenly as the world of womanhood unfolded in front of me, women sharing their near-uniform stories of failure or partial success (also experienced as failure). Some wept as they spoke of their lack of willpower and the ways they knew their lives would transform if and when they lost weight. Marriages would rekindle, careers would flourish, lives would blossom into glorious futures. These women, brimming with grief, spoke of the lives that lay ahead of them, gleaming and pristine. If they could just beat their bodies into submission, their lives would change and their problems would melt away. This had been promised: *The thinner, the winner. Nothing tastes as good as skinny feels.*

As a fat kid, Weight Watchers was my primary nutrition education, and it was by way of points calculation. I learned to search food labels for calories, fat, and fiber, ignoring information about vitamins, minerals, sugar content, and more. A dog-eared points slider lived in my Jansport backpack. I memorized a list of "free" foods, reminding myself in my deepest moments of body shame that I could eat as much celery and egg whites as I wanted.

Weight Watchers ushered in a new era in my life just in time for adolescence: one of endless yo-yo dieting, flirting with eating disorders, and a seemingly never-ending war with the body I had always had and the food I always needed. Little did I know that those endless diets would later be shown to cause permanent damage to my metabolism,[26] ensuring a lifetime as a fat person whose efforts to lose weight would prove increasingly futile over time.

Weight Watchers was also my introduction to diet culture, a system of cultural beliefs and practices that equates thinness not just with health, but with moral virtue, and which advocates for weight loss at any cost. Diet culture isn't just a matter of being on a diet, but of the social forces that make dieting (or *lifestyle changes* or *wellness*) culturally mandatory for so many of us. And for decades now, Weight Watchers has been an exemplar of diet culture. In 1963, Joan Nidetch founded Weight Watchers to spread the gospel of the New York City Board of Health diet that had helped her lose weight.[27] Nidetch, a working-class white woman from Queens, had tried diet pills and fad diets before creating the peer support network that she credited with her lasting weight loss. By 1968 the company had gone public, selling out at its initial public offering.[28] At the height of the women's liberation movement and the fight for a proposed Equal Rights Amendment, many women simultaneously decried impossible standards of beauty and femininity and still doggedly pursued the promise of feminine thinness.

In 1978 Nidetch sold the company to the H. J. Heinz Company, which today owns and operates not only the United States' largest ketchup manufacturer but also Kraft Foods, Oscar Mayer, Philadelphia Cream Cheese, Grey Poupon, and diet foods like the paleo-friendly Primal Kitchen, Oprah Winfrey's O, That's Good!, and Weight Watchers–branded foods. By 1999 Heinz had sold its shares of Weight Watchers to a Luxembourg-based investment firm for $735 million but retained its retail line of prepared Weight Watchers foods.[29] As the company's profits flagged in 2018, Weight Watchers introduced a new program offering free six-week memberships to teens between the ages of thirteen and seventeen. The company projected major growth as a result of its teen membership initiative, projecting a 67 percent increase in sales in under four years. Upon the announcement of the new program, shares jumped roughly by 16 percent, according to *CNN Business*.[30]

But like so many weight-loss programs, Weight Watchers (now rebranded as the more wellness-friendly WW) offers not just diet advice, but an induction into diet culture and the weight stigma that bolsters it. As a fat middle schooler, desperate to realize the promise of a more real, thinner life, Weight Watchers further trained me in a belief system that was culturally ubiquitous. It taught me that fat people were incomplete, that food was to be feared and mistrusted, that my body was a failure, and that a life in a body like mine was no life at all. At eleven, I clung desperately to the idea that my body could and would change—that, somehow, I would become thin. Then and only then could my real life begin.

I stayed in Weight Watchers off and on through high school and college. During high school, I took Fen-Phen and Redux, two prescription diet drugs rushed to market. Within a year, the FDA announced a ban on the drugs, prompted by a growing number of reports that these two widely touted miracle drugs caused heart failure in an alarming number of patients. Family members and adult friends groused about the ban. *Sure, it wasn't good for some people, but it was the only thing that worked for me. Now what was I supposed to do—just stay like this?*

During my senior year, I began the Atkins diet, gingerly monitoring which vegetables were low enough in carbs to eat while longing for a cool, sweet cup of strawberry yogurt. I lost a moderate amount of weight before gaining it, and then some, all back.

By the end of high school, I was fatter than ever. With each diet, I would lose a small or moderate amount of weight before gaining it all back, like so many dieters before me. At my high school graduation, I wore a size 24—the largest size offered in my local department store's plus-size section. I couldn't fathom what came after that. I had never seen it. But I knew that even minor weight gain would throw me into the netherworld of clothing and, I assumed, personhood. Who could clothe someone so fat? And who could respect her?

Through all those diets, my body never changed, at least not for long. And my life—real or otherwise—proceeded without me.

It was years before I realized the emperor had no clothes—that dieting rarely worked, if ever, and that some people were just built fat.

For years, strangers, acquaintances, friends, and family alike would shame me in the name of reaching a healthy weight. When they talked about their own diets, they wouldn't refer to weight loss but to getting healthy so that they would no longer be overweight or wouldn't become obese. And like so many before me, I thought of these categories—healthy weight, overweight, obese, morbidly obese, super morbidly obese—as some kind of objective standard of health passed down from up high. They were all rooted in the BMI, the primary tool used to measure each person's size—and, therefore, their health—by doctors, school nurses, and diet programs. The arithmetic of the BMI was simple: weight in kilograms divided by height in meters squared. But it wasn't until I was in college that I learned the bizarre, and racist, roots of the now ubiquitous and deeply flawed BMI.

The BMI was never intended as a measure of individual health. It was developed in the 1830s by a Belgian sociologist, astronomer, and statistician, Lambert Adolphe Jacques Quetelet. Quetelet, in the search for *l'homme moyen*—an idealized average man—took the measurements of different populations over time, searching for some universal average. For Quetelet, "this average man was hardly the 'average' (read 'mediocre') that is our present connotation. [. . .] If the average man were completely determined, we might consider him as the type of perfection; and everything differing from his proportion or condition, would constitute deformity or disease...or monstrosity."[31] That is, *l'homme moyen* was Quetelet's way of determining bodily perfection for the purpose of creating outsider bodies, the contrasting forms that could be proclaimed diseased or disfigured.

The BMI, then eponymously referred to as Quetelet's Index, wasn't used to measure individual health. To the contrary, the calculation was used sociologically, to assess populations overall at a time when sociology, anthropology, and medical science were all rife with racist and misogynist research. Shortly after the development of Quetelet's Index, Samuel Cartwright, a physician, wrote *Diseases and Peculiarities of the Negro Race*, in which he asserted that a new mental illness, drapetomania, was what caused enslaved Africans to flee captivity. In 1869, neurologist George Miller Beard popularized neurasthenia, a "weakness of the nerves" widely diagnosed in women and used by wealthy men to institutionalize their wives. (Neurasthenia remains a diagnosis on record with the World Health Organization to this day, though it is no longer included in the American Psychiatric Association's *Diagnostic and Statistical Manual of Mental Disorders*.) Hysteria, literally meaning uterus madness, stemmed from an ancient Greek belief that uteruses moved freely through the body, eventually inducing disease or causing strangulation.[32] But at the time of Quetelet's work, hysteria was a medical diagnosis typified by anxiety, irritability, and the desire and pursuit of sex.[33] Notably, hysteria was best treated by "genital massage," which led to the invention of the vibrator, initially utilized as a medical treatment to be administered in a doctor's office. Doctors noted that the treatment would be successful upon paroxysm, which was assumed to be purging the body of its uterine insanity.[34]

Later in the same century, Cesare Lombroso, an Italian criminologist and physician, asserted that crime wasn't the work of *Homo sapiens* but the work of a separate species he called *Homo criminalis*, who were marked by the physical features of primates and apes—which he predominantly ascribed to people of color. White scientists in Europe and America focused significant energy on establishing and popularizing diagnoses that specifically marginalized women, people of color, queer people, trans people, poor people, and disabled people, and that underscored what they believed was the inherent supremacy of class-privileged, able-bodied, heterosexual white men.

By the early twentieth century, studies were published linking fatness to poor health outcomes and, in short order, those poor health outcomes found their scapegoats. Anti-fat sentiment, long targeted at white women, quickly became a tool for racism, antisemitism, and xenophobia. In the *Journal of the American Medical Association*, Dr. Elliott Joslin regularly wrote about a purported connection between people of Jewish descent and diabetes, which Joslin attributed to the weight of Jewish people.

> One has only to visit the Jewish quarter of a large Jewish city to be impressed with the frequency of obesity. [. . .] Very likely with the increasing affluence of the Jewish race in this country, permitting indulgence of their well-known fondness for style, obesity will tend to diminish along with diabetes.[35]

Anti-fat bias was also used to police the line of whiteness—that is, which immigrants could be considered white in the United States and which would remain an underclass. That boundary, and the anti-fatness used to reinforce it, often broke along lines of skin tone, painting darker-skinned Southern European immigrants as fatter and, therefore, less white.[36] As the obesity epidemic emerged in the 1990s and early 2000s, anti-fat panic gripped the nation—and it disproportionately targeted Black women. In 2003 the CDC released a report finding higher rates of fatness among Black women. It would later be revealed that, despite higher rates of fatness in Black communities, those rates did not correlate to an increased risk of disease or mortality. That is, Black women were more likely to be fat, but they were not more likely to be sick as a result of being fat. In her indispensable *Fearing the Black Body: The Racial Origins of Fat Phobia*, sociologist Sabrina Strings draws a troubling historical connection. "Since the height of the slave trade and the growth of Protestantism, black women had been symbols of 'savage' aesthetic inclinations and amoral appetites. Now that researchers found that black women had among the highest BMIs in the country, their size was also evidence of disease."[37]

Like so much of the science of the time, Quetelet's Index was rife with problems. Because Quetelet's research largely took place in Western Europe, the index is focused on predominantly white bodies and has repeatedly been shown to be less applicable—or not applicable at all—to people of color. In 2017 *Newsweek* magazine's article "There's a Dangerous Racial Bias in the Body Mass Index" detailed the ways in which people of a "healthy" BMI are assumed not to be at risk for cardiovascular or pancreatic issues, leaving people of Asian descent at a disproportionate risk of undiagnosed heart disease, diabetes, and other illnesses.[38] Similarly, according to the Endocrine Society, the popularization of the BMI as a measure of body fat has led to an overestimation of "obesity" among Black people.[39] Notably, race-informed studies have found that African-American people with an "overweight" BMI have the lowest mortality rates of any BMI category. But then, the BMI isn't a reliable indicator of the fatness or health of people of color—not by accident, but because it was never designed to be.

And, for the most part, Quetelet's Index wasn't used to measure individual health. That is, not until insurance companies got involved. The Metropolitan Life Insurance Company (now known as MetLife) developed an actuarial index to identify "desirable weight" in order to determine what individual policyholders would be charged (presumably so that the company could increase its profits by charging some policyholders more than others).[40] MetLife's charts made no mention of age, gender, or race; it simply identified "desirable weight" based on height and "frame" of the policyholder—"small frame," "medium frame," or "large frame," all of which were undefined. These tools were routinely used by insurers, though they were not based in any medical standard.

Despite its creator's clear direction, the BMI wasn't proposed as a measure of individual body weight until 1972. That's when one researcher, Ancel Keys, published a study asserting that the BMI was a more effective measure of body fat than using calipers or water displacement. "In that paper, Keys and colleagues refer to Quetelet but ironically, despite an extensive bibliography, do not directly reference any of Quetelet's many papers. They also note Quetelet never actually advocated his ratio as any kind of general measure of body 'build' or fat."[41] Despite that, the BMI has since risen to prominence as Western medicine's primary measure of fatness—and fatness has since risen to prominence as its primary indicator of health.

But 1972 wasn't the end of the BMI's strange story. In 1998 the US National Institutes of Health (NIH) redefined BMI categories, significantly lowering the threshold for Americans to be classified as "overweight" or "obese." "Millions of Americans became 'fat' Wednesday—even if they didn't gain a pound," CNN reported at the time. "25 million Americans who weren't fat before, are now. Even under the previous standards, more than half of all adult Americans are overweight."[42] The new NIH standards were hotly debated by healthcare experts, in part because in the two-and-a-half decades since establishing the BMI as a measure of individual health, diagnostic guidelines and prescription regulations had been written to be anchored in the now-shifting BMI categories. A diagnosis of anorexia nervosa required an "underweight" BMI. And risky diet drugs could now be prescribed to people previously considered to be of a "normal weight."

Despite its dubious origins, the BMI has become a cornerstone of healthcare provision in the US. Obesity, as determined by the BMI, serves as an insurance code in and of itself. Fat bodies were reclassified as a disease by the American Medical Association in 2013.[43] Employers host weight-loss challenges and issue bonuses to thinner workers. Whole Foods announced in 2010 that it would offer larger discounts to employees with lower BMIs, blood pressure, and cholesterol.[44] (Paradoxically, thinner employees would be allowed to purchase more food at a lower cost.) Petroleos Mexicanos, Mexico's state-run oil company, announced in 2019 that they would offer more than five million pesos (or $287 USD) to employees with a BMI of less than twenty-five. "The so-called health bonus is a 4.6 percent increase from the last union contract," said *Time*.[45] According to the Kaiser Family Foundation, 50 percent of large employers operate some kind of "wellness program" that disproportionately focuses on monitoring and controlling employees' weight.[46] Whether employees are lifelong thin people doesn't matter to programs like these—fat people are categorically penalized and thinness is rewarded. Today, the BMI isn't just one in a suite of health indicators—for many, it directly determines their wages and their worth.

Despite being designed as a sociological tool to identify shared characteristics of nineteenth-century Belgians, the BMI was now the predominant tool for measuring individual weight. And even 170 years later, an ocean away, where height and weight have both increased, this relic of a measure wasn't just utilized—its thresholds for a "healthy weight" were reduced. When people got bigger in every way, the medical standard for body size got smaller. And just a few years later, Surgeon General Richard Carmona declared a public war on obesity, citing skyrocketing fatness among Americans—all without noting that the goalposts had been significantly moved. Even today, the bulk of the data on the so-called obesity epidemic fails to account for this change in standard, showing a sharp spike in fatness in 1998, as if everyone in the US suddenly gained dozens of pounds.

The BMI's problems aren't just in its past—they ripple throughout our popular cultural understandings of size and health. Our oversimplified conversation about the BMI tricks us into believing that nearly every thin person is healthier than nearly every fat person. Type 2 diabetes, we're told, is reserved for those we see as grotesquely fat, conveniently overlooking the fact that "healthy weight" diabetics have "double the risk of dying from heart disease and other causes than overweight people with type 2 diabetes," according to the *Journal of the American Medical Association* and Harvard Medical School.[47]

Despite alarmist news headlines and rote beliefs about the unhealthiness of fat, even a cursory look into the newest science of weight paints a much more complex picture. While medical guidelines describe fatness as a disease, Dr. Lee Kaplan, director of the Obesity, Metabolism, and Nutrition Institute (OMNI) at Massachusetts General Hospital, says it's not a monolith. "'One focus of research is to figure out how many types of obesity there are—Dr. Kaplan counts 59 so far—and how many genes can contribute. So far, investigators have found more than 25 genes with such powerful effects that if one is mutated, a person is pretty much guaranteed to become obese,' said Stephen O'Rahilly, head of the department of clinical biochemistry and medicine at Cambridge University."[48] With fifty-nine types of obesity and twenty-five contributing genes, *calories in, calories out* can hardly be a "cure" for them all. Still, thanks to our BMI-fueled unforgiving cultural attitudes toward fatness and fat people, we are regularly held to account for the only bodies many of us have ever had.

And perhaps most critically, even the research that does illustrate a compelling correlation between size and specific health conditions doesn't differentiate what the result of having a fat body is and what the result of the social stress of discrimination is. Anti-fat bias has been found in academic research to be a major problem among social workers, nurses, doctors, medical students, and parents.[49] Despite growing evidence to the contrary, we all share a cultural belief that fat bodies are an individual failing that each of us can and must control. Despite a mountain of evidence linking physical and mental health to social discrimination, the conversation about fat and health stubbornly refuses to acknowledge the possible influence of stigma in determining fat people's health. Decreasing stress improves blood pressure and our reactions to stress can significantly increase the risk of high blood pressure, heart attack, stroke, and other medical problems.[50] Some heart attacks are the direct result of sudden emotional stress.[51] And stress hormones, such as cortisol, can influence the endocrine system, which also manages blood sugar levels.[52] Similarly, research on fat health only rarely accounts for the impacts of extreme dieting on individual health—despite ample evidence that diet drugs, for example, can significantly increase blood pressure.[53] A growing body of NIH research, too, illustrates that extreme dieting may permanently damage our metabolisms, in some cases guaranteeing a lifetime of fatness.[54]

The oversimplicity of the BMI has also fed into a ruthless, black-and-white cultural conversation about health and weight loss. The logic goes like this: every thin person is healthier than every fat person, every fat person can become thin if they try hard enough, fat people simply eat too much, and our greed and gluttony have made us fat. As such, size becomes an indicator of character and willpower—and even nefarious intentions. "Americans believe that obesity is tied with cancer as the biggest health threat in the nation today," reported the *New York Times* in 2016. "But though scientific research shows that diet and exercise are insufficient solutions, a large majority say fat people should be able to summon the willpower to lose weight on their own."[55] The *Times* article cites a University of Chicago survey, funded by the American Society for Metabolic and Bariatric Surgery, of over 1,500 Americans about their beliefs about fatness. Ninety-four percent of the fat people surveyed said they had tried dieting and exercise, and that those changes hadn't resulted in weight loss. "Researchers say obesity, which affects one-third of Americans, is caused by interactions between the environment and genetics, and has little to do with sloth or gluttony." According to researchers, environmental causes have a major impact on our size, and include things like where we live, where we can most easily access food, our income level, and the stress we shoulder as a result of the forms of oppression and discrimination we may face. These findings bear little influence on public opinion; still, those surveyed insisted that a fat body was a sign of these venal sins.

In many ways, those unforgiving attitudes make sense in a nation built upon puritanical ideals. Americans have long prided ourselves on a sense of self-reliance: with a little elbow grease and a lot of effort, we can be whatever we want. We tell ourselves that the United States is a classless society, defined not by some rigid class system but of the willingness of individuals to pull themselves up by their bootstraps. America is a meritocracy, we insist, defined by hard work and tenacity, the hallmarks of a true Protestant work ethic. Bodies become a symbol of that work ethic, the American exceptionalism that we have long believed defines Americanness itself. Fat bodies fly in the face of the work ethic that distinguishes us. And, as Paul Campos notes in *The Obesity Myth*, white and class-privileged people's harsh judgment of fat bodies in particular can often serve as a rerouting of the negative attitudes toward poor people and people of color that are no longer acceptable for predominantly wealthy, predominantly white people to voice aloud.

> The feelings of disgust elicited in others by traditional pariah-class individuals do not simply disappear as soon as it becomes unacceptable to express those feelings openly. [. . .] The disgust the thin upper classes feel for the fat lower classes has nothing to do with mortality statistics, and everything to do with feelings of moral superiority engendered in thin people by the sight of fat people. Precisely because Americans are so repressed about class issues, the disgust the (relatively) poor engender in the (relatively) rich must be projected onto some other distinguishing characteristic.[56]

Throughout the twentieth and twenty-first centuries, fat bodies have been repeatedly used as class-related metaphors, both underscoring and complicating Campos's assertions. In the liberal imagination during the era of President Donald Trump, poor fat people are to blame for the president's electoral success, though fat bodies have been used as political metaphors and social scapegoats long before that. In 2019 comedian Bill Maher famously took aim at fat people as scapegoats for America's health insurance woes, insisting that "fat shaming should make a comeback." Throughout the nineteenth and twentieth centuries, wealthy bureaucrats, politicians, and business leaders were referred to as "fat cats," a stark contrast to the lean, hardworking and virtuous proletariat. In books, political cartoons, films, and

TV shows, fat bodies make up the failings of America, of capitalism, beauty standards, excess, and consumerism.

At a time when overt bias is frowned upon, fat people continue to bear the brunt of a proud and righteous kind of prejudice, whether it be under the banner of healthism, ableism, racism, or classism. Whatever its roots, anti-fat bias is only increasing over time, despite a growing body of evidence illustrating the substantial harm it can cause. But instead of confronting our own biases, even when faced by a mountain of evidence to the contrary, we choose to reaffirm them. When we see fat people, we loose all those biases on their bodies and their character. And in the war on childhood obesity, we have made children the site of so much public abuse.

Despite dedicating federal and state funding, launching national public health campaigns, and a slew of television shows, neither the federal war on obesity nor the war on childhood obesity appear to be lowering Americans' BMIs. There are no fewer fat adults or children now than there were twenty years ago, at the outset of this thoughtless war. Since the rewriting of BMI categories in 1998, more Americans have gotten fat: adults have seen a 29.8 percent increase in obesity, while children have seen an increase of 33.1 percent, according to the CDC, as outlined in the graph on the following page. The war on obesity might not be helping—and given those numbers, it might even be hurting.

Despite constant insistence that we lose weight *for our health* and track the simple arithmetic of *calories in, calories out*, there is no data illustrating that dieting achieves long-term weight loss. To the contrary, constant dieting may make weight loss more difficult, as our metabolisms fight back, searching for the stasis of a familiar, fatter body.[57] A major study following contestants from the television show *The Biggest Loser* showed that despite their dramatic weight loss on camera, most contestants were unable to maintain their smaller size, despite hours of working out each day. The study's results were staggering: after their extreme televised dieting, *every* contestant's body burned fewer calories at rest than it did at the beginning of the competition—and one contestant was shown to burn eight hundred fewer calories each day than expected for a peer of the same gender and size.[58] Those results aren't limited to reality TV contestants. As one *Slate* writer put it, addressing dieters, "You'll likely lose weight in the short term, but

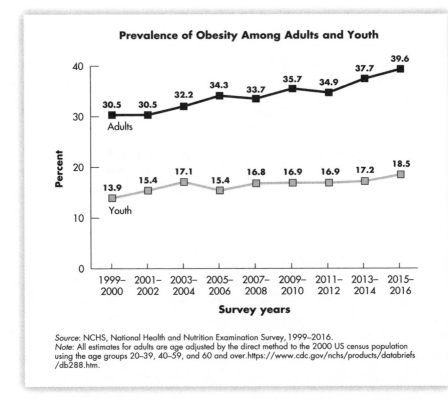

Prevalence of Obesity Among Adults and Youth

Source: NCHS, National Health and Nutrition Examination Survey, 1999–2016.
Note: All estimates for adults are age adjusted by the direct method to the 2000 US census population using the age groups 20–39, 40–59, and 60 and over.https://www.cdc.gov/nchs/products/databriefs/db288.htm.

your chances of keeping it off for five years or more is about the same as your chance of surviving metastatic lung cancer: 5 percent. And when you do gain back the weight, everyone will blame *you*. Including you."[59]

Now, thanks in no small part to the war on childhood obesity, that shame cycle—and its accompanying isolation, health risks, and trauma—starts earlier than ever. If we aren't going to be thin, at least we'll be ashamed.

CHAPTER 3

WHAT THINNESS TAKES

In January 2020, Oprah Winfrey announced a new nationwide tour. Oprah's 2020 Vision: Your Life in Focus tour would include nine stops around the country, from Fort Lauderdale to Denver, St. Paul to Dallas. According to *O, the Oprah Magazine*, the 2020 Vision tour would introduce attendees to "powerhouse leaders in wellness" and "make 2020 the year of transformation for you—mind, body, and spirit." The tour took place in giant arenas, with tickets costing anywhere from $69.50 to $299.99.[1] The all-star guest lineup included Lady Gaga, Tina Fey, Amy Schumer, Michelle Obama, Dwayne Johnson, Tracee Ellis Ross, Kate Hudson, Jennifer Lopez, Gayle King, and Julianne Hough. It was all very *remember your spirit* and precisely what longtime fans look to Oprah Winfrey for: intimate facetime with their favorite celebrities, a sense that personal transformation was possible, and the tools to make their best lives a reality. "This is going to be a day-long party for everyone," said Winfrey.

But despite its messaging of empowerment, the 2020 Vision tour wasn't just Oprah's usual lifestyle leadership. It was presented by WW (formerly Weight Watchers) as part of the rebranding for a struggling company that had fallen out of favor as public opinions of weight-loss diets took a downturn. It was a bold move for a company that, just five years earlier, was "having one of the worst Januaries that anyone could have imagined," according to its senior leadership.[2] By 2019 headlines announced that Weight Watchers "shares crater[ed] 30 percent."[3] Weight Watchers was in trouble, and it needed an infusion of cash and customers.

At the time of the 2020 Vision tour, Winfrey herself owned 8 percent of the company. The tour wouldn't just sell tickets—it would boost the value of Winfrey's then 5.4 million shares in the floundering company.[4]

Like the diet industry before it, this wellness tour would line its shareholders' pockets on multiple levels. And like the diet industry, it didn't promise data-driven, long-term, major weight loss—only anecdotal successes that preyed on members' long-standing sense of failure for simply *having the bodies they have.*

It wasn't the company's first attempt at bolstering sales. In 2019, the company introduced Kurbo, a diet app for children as young as eight. A year earlier, in 2018, Weight Watchers announced that it would offer free membership for teens thirteen to seventeen. In both cases, the backlash from eating-disorder advocates and registered dietitians alike was swift and strong. On Twitter, the response came with a hashtag: #WakeUpWeightWatchers.[5]

> To anyone wondering why we're tweeting about #WakeUpWeight Watchers: Scientific research has shown that putting kids on diets and commenting on their weight puts them at risk of #eatingdisorders and a lifetime of behaviors FAR worse for their health than being at a high weight.
>
> Christy Harrison, MPH, RD
> @chr1styharrison

> The link between dieting & #eatingdisorders is clear and we are concerned about the new @WeightWatchers promotion for teens. Our voices are being heard. They have reached out to us. Stay tuned for updates. #WakeUpWeightWatchers
>
> The National Eating Disorders Association
> @NEDAstaff

Despite this moment of hope, Weight Watchers' Twitter response offered a simple acknowledgment of the controversy, but no change to the program it had introduced.

> Earlier this week, we shared the future vision of Weight Watchers, including some changes we are making to bring health and wellness to

all, not just the few. As part of that, we announced we would open WW
to teens for free. We hear you NEDA and take our responsibility seriously.
We know that the teenage years are a critical life stage and opening WW
to teens with consent from a parent/guardian is about families getting
healthier. What we will be providing for teens is a program that guides
healthy habits for life, not a diet. We have and will continue to talk with
healthcare professionals as we get ready to launch this program.[6]

Like its diet app for children and its free memberships for teens, the
2020 Vision tour aimed to make the company relevant again by boosting
press and memberships. And like its other programs, it illustrated some
troubling aspects of diet culture's transformation into "wellness."

Yes, the 2020 Vision tour trumpeted a holistic approach to wellness and
personal transformation. It offered attendees a workbook, asking them to
identify their goals for "2020 and beyond." At its New Jersey stop, Winfrey
welcomed NYPD officers on stage to congratulate them for their "wellness
transformations," including a video component highlighting those who lost
the most weight. Even as it rebrands itself, diet culture's "wellness transformation" is overt at best and clumsy at worst—a clear search-and-replace
substituted "wellness" for "weight loss."

But more than that, the 2020 Vision tour featured a perplexing set of
celebrity guests for a tour sponsored by a weight-loss company. Guests such
as Jennifer Lopez, Julianne Hough, and Dwayne Johnson owed their celebrity, at least in part, to their thin, muscular bodies. Others, such as Lady
Gaga and Tracee Ellis Ross, had been thin for the entirety of their life in
the public eye. Despite its attempts to build the customer base of a weight-
loss company, the 2020 Vision tour featured precious few people who had
actually lost significant weight. In the world of diet-culture-turned-wellness,
the experience of weight loss doesn't matter. When it comes to evidence of
"wellness," all that matters is *being thin.*

Throughout the publicity for the tour, few remarked on the bizarre dis-
connect of famously thin people selling an approach to weight loss that they'd
likely never experienced. Instead, most of us take up our expected roles as
disciples in the gospel of thinness. In it, bodies like mine are venal sins. Fat
people are morality tales, our bodies feral prophets of the fatness that would
follow any pious thin person who abandoned their vigilance even briefly.

But the 2020 Vision tour was far from the first attempt by the weight-loss industry to align thinness with moral exceptionalism and self-actualization. That perceived moral high ground of thinness was a project in the making for centuries.

Diets and diet drugs have long been a mainstay of American culture. Dating back to the late nineteenth and early twentieth centuries, publishers have offered an endless parade of diet books billed as "reducing guides." Following World War II, weight loss was further popularized through weight loss "salons," such as the national Slenderella chain. (Slenderella now sells diet supplements.)

Diet drugs themselves have long been a constant in the US, especially for women. In the early 1900s, diet pills claiming to be miracle cures flooded the market. "Figuroids" were billed as "the scientific obesity cure" and were marketed alongside pills such as Bile Beans, Gordon's Elegant Pills, and Corpu-lean.[7] Many were laxatives, though others had strikingly dangerous side effects, including "the industrial chemical dinitrophenol, which raises body temperature and can cause blindness. Drugs based on thyroid extract increase the body's rate of energy burning but cause heart problems. Deaths were reported from both."[8] America's obsession with weight loss only strengthened over time. The nation's first amphetamine epidemic was ushered in by the prescribed use of drugs for both psychiatric and weight-loss purposes. Within less than ten years of their introduction, by 1945, amphetamines were in use by over half a million Americans.[9]

By the 1990s the diet industry had become a juggernaut, impervious even to increased consumer protection laws. A 1990 lawsuit against Nutrisystem, a weight-loss meal plan, alleged that the meals had caused gallbladder disease in its customers.[10] By the end of the following year, the diet company had quietly settled with all 199 plaintiffs, and remains on the market today.[11]

Perhaps no story better encapsulates the American fixation with weight loss at any cost than the rise and fall of Fen-Phen and Redux. These twin drugs were widely lauded as miracle drugs throughout the 1990s. Fen-Phen, a shortened name for a fenflurmine-phentermine cocktail, rose to prominence following a 1992 study published in *Clinical Pharmacology &*

Therapeutics.[12] Within a few years, ads for Fen-Phen were everywhere, from *Allure* to *Reader's Digest*.[13] Prescriptions for the much touted miracle drug flooded the market. The popularity of Fen-Phen encouraged manufacturers to push for an accelerated approval by the Food and Drug Administration in 1995. An FDA advisory committee hotly debated the safety of the drug, citing the International Primary Pulmonary Hypertension Study, which linked the drug to "primary pulmonary hypertension, a disease that thickens the capillaries in the lungs and makes breathing very difficult."[14] "What was particularly shocking to me was that on the heels of reporting that this drug caused a fatal, incurable disease in Europe, the company was planning to put it on the American marketplace," says Stuart Rich, who co-authored the pulmonary hypertension study.[15] Despite testimony from Dr. Rich and the opinions of two experts on neurotoxicity, the FDA approved dexfenfluramine in April 1996. "Just three months after the introduction of Redux, doctors are writing 85,000 prescriptions a week," *Time* reported in a cover story titled "The New Miracle Drug?"[16] Ultimately, the drug was approved. Its manufacturer, now known as Wyeth, launched a $52 million marketing campaign and grossed $300 million in 1996 alone.[17] At age fourteen, I was among its eighteen million users.

Just two years later, in August 1997, the *New England Journal of Medicine* published an article by Heidi Connelly, a doctor with the Mayo Clinic, which reported "24 cases of unusual valvular disease in patients taking fenfluramine-phentermine," with some patients seeing onset within just one month of taking the drug. Patients' heart valve problems sometimes required risky and costly heart surgery. In the coming months, another seventy-five cases were reported to the FDA. By the end of 1997, Wyeth had withdrawn both drugs from the market. A 2003 *Forbes* article reported that the company had paid $13 billion in settlements for heart problems caused by Fen-Phen and Redux.[18] When the drugs were removed from the market, a family friend sighed. "Sure, they caused trouble for some people," she said woefully, referring to patients' heart failure, "but they were the only thing that really *worked*."

Many Americans were willing to try *anything* to lose weight, including drugs. While amphetamines are less present in today's diet landscape, laxatives have become increasingly popular, with A-list celebrities like Kim Kardashian and Cardi B endorsing products like "flat tummy tea," a laxative that causes temporary weight loss.

Americans have long sought miracle diet foods, too, longing for the al-chemical power to turn food into weight loss. Nutrisystem and Jenny Craig gained popularity in the 1980s by focusing on providing precooked, pre-packaged meals designed to provide dieters with an easy way to manage their food intake—and to build corporate profits. Brands like SnackWell's promised low-fat cookies and desserts, replacing their then-demonized fat content with staggering amounts of sugar. The 1990s saw the introduction of Olestra, then celebrated as a miracle ingredient that could make potato chips "fat free." What consumers didn't know was that Olestra wasn't fat free—it was a kind of fat so saturated that the human body couldn't digest it. As such, the FDA required, in a 1996 ruling, that Olestra products be labeled with a warning that it "may cause abdominal cramping and loose stools (anal leakage)." Later, scientists found that consumption of Olestra potato chips led to greater weight gain than traditional potato chips.[19] Like so many miracle weight-loss products, Olestra had proven to be a mirage.

Despite decades of trying (and failing) to lose weight, Americans still line up for self-proclaimed miracle drugs and foolproof diets. Since the 1990s, we have known about the dismal success rates of weight-loss programs of all stripes. A wide range of mainstream scientific and medical studies have demonstrated, time and time again, the ineffectiveness of dieting to lose weight. Some studies indicate a weight-loss failure rate of 95 percent, while others paint an even more dismal picture, with 98 percent of dieters failing to lose weight and failing to keep it off.[20] Studies based on twins show that genetics could account for as much as 80 percent of a person's size.[21] One landmark study, published in 1986 in the *New England Journal of Medicine*, found that adopted children overwhelmingly ended up with body types like their birth parents—despite being raised by a family with different body types who predominantly shaped their eating and exercise habits.[22] Others show that the body *defends* against weight loss by significantly slowing the metabolism.[23, 24] A handful of studies have found more favorable conclu-sions for dieting (or other nonsurgical weight-loss methods) that have since been found to be bankrolled by diet pill manufacturers, diet food delivery services, and other corporations that stood to profit from more dramatically advantageous findings.[25] Despite their questionable origins, bankrolled diet industry studies have been published in the *New England Journal of Medicine*, the *Journal of the American Medical Association*, and other prominent and well-regarded medical journals.[26]

Not only is long-term weight loss extremely unlikely, dieting for weight loss may actually be hazardous to our health. What we have long considered the health conditions associated with being fat in actuality may be the effects of long-term dieting, which very fat people are pressured heavily to do. One Yale University study found that adult women (ages eighteen to forty-nine) who have used common, over-the-counter appetite suppressants faced a 1,558 percent increased risk for hemorrhagic stroke.[27] Even in the absence of appetite suppressants, weight cycling—that is, a history of gaining and losing significant amounts of weight, sometimes referred to as yo-yo dieting—has been associated with an increased risk of heart disease and cardiac arrest in women,[28] and an increased risk of death regardless of gender.[29] Still, given the US's cultural obsession with the societal war on obesity and the individual battle of the bulge, weight cycling has become a way of life for most Americans and a cultural mandate for those of us who are fat by every measure. Despite extraordinarily small odds of success and a lack of proven nonsurgical methods for safe and lasting weight loss, Americans remain fixated on the dogged pursuit of a near-impossibility, a nation of Don Quixotes tilting at windmills.

Dieting doesn't work, nor do diet drugs, but they do contribute to a growing wave of eating disorders in the US and worldwide. According to the Center for Eating Disorders at Sheppard Pratt in Baltimore, "Dieting is the most common precipitating factor in the development of an eating disorder. [. . .] Restrictive dieting is not effective for weight loss and is an unhealthy behavior for anyone, especially children and adolescents. For individuals who are genetically predisposed to eating disorders, dieting can be the catalyst for heightened obsessions about weight and food."[30] The National Association of Anorexia Nervosa and Associated Disorders report that a minimum of "30 million people of all ages suffer from an eating disorder in the U.S."[31] and roughly once an hour "at least one person dies as a direct result from an eating disorder."[32] A total of 0.9 percent of American women will have anorexia nervosa in their lifetime and 1.5 percent will have bulimia nervosa, while 2.8 percent of Americans of all genders will have binge eating disorder at some point in their lives, though these numbers are limited by reporting structures.[33] For example, estimates may only reflect people who have health insurance that covers eating disorder treatment, those who have enough awareness and support to seek that treatment, and those who are willing to acknowledge that treatment to researchers. For thinner people, these disordered behaviors are cause for a caring kind of concern, immediate treatment, and lasting emotional support. But for fat people, they are cause for a cold kind of congratulations, a carrying out of our duty to become thin at any cost. When you're fat, restrictive eating is a cultural mandate, which consequently means that many fat peoples' eating disorders go undiagnosed and untreated. Adolescents with BMIs in the overweight or obese ranges make up a significant slice of young people with eating disorders, but those disorders frequently take years longer to be identified and treated in fat patients than in thin ones.[34] Even the diagnosis for anorexia nervosa requires an underweight BMI of seventeen or lower, relegating fat anorexics to a lesser known diagnosis of atypical anorexia and reinforcing the idea that fat people simply cannot have restrictive eating disorders—that is, not until we're thin.

In recent years, as "wellness" has come to replace "dieting," it's created the potential for more thoughtful, anchored conversations about size, eating, and health. But as "health" has come to take the place of "thinness" in the search-and-replace of diet culture, little has changed. The world of "wellness" doesn't address "dieting"; it instead refers to "cleanses" and "detoxes" while using the same restrictive practices and pseudoscience to claim untenable and unrealistic weight-loss goals. The wellness industry, far-reaching and ill-defined, includes trends as wide ranging as athleisure, essential oils, "wellness real estate," "wellness tourism," and even Weight Watchers. As of 2018 its worth is estimated to be a staggering $4.5 trillion worldwide.[35] With these cultural changes has come an emerging new eating disorder diagnosis: *orthorexia*. The term, coined in 1998, refers to an obsessive focus on "healthy eating," often marked by an increasingly specific and restrictive set of rules. Though orthorexia has yet to be codified in the *Diagnostic and Statistical Manual*, advocacy organizations and treatment centers have embraced it as a growing concern within the eating disorder community. According to the National Eating Disorder Association, symptoms include the following:

+ Compulsive checking of ingredient lists and nutritional labels
+ An increase in concern about the health of ingredients
+ Cutting out an increasing number of food groups (all sugar, all carbs, all dairy, all meat, all animal products)

+ An inability to eat anything but a narrow group of foods that are deemed "healthy" or "pure"
+ Unusual interest in the health of what others are eating
+ Spending hours per day thinking about what food might be served at upcoming events
+ Showing high levels of distress when "safe" or "healthy" foods aren't available
+ Obsessive following of food and "healthy lifestyle" blogs on Twitter and Instagram
+ Body image concerns that may or may not be present[36]

As diet culture disguises itself, shapeshifting into a more palatable "wellness" approach with the same old goals, orthorexia emerges as its corollary eating disorder. At a time when cleanses and detoxes are increasingly de rigueur, orthorexia often manages to fly under the radar, masquerading as an understandable and even laudable concern for health. But as with so many eating disorders, it is hardly so benign. For each of these eating disorders, genetics are significant contributors, often accounting for 50 percent or more of the risk of a given eating disorder.[37] Genetics are the gun, and for many, dieting is its trigger.

Even as the language of weight loss changes from *dieting* to *wellness*, consumers remain vulnerable to unscrupulous claims for dietary supplements that are significantly less regulated than prescription drugs. One 2011 survey by the Federal Trade Commission, which is charged with regulating accurate advertising, found that more Americans had fallen prey to false weight-loss advertising than any other kind of fraud tracked by the Commission.[38]

Dr. Mehmet Oz, whose television career got an early boost from weight-loss evangelist Oprah Winfrey, has made frequent and sweeping proclamations about the effectiveness of weight-loss supplements on his daily afternoon talk show. At first blush, Dr. Oz seems like a perfect, impartial source for accurate weight-loss information: a cardiothoracic surgeon, Columbia University professor, with a bachelor's degree from Harvard and an MD and MBA from the University of Pennsylvania. Oz became a mainstay on television in 2003 when *Second Opinion with Dr. Oz* premiered with Oprah Winfrey as the show's first guest. In 2009 he became a phenomenon with a syndicated, daily network health talk show, *The Dr. Oz Show*, where he regularly recommended supplements and treatments to his viewing audience and frequently focused on the obesity epidemic, the dangers of fatness, and remedies for it.

In 2016, those claims caught up to him, and Dr. Oz was called to testify in front of the US Senate's Subcommittee on Manufacturing, Trade, and Consumer Protection for his constant endorsements. Dr. Oz was a longtime proponent of green coffee extract, leading to a boom in production of the supplement.

> Within weeks of Dr. Oz's comments about green coffee—which refers to the unroasted seeds or beans of coffee—a Florida-based operation began marketing a dietary supplement called Pure Green Coffee, with claims that the chlorogenic acid found in the coffee beans could help people lose 17 pounds and cut body fat by 16 percent in 22 weeks. [. . .] [T]he Federal Trade Commission sued the sellers behind Pure Green Coffee and accused them of making bogus claims and deceiving consumers.[39]

Press coverage of the doctor's appearance on Capitol Hill led with splashy headlines: "The 'Dr. Oz Effect': Senators Scold Mehmet Oz for Diet Scams," trumpeted NBC News;[40] "Watch Congress Make 'An Example Of' Dr. Oz," read *Business Insider*;[41] "Senators to Dr. Oz: Stop Promising Weight-Loss Miracles," said *The Atlantic*.[42] And true to the headlines, Senator Claire McCaskill took the doctor to task.

> McCaskill read Oz's words from past segments of *The Dr. Oz Show* back to him with a clinical formality that underscored their absurdity:
>
> "You may think magic is make-believe, but this little bean has scientists saying they've found the magic weight loss cure for every body type: It's green coffee extract."
>
> "I've got the number-one miracle in a bottle to burn your fat: It's raspberry ketone."
>
> "Garcinia cambogia: It may be the simple solution you've been looking for to bust your body fat for good."
>
> McCaskill continued, as if reproaching a child. "I don't know why you need to say this stuff, because you know it's not true. Why—when you have this amazing megaphone and this amazing ability to communicate—would you cheapen your show by saying things like that?"[43]

Despite broad coverage and damning admissions, Dr. Oz's questioning on Capitol Hill doesn't appear to have shifted Americans' consciousness or our buying habits when it comes to diet products. Weight-loss supplement Hydroxycut remains in business despite class-action lawsuits and consumer deaths.[44] While diet pill sales are down, meal replacements and other weight-loss products are up, leaving the industry worth $72 billion in the US alone in 2019.[45] By the end of 2023, researchers predict, the global weight-loss market will be worth a staggering $278.95 billion worldwide.[46] Despite overwhelming evidence to the contrary, American consumers seem too desperate for a miraculous, lasting weight-loss solution, and many of us are willing to pay top dollar for even moderate weight loss. No matter how damning the evidence against it, the weight-loss industry remains a juggernaut. It may just be too big to fail.

This cultural obsession with weight loss doesn't just impact our physical and mental health; it also impacts our sense of self and, consequently, our relationships with others of different sizes. Women of all ages report astronomical levels of body dissatisfaction, ranging from a low of 71.9 percent of women ages seventy-five and up to a high of 93.2 percent of women between the ages of twenty-five and thirty-four.[47] According to a survey conducted by Yale University's Rudd Center for Food Policy and Obesity, nearly half of respondents would rather give up a year of their lives than be fat.[48] "The 4,000 respondents in varying numbers between 15% and 30% also said they would rather walk away from their marriage, give up the possibility of having children, be depressed, or become alcoholic rather than be obese."

But our insecurities don't stop at our own skin. The ways in which straight-size people see fat people are increasingly limited by their own insecurity. In body positive spaces, for example, thin people will often struggle to hear fat people's stories of discrimination. The concrete, external harms of anti-fatness are often reframed and reinterpreted as insecurity by thinner people, especially women. After all, thinner women simply aren't subjected to the same levels of societal prejudice, harassment, bullying, and overt discrimination as fatter people. As such, *feeling insecure* is among the worst things many thinner women can imagine, so many interpret fat people's stories of *explicit, interpersonal,* or *institutional anti-fatness* as *insecurity*. The phenomenon of repackaging a fat person's discrimination as a more palatable, more understandable kind of internal struggle with body image is one I've come to refer to as *thinsecurity*.

Thinsecurity-driven misinterpretations of fat activism are constants. Frequently, when I share my experiences with thinner people, I'm met with a confidential nod and a misplaced sense of shared experience. I'll tell a thin man about my experience being reseated on a plane, and he'll say, "I get it. We all have our insecurities." A thin woman will meet my story about a stranger shouting slurs at me with a hand over her heart. "Bad body image days are the *worst*." Thinsecurity is a seductive thing. It tells thin people that *feeling badly about one's own body* is the worst—and only—outcome of difficult experiences with our bodies. They cannot fathom what are such commonplace experiences for very fat people: A stranger recommending a surgeon. A family member withholding food *until you look like you need it*. Fat camp. Being recommended for *The Biggest Loser*. And on and on and on. Those experiences are too far from their own, unimaginable to someone who has so long been locked in place by their perception of their own body. So straight size people reinterpret them, make them something easier to understand. Rather than talking about body-based oppression, they revert the conversation to their thinsecurities.

But the misinterpretation doesn't stop there. When fat activists talk about body-based oppression, thinner body positivity activists paint it over, replacing it with a more palatable *insecurity*. But when we don't talk about body-based oppression, we're strangely lauded for our *confidence*.

"You're so brave to wear that," a stranger tells me at a bus stop. "I wish I had your confidence. Get it, girl!"

I am covered from head to toe in a purple knit cotton dress with a high neckline and a knee-length hem. Beneath it, I wear opaque tights and boots. By any measure, I am dressed conservatively and, frankly, unremarkably. But thinsecurity has rerouted the way this stranger sees me. She cannot imagine living in a body like mine, cannot imagine being seen in public, cannot imagine daring to leave the house in skin that is so obviously and objectively hideous. She imagines that I am wildly insecure and in desperate need of immediate comfort. And so, without asking about my experience, she offers an unsolicited compliment for braving the fear she's mapped onto my scrim of a body: *You're so brave. I wish I had your confidence.*

Sometimes, those compliments—meant to assuage unconfirmed insecurities—don't end with a simple, awkward remark. Increasingly, strangers, friends, and family will enlist me in the work of breaking down their own insecurities, often without my consent. Thin people—especially thin women—expect fat people like me to act as midwives for their confidence. *How do you do it? Teach me your ways!* They expect fat women in particular to become midwives for their waning self-confidence. We are the hired help who never asked for the job and are certainly not paid for it. We are expected to accompany thinner friends to stores that do not carry our sizes, watching as they try on clothing that makes them feel insecure and boosting their confidence with constant reassurances. We become set pieces, two-dimensional props for their more real lives. More than that, we reflect their bodies back to them, their imperfect thinness made beautiful by its proximity to the abject failure of our fatness. We are reminders of what could be. Thinner people embrace fatter people as a way of finding their relative virtue. *At least I'm not* that *fat.*

Thinness is a bizarre and alienating construct. Plus size or straight size, seemingly none of us believe that we qualify for the distant perfection of thinness. Straight-size people do verbal acrobatics to avoid describing themselves as thin, opting instead for scare quotes around words like *slim* and *average*, while simultaneously endlessly dieting to realize the promise of the impossible thinness that is just out of reach. Plus-size people forgo even the cold comfort of proximity to thinness and are left to fend for ourselves in a world that tells us that our bodies, hopelessly and irredeemably fat, cannot be named and cannot be saved. Thinness takes from all of us.

Thinness takes so much from so many straight-size people. It takes their money for diet pills, meal delivery, workout tapes, and weight-loss supplements. It takes away their ability to see their own bodies as they are, replacing that image with some distorted funhouse mirror reflection—and in so doing, it takes so much of their self-esteem along with it. It takes away interesting conversation, relegating us to the rote and interminably boring script of weight loss: who's on what diet, who was *good*, who was *bad*. Thinness takes away so many straight-size people's ability to hear fat people, to acknowledge our experiences even when they differ from those of straight-size listeners. And when it takes away our ability to hear one another, it slowly erodes straight-size people's relationships with fat family members, friends, colleagues, and others, quarantining core conversations as off-limits and forever maintaining an unspoken and uneasy distance.

Thinness takes so much from fat people too. It takes away those same relationships with thinner people, teaching us that we will never truly be heard or understood. It takes away our ability to describe our own bodies, replacing our own descriptions with something thin people can understand—something that makes them feel comfortable, less threatened, and less privileged. And when it takes away our descriptions of our own bodies, it also takes away our ability to describe our own experiences and know that they'll be heard on their own terms. It takes away quiet, everyday activities too: eating, working out, buying groceries, and shopping for clothes all become seen as unspoken invitations to comment on our bodies, our practices, the weight loss in which we must be in hot pursuit.

All of us deserve better than what thinness takes. We deserve a new paradigm of health: one that acknowledges its multifaceted nature and holds t-cell counts and blood pressure alongside mental health and chronic illness management. We deserve a paradigm of personhood that does not make size *or* health a prerequisite for dignity and respect. We deserve more places for thin people to heal from the endless social messages that tell them at once that their bodies will never be perfect enough to be beautiful and simultaneously that their bodies make them inherently superior to fatter people. We deserve spaces for thin people to build their self-confidence with one another so that the task no longer falls to fat people who are already contending with widespread judgment, harassment, and even discrimination. We deserve more spaces for fat people too—fat-specific spaces and fat-only spaces, where we can have conversations that can thrive in specificity, acknowledging that our experiences of external discrimination are distinct from internal self-confidence and body image issues (though we may have those too). We deserve those separate spaces so that we can work through the trauma of living in a world that tells all of us that our bodies are failures—punishing thin people with the task of losing *the last ten pounds* and fat people with the crushing reality of pervasive social, political, and institutional anti-fatness.

We deserve more spaces to think and talk critically about our bodies *as they are*, not as we wish they were, or as an unforgiving and unrealistic culture pressures them to change. We deserve spaces and movements that allow us to think and talk critically about the messages each of us receive about our bodies—both on a large scale, from media and advertising, and on a small scale, interpersonally, with friends and family. But we can only do this if we acknowledge the differences in our bodies and the differences in our experiences that spring from bodies. We deserve to see each other as we are so that we can hear each other. And the perfect, unreachable standard of *thinness* is taking that from us.

Thinness takes so much, and we deserve to take it back.

CHAPTER 4

ON CONCERN AND CHOICE

It happened at the grocery store.

It had been a busy week and I was looking forward to decompressing by way of my weekly meal prep. There was something meditative in listening to a new record while my hands did the tender work of cleaning, peeling, chopping. There's a mindfulness necessary for cooking—should my anxious mind wander to the challenges at work or the housework left to be done, I might overcook the pasta, burn the temperamental maple syrup roasting on squash, let a sharp blade slice into my own soft flesh. I had to pay attention, had to breathe deeply and stay focused on the task at hand, so I did. It was a welcome relief.

At the grocery store, I happily wound through aisles and refrigerated cases. I spent the most time in the produce section, picking emerald zucchini from pristine piles, papery purple shallots, and perfumed cantaloupe from atop a pyramid display. As I shopped, I noticed another woman stealing glances at my cart, then my face. Like many people in my neighborhood, she was a baby boomer—in her sixties, white, and with the trappings of class privilege popular in a city that eschewed displays of wealth. She looked like many of the parents from the private high school I'd attended on a faculty discount. Her clothing was expensive without being flashy, her graying hair was cropped into a short, straightforward haircut I recognized from so many of my mother's friends. In the Pacific Northwest of my childhood and young adulthood, money didn't call attention to itself.

As I moved on, her cart followed mine, her glances turning to stares. I smiled, hoping to nudge her into looking away, but her eyes were no longer on me. Instead, they were fixed on my cart, her brows now stitched together as she openly stared. I turned away from my cart to pull spinach from the refrigerated case. When I turned back, she was plucking the cantaloupe from my cart. Her eyes met mine and she smiled.

"It's got too much sugar for you, and that's the last thing you need," she said happily. Her voice chirped, buoyed by the self-satisfaction of doing such a good deed for a stranger who so clearly needed her help. She turned away with my melon in her hand and returned it to its display, and then she was gone.

I retreated to the baking aisle, pretending to peruse dry spices while I gathered myself and waited for her to leave the small market. I was stunned. Over time, I had become used to long glances, open stares, suggestions, and mandates about my food. I had grown accustomed to catcalls and street harassment. I had come to expect open commentary on what I ate, how much, and how often. But never had I encountered someone who thought to take physical control of what I was eating—much less a *fruit*—and, more than that, to so clearly think it was a service to me. I wondered if, in the BMW X5 I imagined her driving, she had taped a "my body, my choice" sticker in the rear window.

As the shock wore off, something wilder emerged: a deep and sudden anger. I simmered with frustration and resentment as I drove home, uncertain how to manage such an untamed and foreign reaction. I knew how to handle tears, melancholy, resignation—but what to do with such fresh, live rage writhing so violently in my chest?

The anger stayed with me all day. That evening, I told a friend over drinks.

"Are you sure?" the friend asked, face tangled with skepticism. "Maybe she thought it was her cart."

"She didn't. It was mine."

"She could've made a mistake."

"Then why would she explain that I don't need more sugar?"

"Maybe she was leading by example—like, 'hey, neither one of us needs more sugar, so I'm putting mine back.'"

"That's not any less condescending," I snapped, voice cracking under the weight of my frustration, anger rising through my shoulder blades once again.

"But you have to understand, it's coming from a good place," my friend pleaded, now gesturing with willowy fingers and delicate wrists. "She was just concerned for your health."

There it was—the salt on such a fresh wound. I was frustrated, deflated, exhausted, and done. So much of my experience as a very fat person had been defined by others' bias against bodies like mine. And when it came from those closest to me, even the most explicit judgment was reliably shielded by a missionary claim of *concern for my health.*

As a fat person, I have faced constant judgment, harsh rejection, and invasive questions, which always close with the same stale phrase: *I'm just concerned for your health. I'm concerned for your health,* so I have to tell you, again and again, that you're going to die. *I'm concerned for your health,* so I have to tell you that no one will love you at your size. *I'm concerned for your health,* so I cannot treat you with basic respect.

But those conversations rarely bear the hallmarks of concern. Concern is curious, tender, loving. Concern is direct and heartfelt. Concern does its work delicately, with great care. It looks after the people we hold dear. Concern is rooted in love—not, as in so many of these conversations, rooted in power, paternalism, and open contempt.

Concern for fat people is understandable. Every day, local and national news coverage features stories about the obesity epidemic, accompanied by footage of disembodied fat torsos, presuming that showing our faces—like real people, with real lives—would cause too much shame. After all, who could bear to be seen in a body like ours? Concern has been proposed everywhere, time and time again, as an appropriate and even virtuous reaction to the scourge of bodies like mine. But concern—true concern—shows itself vulnerably. It does not insist upon itself, shouting down the din around it. Concern asks tenderly, walks softly. Concern brings the soft brushes of an archeological dig, not a steamroller to pave over what lies beneath. Concern thrives on love, not shame and preening schadenfreude.

Fat people—especially very fat people, like me—are frequently met with screwed-up faces insisting on *health* and *concern.* Often, we defend ourselves by insisting that concerns about our health are wrongheaded, rooted in faulty and broad assumptions. We rattle off our test results and hospital records, citing proudly that we've never had a heart attack, hypertension, or diabetes. We proudly recite our gym schedules and the contents of our refrigerators. Many fat people live free from the complications popularly associated with their bodies. Many fat people don't have diabetes, just as many fat people do have loving partners despite common depictions of us. Although we are not thin, we proudly report that we are happy and we are healthy. We insist on our goodness by relying on our health. But what we mean is that we are tired of automatically being seen as sick. We are exhausted from the work of carrying bodies that can only be seen as doomed. We are tired of being heralded as dead men walking, undead specters from someone else's morality tale.

These defensive assertions about our health aren't wrong, but they don't reflect every fat person's reality. Some of us aren't healthy or able-bodied. Some of us struggle with chronic illness, mental health issues, eating disorders, disabilities, abuse. Some of us have hypertension, diabetes, heart disease. For these fat people, *happy and healthy* is an alienating aspiration and an unreliable narrator of our bodies. And even when we are *happy and healthy*, we're still met with the high-minded bullying of *concern*.

In recent years, Lizzo has emerged as a new kind of pop star, one whose body of work focuses on loving, accepting, and celebrating herself. Lizzo's presence on the national stage has been enthusiastically embraced, a welcome counterpoint to decades of celebrities who only fit (or strive to fit) an ever-narrowing standard of beauty that is almost always predicated on thinness.

But Lizzo's rise as the world's most prominent plus-size pop star has met more than its share of backlash too. And despite her focus on music, the majority of backlash has taken aim at her body. In 2019 *The Biggest Loser* trainer Jillian Michaels discussed Lizzo's body on *BuzzFeed*'s morning show, *AM2DM*. When host Alex Berg brought up her own excitement at seeing "women like Ashley Graham and Lizzo, who are preaching self-acceptance," Michaels quickly cut in. "Why are we celebrating her body? [. . .] 'Cause it isn't gonna be awesome if she gets diabetes. I'm just being honest. I love her music, my kid loves her music, but there's never a moment where I'm like, 'I'm so glad that she's overweight.' Like, why do I even care? Why is it my job to care about her weight?"[1] Berg had not asked Michaels to "care about her weight" or "celebrate her body"—she hadn't even finished her question. Michaels, largely unbidden, asserted herself as the authority on the body of a woman she had never met. In that moment, she became one of the country's most famous concern trolls.

The response to Michaels's remarks was swift. "Unless Jillian Michaels is holding a chart of Lizzo's bloodwork, she has no business speculating what diseases the pop singer is at risk of developing," wrote *Chicago Tribune* columnist Heidi Stevens.[2] Actor and activist Jameela Jamil tweeted, "MY WHOLE DAMN THIN FAMILY HAS DIABETES AND HIGH CHOLESTEROL AND PROBLEMS WITH OUR JOINTS. Why is this woman acting like she's an MRI? Stop concern-trolling fat people and get in the bin." One viral tweet described Lizzo's nightly show as "an incredible athletic feat." "Try running 7MPH in heels on a treadmill clearly singing the words to Truth Hurts without sounding out of breath. Stop halfway to play the flute for a minute. Now start running again and finish the song. Now do this for two hours."[3]

When called upon to respond to the backlash, Michaels doubled down. "I'm a health expert. For decades I have said repeatedly that your weight and your size have no bearing or merit on your value, your beauty, your worth, your ability. Where it does have relevance is *your health*. To pretend that it doesn't is not only irresponsible, it's dangerous—and it's just not a lie that I'm willing to tell because it's politically correct."[4] Despite these recent claims of body positivity, Michaels has made a career out of asserting that fat people are failures, as witnessed by her "tough love" physical training on *The Biggest Loser*. In 2016 *The Guardian* reported on Michaels's behavior under the headline "It's a Miracle No One Has Died Yet" and included direct quotes from Michaels from past seasons of the show:

> "I don't care if people die on this floor. You better die looking good."

> "If you don't run, I will pull Alex on the floor and I will break every bone in his body."

> "The only way you're coming off this damn treadmill is if you die on it!"

> "It's fun watching other people suffer like that."[5]

Michaels's unbidden comments on Lizzo's body illuminate a simple, difficult truth: that no amount of *health* or *happiness* will deliver our humanity, our dignity, or a safe haven from abuse. Whoever we are, however our bodies came to be, *health* does not deliver us from the well-intentioned bullying of *concern*. Our delivery from concern lies only with the stranger who asks about diabetes or the acquaintance who recommends bariatric surgeons. The family member who believes we will never find a partner because *who could love a body like ours*. The coworker who offers diet advice that's never been requested. The friends who complain over breakfast about a friend's size. The person who removes groceries from a fat stranger's cart. Our delivery from concern lies with you.

We don't often ask ourselves what our response to fatness says about us, but it says so much about our empathy and our character. We spend so much time examining fat bodies in front of us that we fail to examine our response to them. We learn not to feel the heat and pressure that so many fat people face, and in so doing, we ignore our contributions to it. We can't understand how our actions undercut our love for the fat people in our lives.

No, we don't often ask those questions. Instead, we push away examinations of ourselves in favor of *health* and *concern*. Instead, we avoid saying *fat*. Instead, we defend those who hurt the people we love, insisting on their steamroller of *concern*. Instead, we push aside the hard work of empathy and opt for the ease and satisfaction of judgment. Instead, we take comfort in thinness, believing it to be a sign of mastery and will. Instead, we walk away from the bigger question: In sickness and health, who do you want to be?

Instead of looking at yourself, you look at me.

Concern for your health is a cardinal sign that a fat person is experiencing what's often referred to as concern trolling. Concern trolls are a different breed than the gleeful Redditors and 4chan users who so often hunt women, people of color, fat people, autistic people, and disabled people for sport. Concern trolling is defined more by its impact than its intent—many concern trolls would balk at being described as trolls at all. Rather than "playing devil's advocate" or directly provoking marginalized people, concern trolls position themselves as sympathetic supporters who "just have a few concerns." Concern trolls are experts at erecting strawmen, insisting that they *want* to be supportive, as if their support is a vote a marginalized person needs to win. Concern trolls tell people of color that they'll *never win anyone over if they're so angry all the time*. They insist on making sure transgender people are *really sure about transitioning, because you know it's not reversible, right? I just don't want you to do something you'll regret.* As if the humanity of marginalized people is a campaign and we've put our own experiences up for debate. As if our hurt, harm, and trauma were simply *fair game.*

But that's just one form that the well-intentioned bullying of concern trolling takes in the lives of fat people. Concern trolls are shapeshifters, changing their arguments and excuses to evade both accountability and direct conversations. Concern trolls talk about *tough love* as they withhold food, clothing, affirmation, love in the name of pressuring a fat person into thinness. They imagine our bodies as coal and that their pressure will make us diamonds. Concern trolls lament our size, offering compliments only with judgmental caveats attached. *You've got such a pretty face. If only you'd lose some weight.* Their eyes follow our fork from our plate to our mouth and back again, sometimes even freely commenting on what we eat, whether we eat, and how much. When challenged, many become defensive, even indignant. *I'm just trying to help.* Food surveillance and policing are especially insidious and pernicious tactics of many concern trolls.

For many fat people, concern trolling doesn't end at overt comments about our food, size, or perceived motivation. Sometimes, that concern turns into invasive, deeply personal cross-examinations that I've come to call *thinterrogations.* Some thinterrogations are confined to dieting. *Have you tried paleo? What about keto? Did you track your macros? Did you work out? Did you cut out bread? Did you cheat? You must have been sneaking sugar. You probably aren't doing it right.* Others become deeply intimate, with thinterrogators asking after the trauma they're certain must be at the root of my size. *Were you abused? Molested? When did it happen? How? Are you in therapy? Is it comfort eating? I'm an emotional eater, too, and here's how I beat it. Have you tried Overeaters Anonymous? EMDR?* These trauma voyeurs, often strangers or acquaintances, have invented an etiology of my body: a troubled past, a mental or experiential defect that has led me to maladaptive behavior. A fat body must be the result of some tragedy. A fat body is deviant, aberrant, troubling. A fat body can never simply *be.* A fat body must be explained, and thinterrogators *just ask what everyone's thinking.*

Whatever the behavior—strawman debates, food policing, trauma voyeurism, "tough love," or "motivation"—concern trolling relies on the logic and tactics of abuse. Concern trolling tells fat people that whatever befalls us is our fault and that no thin person can be held accountable for their own behavior when faced with the sight of a fat person's body. It tells fat people that concern trolls *wouldn't have to hurt you if you didn't make me.* Concern trolling is the trojan horse of anti-fatness, seductively telling thinner people that everything they're doing is *for a fat person's own good.*

The simple fact, though, is that concern harms fat people. It wrests our bodies from our control, insisting that thin people know our bodies best and that, like a car accident or child abuse, fatness requires a mandatory report. As if fat people don't know that we're fat, and that fatness is at once reviled and luridly surveilled.

Nearly all academic and scientific research that has looked for a link between weight stigma (including concern trolling) and ill health has found it. One such study, published in *Obesity: A Research Journal,* asked a predominantly white group of 1,013 women about their experiences with weight stigma and stereotypes of fat people. People who had internalized anti-fat stereotypes were more likely to binge eat, and neither believing anti-fat stereotypes nor directly experiencing stigma "motivated" participants to lose weight.[6] Another study found that Black and white "adolescents who indicated that the primary reason for unfair treatment was their physical appearance had elevated ABP," or ambulatory blood pressure.[7] A third studied the mental health of ninety-three fat people in a "residential weight-loss facility," focusing on assessing depression, self-esteem, body image, overall psychiatric symptoms, and how mental health related to patients' experiences of weight stigma and internalization of anti-fat beliefs. Concern trolling—including "tough love"—was overwhelmingly experienced by participants, with 97.9 percent having experienced nasty comments from family, 89.1 percent reporting inappropriate comments from doctors, 86 percent reporting that loved ones were embarrassed to be associated with a fat person, and 78.3 percent reporting that others had made negative assumptions about them.[8] The psychological findings were striking:

> Participants' anti-fat beliefs significantly predicted mental health symptoms. Specifically, the regression models accounted for substantial portions of the variance in psychological outcomes, ranging from 22% in general psychiatric symptoms to 13% in depression scores. Furthermore, antifat attitudes uniquely predicted mental health symptoms after taking into account possible mental health differences due to age, age of onset, gender and BMI.[9]

A 2014 research review in the *Journal of Obesity* outlined the health impact of weight stigma, including direct aggression, institutionalized stigma, and even seemingly well-intended microaggressions and "complimentary weightism" (that is, complimenting weight loss).

> Schafer and Ferraro found that weight stigma was related to increased health risks that are typically attributed to being obese, such as functional disability and decreased self-rated health, over a 10-year period. The evidence further indicates that weight stigma is related to elevated ambulatory blood pressure, unhealthy weight control and binge eating behaviors, bulimic symptoms, negative body image, low self-esteem, and depression among children, adolescents, and adults.[10]

Research increasingly demonstrates that fat peoples' experiences with weight stigma and our internalization of anti-fat stereotypes worsen our health on all fronts, from the functioning of our brains to the very blood in our veins. Contrary to popular belief, the constant stream of cruel and judgmental comments and tactics aimed at fat people cannot be simply brushed off, nor are they without repercussions—even when they're cloaked in a *concern for our health*.

Messages seeking to make fat people thin, whether through shame or concern, simply don't work. One randomized control study from the *American Journal of Preventative Medicine* assessed reactions to anti-fat health campaigns and found that "stigmatizing campaigns were no more likely to instill motivation for improving lifestyle behaviors among participants than campaigns that were more neutral," regardless of their body size.[11] Another study, this one published in the *International Journal of Obesity*, engaged people of all sizes and assessed their perceptions of "obesity-related" public health campaigns.

> Participants responded most favorably to messages involving themes of increased fruit and vegetable consumption, and general messages involving multiple health behaviors. Messages that have been publicly criticized for their stigmatizing content received the most negative ratings and the lowest intentions to comply with message content. Furthermore, messages that were perceived to be most positive and motivating made no mention of

the word 'obesity' at all, and instead focused on making healthy behavioral changes without reference to body weight.[12]

Regardless of the topic, shame doesn't motivate change; it instead conveys that the shamed party is simply a bad *person*, and nothing can be done about that.[13] The article "Status Syndrome," published in the *Journal of the American Medical Association*, lays out the evidence that stigma and social status are major drivers of health, especially for poor people. "Socioeconomic differences in health are not confined to poor health for those at the bottom and health for everyone else. Rather, there is a social gradient in health in individuals who are not poor: the higher the social position, the better the health."[14] Researchers are learning what fat people have long known—that discrimination and stigma are major drivers of health outcomes and that all that *concern* is harming us more than it's helping.

Ultimately, anti-fatness isn't based in science or health, *concern* or *choice*. Anti-fatness is a way for thinner people to remind themselves of their perceived virtue. Seeing a fatter person allows them to remind themselves that *at least I'm not that fat.* They believe that they have *chosen* their body, so seeing a fat person eat something they deem unhealthy reminds them of their stronger willpower, greater tenacity, and superior character. We don't just *look* different, the thinking goes; we *are* different. Thinner people outwit their bodies. Fatter people succumb to them. Encounters with fatter people offer a welcome opportunity to retell that narrative and remind themselves of their superiority.

Over time, I have come to learn that these moments—the threats, the *concern*, the constant well-intentioned bullying—run even deeper than a simple assumption of superiority. It is a reminder so many thin people seem to desperately need. They don't seem to be talking to me at all. They seem to be talking to themselves.

Thin people don't need me to know about a diet or a surgeon. They don't need me to hear them expound on the evils of the obesity epidemic or the war on obesity. They need to remind themselves to stay vigilant and virtuous. The ways that thin people talk to fat people are, in a heartless kind of way, self-soothing. They are warnings *to themselves from themselves.* I am the future they are terrified of becoming, so they speak to me as the ghost of fatness future. They remove food from my cart as if it is their own. They offer diet advice forcefully, insisting that I take it. If I say that I have, they insist

I must have done it wrong, must not have been vigilant enough, must not have had enough willpower. They beat me up the way most of us only talk to ourselves. As if in a trance, they plead with me, some terrifying future self.

Sometimes, the trance breaks. Maybe it breaks because they realize, with great discomfort, that they have made extraordinary judgments, issued intrusive mandates like some petulant prince. Maybe it breaks because a fat person asks them to stop. But whatever breaks the trance, the thinner person seems to return to themselves, recognizing that they may have overstepped. And without fail, they will offer the same rote caveat, a hasty waiver, unsigned, disclaiming any injury caused: *I'm just concerned for your health*. And just like that, all that judgment, all those assumptions, all that cruelty suddenly becomes a humanitarian mission. *Concern for your health* is yet another example of the superior nature of thin people. They look better because they *are* better, and they're even generous enough to publicly shame you into being better too. It is the burden of thinness, saving so many poor, wretched fat-asses. Heavy is the head that wears the crown.

Each time I ask a concern troll what's behind their comments—why they see themselves fit to so readily judge fat people, then somehow transform that judgment into a public service—their responses echo one another. "Maybe it'll motivate you to change." As one commenter wrote in response to one of my essays, "People are born Black or white, gay or straight, but NO ONE is born fat."[15] In spite of overwhelming evidence from mainstream sources that body size is largely out of our control, nearly every concern troll I've asked shares one simple belief: that fat people *choose to be fat*.

As a queer person who grew up and came out in the 1990s, I find the contours of this argument are familiar, and they echo ones I've heard before. Parents of queer and trans kids don't want their kids to come out because they're *concerned* about their safety. Straight people aren't homophobic; they're just *concerned* about queer and trans people contracting HIV. Homophobic faith leaders love the sinner but hate the sin and believe that queer people will recruit unsuspecting straight children who will then *choose a homosexual lifestyle*. With a couple of decades of hindsight, many of us can now see these for what they were—smokescreens for straight people's discomfort with queer people, and their fear of having to accept something they'd so long feared or derided. As comfort with LGBTQ people continues to grow, these concerns have largely fallen away. Worries about LGBTQ people "re-cruiting" children are now largely laughed off as relics of a bygone era. HIV is understood to impact people of all sexual orientations; indeed, according to HIV.gov, the rates of new HIV diagnoses are falling nearly twice as fast in queer communities than straight ones.[16] Policy changes, culture changes, and large-scale public education campaigns have allowed many straight peo-ple to change their attitudes toward LGBTQ people, while simultaneously freeing themselves from any reflection on the impacts of that behavior. Cul-turally, it's allowed many of us to identify homophobia and transphobia in the rearview mirror as it recedes into the distance, some nasty force tied only to the figureheads of anti-LGBTQ movements and not to the many straight and cisgender people whose discomfort allowed their leadership to thrive.

We don't have the benefit of that distance when it comes to understand-ing anti-fatness. It is the polluted air we breathe, invisible and everywhere. Over time, its ubiquity changes how each of us operates, and we reproduce anti-fatness everywhere: in our internalization of anti-fat stereotypes, in our treatment of fat people, in our assessments of our own bodies, in the media we consume, and the stories we tell. Anti-fatness has turned so many of us into perpetual-motion machines, forever doing its work on its behalf, all of which is powered by the certain and baseless belief that *being fat is a choice.*

For some fat people, being fat *is* a choice. Gainers proudly and intention-ally get fatter, with many saying they feel their most beautiful, most power-ful, and most like themselves at their fattest.[17] Feeders seek feedees, partners who consent to being fed for the purposes of gaining weight.[18] Some people simply prefer how they look when they're fatter. For a wide range of reasons, there are fat people who choose to be fat.

Scientifically, most of us cannot appreciably change our body size or shape. Whether a diet, a cleanse, a "weight-loss journey," or a lifestyle change, the many methods we use to lose weight simply don't lead to sig-nificant, sustained weight loss for the vast majority of people. In 2007, re-searchers at the University of California at Los Angeles (UCLA) made a splash with the release of a meta study that analyzed thirty-one longitudinal studies. "We found that the majority of people regained all the weight, plus more. Sustained weight loss was found only in a small minority of partici-pants, while complete regain was found in the majority. Diets do not lead to sustained weight loss or health benefits for the majority of people."[19] Ninety-five percent of those who attempt to lose weight through dieting gain that weight back—and often more—within just a few years.[20] Indeed, those same UCLA researchers plainly noted that among the greatest predictors of future weight gain were *recent attempts to lose weight*.[21] The data is clear: diets simply don't work.

The other mainstay of weight-loss attempts, of course, is exercise. The old truism of dieting is that it's as simple as *calories in, calories out*—so if a person limits their caloric intake and increases calorie-burning activities, they'll *have* to lose weight. But despite being beneficial for cardiac health, circulation, mental health, and other areas of personal health, exercise has long been known to be ineffective as a weight-loss method.[22] It simply doesn't burn enough calories to lead to significant weight loss, and many types of physical activity lead to an increase in muscle mass—which won't lower the number on the scale. And on top of that, many of us eat *more* after working out, offsetting the few calories we just burned.[23]

While many of us know people who have undergone major weight loss through diet or exercise, those anecdotal cases are an extreme statistical minority, making up less than 5 percent of all dieters. Contrary to popular opinion, neither diet nor exercise leads to long-term weight loss for the vast majority of us. That's borne out by larger-scale data too. According to the *American Journal of Public Health*, women with BMIs categorized as obese have an extraordinarily slim chance of reaching their BMI-mandated "normal" weight. Just 0.8 percent of fat women become thin in their lifetime.[24] The few that do will face a grueling uphill battle, since weight cycling and dieting may dramatically and permanently alter their metabolisms, making it harder to maintain weight loss.[25] According to the CDC, despite a deluge of federal funding for the war on obesity, Americans are fatter now more than ever before.[26] People who were thin are now fatter and people who were fat are fatter still. Our war on obesity has unquestionably failed—in large part because we don't have nonsurgical, evidence-based weight-loss treatments that are proven to work for more than a short time.

On top of that, our understanding of the nature of fatness is becoming increasingly complex and nuanced. Many of us have a wildly oversimplified understanding of fatness. Obesity is culturally understood as one condition with two causes—eating too much and moving too little. When pressed to explain *how* we know what we know, most of us will come up with some variation on *It's just science*. But the science of weight couldn't be more different. As of 2016, researchers at OMNI have catalogued fifty-nine different types of obesity—each with their own causes, contributing factors, unknowns, and possible treatments.[27] According to the head of the department of clinical biochemistry and medicine at Cambridge University, "investigators have found more than 25 genes with such powerful effects that if one is mutated, a person is pretty much guaranteed to become obese[.]"[28]

Despite so much overwhelming evidence, most of us are staggeringly incurious about the nature of such a complicated condition. We remain recalcitrant, holding onto our outdated, disproven, and destructive cultural beliefs about fatness and fat people. Besides, if we acknowledged that fatness might not be a personal failing, we might have to treat fat people differently, with less condescension and disdain. And if we couldn't look down our noses at people fatter than us, how will we make ourselves feel better about our own bodies? Who would we pity, lament, mock, malign? And what would become of our lesser selves?

His first email seemed pointed, but innocent enough. He asked if I had tried to lose weight and why I didn't just do that instead of writing about what it was like to board a plane as a fat person. I had set a rule for myself of responding to every reader email in good faith, and I followed it here. I told him that while I heard people openly complain about fat people on airplanes, I didn't think they had reckoned with the impacts of their actions. The exchanges that followed were short, and increasingly terse.

HIM: Why do you want sympathy for being a fat tub of shit? Eat less . . . exercise . . . self-control. It's easy.

ME: I didn't ask for sympathy. I just wrote about what I did to prepare for a flight. I also wrote that I lost 60 pounds. What's your goal in writing to me? What outcome were you hoping for?

HIM: Don't have a goal . . . So on twitter I see you post about "abuse" . . . you're a fat tub of shit and should be embarrassed. Work in yourself and then you won't be a lard ass any more.

He closed his email with three smiling shit emojis.

I blocked his email address. In the coming days, he created five additional email addresses, sending me missives each day from a new account.

Obesity as a human right? Absolutely not, slob!!! Graphic gifs of hippos shitting. Lists of terrible, tired fat jokes cut-and-pasted from websites. *Don't you want to see your kids grow up? Or do you hate them so much you'd eat yourself to death? Or maybe they want you to die too?* Each morning, I looked for emails sent from new, anonymous accounts, eventually blocking them without opening them. And the next day, the cycle would begin again.

Eventually, he grew tired of sending emails and began sending comments through Twitter, through anonymous question-asking apps, through any contact method he could find.

> Ban this you fat fuck. I will never stop until the obesity rates start lowering. You advocate unhealthiness. You advocate death. All under the sham of it being acceptance and positivity.

> Thanks for mentioning where your doctor is to some random person on Twitter. "Just a few blocks away." We'll find you.

> Weak manatee can't lose weight and makes excuses.

> Last warning. You keep on with this unhealthy preach, and we'll make sure you won't even be able to type any more.

> Hello silly overgrown manatee. Why not just admit that obese people live a life that's shorter and of worse quality?

> I use you as motivation to exercise and eat healthy. I would never want to end up as fat as you. I can only imagine how poor your life quality must be. To not fit in a plane, not wear normal clothes, not have enough stamina as most people, etc… that is something I would never want for me, my kids or anyone in my family. Care about your body, it doesn't deserve clogged arteries and sore joints.

> Fat will always be considered ugly by the majority of society. Even by Ancient Greeks, chiseled thin muscular bodies were adored and the beauty standard catered to it. You will always be ugly and fat. Unless you change the fat part.

The comments were endless and ruthless. To him, my body was an undeniable choice, evidenced in so many of his missives. *Work in yourself and you won't be a lard ass anymore. Eat less . . . exercise . . . self-control. It's easy. You will always be ugly and fat. Unless you change the fat part.* The fact that I was urging others to treat fat people with respect and to look critically at their own harmful behaviors felt, to this stranger, like a shirking of my own responsibility to get and stay thin. Because fatness was, in his mind, a willful choice anchored in gluttony and sloth, requests to respect fat people's dignity felt not just premature, but delusional. To him, I had fallen off the deep end, into a kind of fat madness.

I reminded myself of what I knew, that these were his judgments and not mine, but each time the reminders worked a little less. As the comments flooded in (dozens each day), they wore at me like water on a rock. I could feel myself eroding. After weeks of unending harassment, they began to cut through me, some sharp, irreducible pain. A fresh wound every day. I needed to know who he was, needed to see his face. I needed to know if he planned to make good on the constant threats, and if he could. It took less than five minutes to find him. His first message came from his personal account, linked to a public Facebook profile.

I had expected some sign, though I don't know what—a sinister grin? Proud bigotry against all manner of people? Posts mirroring the vitriol he'd sent to me? But I found none. There were no alt-right memes, no Pepe the Frogs, no swastikas.

He was forty, lived in Kansas City, was a father of three. In his profile picture, he wore a tattered baseball cap and smiled widely at the camera. For a moment, I felt his eyes meet mine. Surrounding him were the faces of what appeared to be his three young daughters, all elementary school age or younger.

I sat back, disheartened and deflated. He wasn't some snarling beast, some anti-everyone activist. He looked like men in my neighborhood, people on my street, a friend of a friend. These weren't the beliefs of some vocal, cruel minority—he was the voice of the majority. People like him—people with steady jobs, people with kind smiles, people with sweet young children—were all around me. As I stared at his face, so guileless and quietly monstrous, I was terrified.

Then my eyes settled on his daughters. Their faces were sweet and soft, lit up by their trio of bright and broad smiles, each mimicking the next. I ached for what invariably lay ahead of them. What would happen to them in adolescence, when their bodies were sure to grow? What would become of them if one became fatter than their father wanted? How would his rage curdle and what sickness would that cause in his children? Had they already seen the monstrosity in their father, or was that a grief yet to come? Would he speak to his daughters the way he had spoken to me? Or would he insist that their bodies were a choice and that he was just *concerned for their health?*

However anti-fatness shows up, even in ways that seem benign, each paves the way for the next, laying a foundation that makes more overtly anti-fat behavior possible. Laughing at fat jokes lets the people around us know that they're okay to tell. Telling fat jokes makes more room for disregarding fat people's humanity. Disregarding our humanity opens the door to treating us callously, parroting hurtful stereotypes back to us under the guise of *concern for our health.* This callous treatment makes way for overt discrimination, harassment, violence, and death threats, each softening the ground for the next. Whether the wolf (*ban this, you fat fuck*) or sheep's clothing (*I'm just concerned for your health*), the story ends the same way. The wolf bares its teeth, then devours its prey. However anti-fatness presents itself, it will swallow me whole.

Still, this nearly naked contempt doesn't appear from nowhere. *Concern* and *choice* aren't cultural constants because they hurt fat people—they're ubiquitous because they *benefit* people whose bodies are socially accepted: Thin people and some smaller fat people. White or light-skinned fat people. Fat women with hourglass figures and fat men with barrel chests and broad shoulders. Smaller fat people who look white, look able-bodied, and who perform their gender "correctly." Fat people who aren't *that fat.*

Anti-fatness isn't about saving fat people, expressing *concern for our health*, or even about hurting us. Hurting us is a byproduct of reinforcing the egos of the privileged thin. Fat people are specters of some haunting future in which thin people become fat, and like any supernatural foe, we must be vanquished. Thinner people conquer fatness by distancing themselves from fatter people—through street harassment, food policing, and voicing constant judgment so that those around them know that they're *not that fat,* not that bad, not that slovenly, not that careless. Fat people are props, set pieces to prove thin people's virtue by contrast. Even the most benevolent thin people simply tolerate bodies like ours. In *Regulating Aversion: Tolerance in the Age of Identity and Empire*, Wendy Brown describes tolerance as "a discourse of power."[29]

> Despite its pacific demeanor, tolerance is an internally unharmonious term, blending together goodness, capaciousness, and conciliation with discomfort, judgment, and aversion. Like patience, tolerance is necessitated by something one would prefer did not exist. It involves managing the presence of the undesirable, the tasteless, the faulty—even the revolting, repugnant or vile. [. . .] As compensation, tolerance anoints the bearer with virtue, with standing for a principled act of permitting one's principles to be affronted; it provides a gracious way of allowing one's tastes to be violated. It offers a robe of modest superiority in exchange for yielding.[30]

In this way, thinness becomes a system of supremacy—a way of organizing the world around us and once again casting ourselves in a graceful light. At every turn, thin people are defined by their virtue: the restraint and vigilance to stay thin, the tenacity and dedication to monitor their bodies at every moment, the goodness to spread the gospel of thinness to wretched fatter people, and the restraint to stop short of death threats.

Everything about hating me reinforces what thin people need to hear about themselves. They don't want to hurt me; they want to stop hurting themselves. They don't want to hurt me, but they do.

Concern and choice are seductive. *Concern* tells thinner people that they are doing me a favor by ignoring my feelings, experiences, boundaries, and needs. *Choice* tells you that any harshness, judgment, and withholding is warranted—after all, I brought my body on myself, which means I asked to become a scapegoat. *Concern* is built on the foundation of *choice*. If a fat person has brought their own ill-fated body on themselves, if she has *chosen fatness*, then her boundaries simply don't matter—including asking those around her to withhold their concern. No matter how much a fat person protests, no matter how cogent her arguments or how urgent her pleas, her requests are always belied by *choice* and overridden by *concern*. Accordingly, these two insidious forces reliably render thinner people the expert on fat people's bodies, experiences, and needs. The duetting siren songs of *concern* and *choice* lure thinner people into a casual kind of abuse, a ready carelessness and heartlessness reserved for the worst of the worst, and the simple sight of my body proves that I'm deserving of their toughest tough love and all the *concern* they've got.

But whatever the explanation, whatever the caveats that follow such intense and constant judgment, pressure, rejection, and discrimination, a simple fact remains: the way that thinner people treat fatter people *is abuse*. *Choice* whispers to thinner people that they wouldn't hurt me if I didn't make them. It tells them they're doing me a favor—more than that, that they'd be doing a disservice if they *didn't* express deep contempt for bodies like mine. Like so much abuse, its cruelty disguises itself as something not only benign, but beneficial.

But the truth is that *concern* and *choice* are cover for a convenient and tempting set of stories that establish a hierarchy of people by establishing a hierarchy of bodies. They are judge and jury so that every thin person may play executioner for any fat person. But by every measure, *choice* is false and unfounded, and *concern* isn't helping. If thin people are *just concerned with our health*, they can tackle the bias that is hurting fat people much more than our bodies themselves.

CHAPTER 5

THE DESIRABILITY MYTH

I am walking home from work when I catch a stranger's eye. She stares openly, slack jawed, looking my body up and down, over and over again.

"Excuse me," she shouts. "Are you big enough yet?"

I keep my head down, eyes fixed on the pavement, walking swiftly, willing the moment to pass.

"Is everyone else seeing how fat this bitch is? Look at her!" She points at me, searches the faces of passersby. I do not respond, nor does anyone else. I walk faster, face searing red, wishing the world away.

Even in my silence, she is provoked, voice transforming itself from a shrill shout to a bared-tooth snarl. "How do you let that happen? Can you even hear me? I deserve an answer!" My heart beats heavy in my throat, stifling any response I might muster.

That evening, I struggle to concentrate or relax. My heartbeat shakes and clatters like a paint mixer in every inch of my skin. I am hopelessly vigilant, distracted by some complex calculus that might help me predict or prevent this stranger's return. What little sleep I get is restless. The next day, I tell my boss I will work from home. I do not tell her why.

For months, I cannot think about what this stranger said—I can only feel it. I remember her constantly. Shame fills my body like a water balloon, fragile in its fullness. The simple act of walking down the street in a fat body called up a deep rage in a perfect stranger.

Our encounter took place across the street from my office. In the afternoons following, I catch myself staring out my window at the corner where it happened, remembering it like some fever dream. I become a knot of muscle memory, with tense forearms and fists, calves flexed and ready to run. Before I leave for the day, I check out the window again, scanning the street for her.

I stop wearing the dress I wore that day, first hanging it in the back of my closet, then giving it away a few weeks later. Its bold, magenta knit draws too much attention to a body that cannot keep me safe. I begin wearing baggy, nondescript clothing. Plain jeans and oversized black tunics. Long sleeves and large coats. Long necklaces over high necklines. But even with my new wardrobe and protocol in place, it happens again.

After a late night in the office, I walk out to my car. I hear light, shuffling footsteps behind me. At the end of the block, I check furtively over my shoulder. There, a sallow, older man is measuring his paces behind mine, stretching behind me like a shadow.

At the crosswalk, I look back again. His eyes are fixed on me.

"No one will ever love you," he says, voice loud and tone plain. "Not looking like that."

I walk faster, feeling for my keys inside my bag. I look back over my shoulder again, glancing back at him. He does not look away.

"No one will ever love you," he says again, louder. The faster I move, the swifter his gait, and the louder his voice, this ghostly prophet following me between warm and distant streetlights.

My feet move quickly, keys locked between my fingers as makeshift brass knuckles that I know I will never use. I look again. He is still following, watching me closely, face slowly twisting into a mask of a grimace.

I round the corner. He matches my pace, then says it again, louder still, "No one will ever love you."

I break into a run, sprinting to my parking garage, running up the stairs past the too-slow hydraulic elevator. I take the stairs two at a time, heart pounding in every inch of my skin, breath strangled by the certain danger behind me.

I start the car and drive out of the parking garage as fast as I can. I make quick calculations about what will keep me the safest. Hiding in my car would make me a sitting duck. Driving further up in the parking garage and waiting for him to leave would only trap me. I decide that the only way out is through this—through him—and I speed down the concrete ramps to the street below.

When I reach the exit, I nervously scan the sidewalk for my phantom aggressor. He is gone.

I drive home as quickly as I can, heart still racing. When I finally reach my street, my breathing slows enough to catch up to what has just happened. Suddenly, when I catch my breath, I am overcome. My tears come in waves, stronger each time, until I can hear myself wailing.

I am not humiliated or ashamed. I am terrified.

All my precautions failed. There is nothing I can do to stay safe. However I dress, whoever is around, I am always vulnerable. My body makes me a target.

Over time, I come to accept that there is nothing I can do to control these moments of unbridled aggression. I tell myself that these two strangers made their own decisions about what to do when they saw me. I tell myself that they alone were responsible for their own behavior, although I cannot quite believe it yet.

I do not tell anyone what happened until finally, weeks later, I work up the courage to disclose these moments to thinner friends. When I tell them, I am met with the reaction I fear: a battery of questions and rejections, a hypnic jerk that keeps them from settling into the difficult truth of things. *What were you wearing? Did you say something to him? Did she look like an addict? Was he homeless?*

The more we talk, the more my straight-size friends reach for any reason to push this information away, excuse it, make it somehow logical, expected, routine. Because to them, this unprompted behavior is unthinkable. Like men hearing about the pervasiveness of catcalling for the first time, thin people cannot quite reconcile the differences in our daily lives. It is too distressing to recognize that their fat friend lives with such a dramatically different reality. And it is too alienating to acknowledge the simple fact that their bodies have spared them from a tumult they never imagined. It is illogical. So, to them, it is impossible.

The world of straight-size people is a reliable one. In their world, services paid for are services procured. Healthcare offered is accessed. Conflict arises primarily from active decisions to provoke and is rarely—if ever—prompted by the simple sight of a stranger's body. The biggest challenges with anyone's individual body are their attitudes toward their own skin, not issues of security, dignity, or safety from bodily harm.

But for fat people, the world we walk through is unpredictable and unforgiving. Even walking down the street becomes complicated, uncertain, unsafe, as we pass through the gauntlet of a Greek chorus singing our tragedies back to us. *No one will ever love you. Can you hear me? I deserve an answer.*

Strangers' interjections about my body, my food, my clothing, and my character are a daily feature of my life as a very fat person. The fatter I become, the more jagged the remarks, a razor wire drawing a ragged cut through the day. At size 20, the comments were insistent and pushy, often offering "helpful" advice on diet and exercise, or on how losing weight would help me "land a man." At a size 26, they began to curdle, souring into strangers spitting their disdain on the bus or at a street corner. And at size 30, they became menacing, a chorus of grim reapers foretelling my death, ferrying me across the river Styx.

This phenomenon became so prevalent that I began to shorthand it to friends as *fatcalling*. Named for catcalling, fatcalling comprises the unending stream of comments, judgments, and commands that inundate the lives of fat people, invited only by our bodies passing into a stranger's field of vision. Like catcalling, fatcalling is fully unearned, uninvited, and counterproductive, and it becomes an exhausting fact of life for those targeted by it. It is a well-known phenomenon, especially among fat activists and very fat people. In 2015, photos of a fat man dancing went viral on the notorious trolling site 4chan. "Spotted this specimen trying to dance the other week," the caption read. "He stopped when he saw us laughing."[1] Author and fat activist Lesley Kinzel faced strangers in a Home Depot parking lot shouting "Damn, bitch, you are huge!"[2] Even *Vogue* has written about the ubiquity of fatcalling.[3]

Like catcalling, fatcalling sometimes masquerades as a compliment but quickly sours. One fat teen shared their story in curriculum from the anti–street harassment organization Hollaback:

> School had just gotten out and, just as I did every other day, I met my girl-friend to walk her home. Holding hands, we passed one of the busiest build-ings where a [guy] with a bunch of his [friends] whistled and called out to us, "Nice! How can I get in on this?" [. . .] I called back, "Lucky for us, you can't." [. . .] At this point, about four large high school boys came towards my girlfriend and I. I could feel my heart rate skyrocket. The one who I

told off continued, "Whatever. You're just a fat, ugly dyke, anyway." They all laughed and I could totally see one hungrily staring at my girlfriend. I pulled her closer and we walked home without another word, but that didn't stop them from shouting at us across the block, calling us dykes and sluts.[4]

Psychologist Jason Seacat conducted a study to determine just how frequently fat women felt judged in the world around them, asking fifty overweight and obese women to write down every instance in which they felt judged or insulted as a result of their weight. On average, the women reported three incidents every day.

Some of those involved inanimate objects, like turnstiles and bus seats that were too small. But many involved interactions with other people. One woman said a group of teenagers made mooing noises at her in a store; another said her boyfriend's mother refused to feed her and commented that she was so fat because she was lazy. Seacat was inspired to do the study after watching a group of teens at his gym loudly harassing a fat woman, who eventually gave up and left the gym.[5]

Like catcalling before it, fatcalling is rarely about compliments, attraction, health, wellness, or any other benefits to the person being harassed. As Lesley Kinzel puts it, "public harassment by a stranger isn't about making you feel good. It's about putting you in your place, and reminding you that as a woman, your social purpose is to look appealing to guys."[6]

But despite these clear lines between our experiences of catcalling and fatcalling, my thin friends still struggle to grasp the latter. And there are so many similarities between these twin phenomena.

Like street harassment facing thinner women, fatcalling is also rooted in a deep sense of entitlement to others' bodies—an entitlement that is affirmed in nearly every aspect of our culture. Women's bodies are always at men's disposal, there to comment on, to ogle, to touch, and to take. Women are expected not to "provoke" men with our style of dress, expected to take men's constant come-ons as compliments, because *boys will be boys*. Women carry mace, learn self-defense techniques, develop networks to notify other women of men who assault and sexually harass us. Catcalling, like assault and harassment, are facts of life that we're expected to account for in our daily lives. And we do, often as a matter of survival.

Fatcalling shapes that unpredictable world in which fat people live. Will a passerby smile warmly, or spit an epithet at my broad, soft body? Will a doctor examine me, offer up treatment options, or will I be ejected from her office? Fatcalling offers only intermittent reinforcement—the uncertainty of abuse, replicated on an all-consuming, societal scale. As a fat person, I have developed a Pavlovian response to situations that may invite fat hate. Left wondering whether or not it would materialize, I have learned to anticipate it everywhere, because it could show up anywhere.

Anticipating and avoiding fatcalling is baked into every aspect of my life as a fat person. It determines how I will get home from work, and when, for fear of running into another of the phantoms that haunt the streets around my office. Should I walk, I may encounter my past assailants. If I take the bus, I will be met with the screwed-up faces of my fellow passengers, all suddenly placing bags on the seat next to them. Some will look up nervously. Others will nod warmly and tell me that standing is good for me. *Give those muscles a chance to do some work, hon.* On rarer occasions, a stranger will become aggressive, demanding I stand or *stay away.* When I reach my stop, I will hear his voice echoing behind me: *It's a wonder the bus doesn't bottom out when she's on it. Don't come back until you're half your size!*

The threat of fatcalling prevents me from wearing short sleeves, even on the hottest summer days, because I remember the passerby that stared at my arms and said plainly *no one needs to see that.* (I turned calmly and said, "It's 102 degrees out. What do you think I should be wearing?" He shrank away. I have not worn a sleeveless dress since.)

Fatcalling determines when and how I buy groceries. I have come to expect the occasional stranger removing items from my cart at the grocery store (*melon is much too high in sugar*), then puffing up with self-congratulatory pride. As I stood in the pasta aisle last year, one man simply stared at me, stunned. *No wonder,* he muttered as I pulled a box of orzo from the shelf. Now I buy my groceries late at night, when the store is emptied of do-gooder critics, or I order them for delivery.

The threat of fatcalling means I stay wary of new jobs, keeping close tabs on the number of straight men in a given organization. A fat friend told me about her male colleagues' lengthy conversation, going on about the women at work they'd like to sleep with. They pointedly told her they'd never sleep with her. *I just wanted to work,* she told me, deflated. As with catcalling, her experience with fatcalling had become a sad reality, a painful truth that was the price of living in the only skin she'd ever had. As she told me, we both knew that no one would stand up to it, no one would stop it, and it was our job to soldier through. So we do.

Because fatcalling, too, is widely anticipated and affirmed. Shows like *The Biggest Loser* and *Extreme Makeover* glorify "tough love" for fat people, while shows like *My 600 Pound Life* feature a never-ending intervention, a Mobius loop of fat suffering. For over a decade, blockbuster comedies were centered around characters played by actors in fat suits. *Norbit, Shallow Hal, The Nutty Professor, Austin Powers: The Spy Who Shagged Me,* and *Big Momma's House* made a meal of fat jokes, shaping their whole cinematic raison d'être around punchlines that ginned up disgust with fat bodies—especially fat women's bodies. Fat jokes are made even by comedians of all political persuasions, even the most politically progressive ones. Trevor Noah, host of *The Daily Show*, famously tweeted about fat women:

> "Oh yeah, the weekend. People are gonna get drunk & think that I'm sexy!" – fat chicks everywhere."
>
> @trevornoah, October 14, 2011

The prevalence of fatcalling in media has prompted life to imitate art— or, at least, real-life practices are validated by widespread media affirmation. Now, most straight-size people default to one of a few reactions to seeing bodies like mine: deep pity, condescending instruction, cruel harassment, or jokes that soften the ground for all of the above.

But despite the many similarities between fatcalling and catcalling, the former is rooted in a different set of cultural impulses. While both flow from a deep-seated entitlement to others' bodies, fatcalling allows harassers to believe that their actions are truly a service to those they harass. When sexualized, fatcalling is meant to throw fat women a bone and provide us with the sexual attention we're never expected to get. If it's diet advice or overt verbal abuse over the size of our bodies, we're expected to greet it with open arms, a much-needed wake-up call to pull us from the rock bottom that we have so clearly reached. Sometimes fatcalling is a series of harsh realities, fancying itself to be tough love. *You're going to kill yourself, is that what you want? I hope you enjoy your foot amputation.* Fat people are expected to greet such remarks as a shock jock kind of truth-telling. *I'm just saying what everyone's thinking.*

Thanks to thin strangers' noblesse oblige, we are freed from our delusion that our bodies are acceptable. We now know that we are fat, that we are repulsive, and we are now freed to become thin.

The sexualized side of fatcalling looks different from catcalling too. As a fat woman, I am not instructed to smile. Catcallers do not consider themselves to be wooing me, concocting faux romances in their minds. I do not face the inconvenience of chivalry. I am not worth that much. Instead, I face the grislier side of sexual harassment: unsolicited disclosures of men's rape fantasies, a violent expectation of full access to my body, and the certainty that any assault will be met with my gratitude.

These attitudes don't just impact fat women. Fat men are expected to be sexually frustrated, starved for attention, impossibly lonely, pathetic with the thin women they must so desperately want. On a 2017 episode of *Family Feud*, Steve Harvey asked contestants to "name a reason a woman might end up with a chubby man."[7] Their responses were a telling outline of popular beliefs about fat men:

Fatty got money!	34
She's fat/digs food	23
She'll look better	12
She's in love	9
He's warm/cuddly	6
He won't cheat	4

Each response indicated a toxic set of underlying assumptions about fat men. Fat men weren't afforded the freedom to be simply handsome, interesting, charming, or a catch. They had to provide some other auxiliary benefit to warrant the attraction of any woman. These men had to be wealthy, they had to make her "look better" by comparison, or they had to be companions in overeating ("she's fat/digs food"). If fat men were worthwhile partners by any measure, it was because they "won't cheat," or, as writer Philippe Leonard Fradet puts it, "either a) he wouldn't do anything to ruin the 'only sure thing' he has in his current relationship, and/or b) no one else would want to be with him."[8] Any physical attraction to a fat man was pronounced in strictly desexualized terms ("he's cuddly"). Of the one hundred respondents, only nine offered that a woman—any woman—might fall in love with a fat man.

Fat men's sexuality remains contested territory in our popular imagination. TV and film comedies in particular act out our conflicted cultural understandings of fat men's sexuality. On one hand, fat men are depicted as bumbling, flawed, and unintelligent, but likeable and partnered with conventionally attractive, thin women (Homer Simpson in *The Simpsons*, Peter Griffin in *Family Guy*, Doug Heffernan in *The King of Queens*, Uncle Phil in *The Fresh Prince of Bel Air*, Jerry Gergitch in *Parks and Recreation*, and so on). On the other hand, fat men are portrayed as sexless, emasculated, socially discomfiting, and repulsive to women (Garrett Lambert in *Community*, Comic Book Guy from *The Simpsons*, Fat Bastard in *Austin Powers: The Spy Who Shagged Me*). On the rare occasion a fat man is depicted as lovable, his appeal is often both nonthreatening and decidedly unsexed (Albert in *Hitch*, Jacob Kowalski in *Fantastic Beasts and Where to Find Them*, Schmidt in 2012's *21 Jump Street* reboot, and even Sir John Falstaff in many of Shakespeare's plays). In comedy, such as in *Family Feud*, while fat men might be loved, they won't be desired.

Fat trans people, too, bear the brunt of fatcalling. Trans people who are fat face constant misgendering, their gender expression inscrutable to the thinner people around them, buried beneath layers of fat that stubbornly genders and desexualizes their bodies. And those bodies—incomprehensible in both gender and size to the smaller, cisgender people around them— put them at the margins of the margins, struggling to stay safe. Writer and journalist Katelyn Burns writes about the dual burdens of fatphobia and transphobia:

> Skinny women are scared to get fat, fat women are depressed by being constantly told that they are not worthy. That fat women are not worthy of love, of affection, or of respect. Not only was I stuck in the wrong gendered body for myself, I was also stuck in a body shape that has been deemed unacceptable by society at large.[9]

Indeed, our cultural imagination seems to cast fat trans and nonbinary people as failures in two rites: failures to embody the thinness that is expected of everybody and failures to uphold a binary understanding of gender as hypermasculine or hyperfeminine. Professor James Burford and illustrator Sam Orchard, in their chapter of *Queering Fat Embodiment*, explore these restrictive narratives. "Often, these values emerge through the figures of the 'trans person trapped in the wrong body' and/or 'thin person trapped in a fat body.'"[10] While these narratives may resonate with some, too often they are our only cultural scripts for understanding fat and trans bodies. In that way, not only are fat trans people desexualized, the very narratives of their own bodies are wrested from them too.

When viewed through the lens of binary gender, the influence of misogyny on anti-fat bias snaps into focus. A 1996 study in the *Journal of Applied Psychology* looked at the attitudes that undergraduate students held toward fat men and women, illuminating a troubling double standard. The study's participants viewed fat men's sexual experiences on a par with those of thinner men, but saw fat women as "less sexually active, skilled, warm, and responsive, and perceived her as less likely to experience desire and various sexual behaviors" than a thinner woman. Participants also viewed fat women as "less sexually attractive, skilled, warm, and responsive" than fat men.[11] That is, while participants viewed fat men's sexual experiences as comparable to thinner men's, fat women were seen as both less desirable and less desiring than both thinner women and fat men. In that way, fat women become sexual objects living in a world devoid of sexuality. We can neither desire nor be desired, which means we'll accept any sexual attention with gratitude. Notably, though, a 1997 study found higher levels of eating disorders and sexual dysfunction in fat men than in their thinner peers. Study participants expressed a "lack of desire for sex, lack of erotic fantasies, and lack of motivation in sexual advances."[12] Like so many fat people, these fat men had internalized the belief that their bodies unsexed them. Indeed, fat people of all genders are expected to be grateful for any sexual attention we get. Because wanting us is unthinkable, we must never be desired.

But it's that precise impossibility of desire that keeps us unsafe, making us colossal targets for sexual harassment and violence. And, in 2017, conversations about sexual harassment and violence took center stage like they never had before.

On October 5, 2017, the *New York Times* broke the story of Harvey Weinstein's constant, systematic acts of sexual assault. Dozens of actors came forward with horrifying stories of rape, blackmail, physical intimidation, and torpedoed careers. In the months following, more titans of industry fell, victims of the circumstance only they created. Politicians, writers, musicians, filmmakers—countless public figures have been publicly accused of sexual harassment and assault by deeply brave individuals from all walks of life.

Together, these survivors reawakened a movement created by activist Tarana Burke some ten years earlier. The MeToo movement showed the chilling prevalence of sexual assault and harassment, especially among women. The movement has led to a sea change in cultural tolerance for sexual violence and misconduct. For once, institutions have begun to publicly decry the behavior of the men who make remarks, who expose themselves, who consolidate and abuse their power, who demand our bodies.

The people coming forward—mostly women—are young and old, rich and poor, famous and unknown. And overwhelmingly, they're thin. But 67 percent of American women are plus size. So, where are they?

In 2017, twenty-one-year-old Quantasia Sharpton filed suit against Usher for failing to share his herpes diagnosis with her before she says they slept together. Quantasia was just one of three people to sue the singer, but she was the only one who appeared at a press conference. And she was a fat Black woman.

The online response was swift and ruthless. Popular figures like comedian Lil Duval lined up to make cruel jokes at Sharpton's expense, often distancing themselves from fat shaming even as they publicly ridiculed a fat woman. Each of the following tweets received over six thousand likes:

I refuse to believe Usher fucked this.

— @lilduval, August 7, 2017

I also hate fat shaming but someone said "okay so did Usher give her herpes or Hershey's?"

— @_AmmBURR, August 7, 2017

somebody said usher went from smashing chili to smashing pork n beans. i hate fat shaming but y'all . . .

— @_lesbiTREN, August 7, 2017[13]

The idea that Usher, a handsome pop and R&B icon, could desire Quantasia Sharpton, a beautiful, young fat woman, was unthinkable. To thousands on Twitter, not only was Usher's desire for Quantasia impossible, but her self-advocacy in the face of his alleged recklessness had to be met with a wall of resistance. It had to be shut down. *The Root* writer and editor Monique Judge wrote, "You look at fat black women as being mothers and aunties. And if we aren't maternal—because the expectation that we must be is some bullshit—that doesn't make us any less desirable."[14] Quantasia had stepped out of those limited, maternal roles and was publicly punished for doing so.

I was fifteen years old and a size 18 when, for the first time, a man told me he'd fantasized about raping me. He told me that he longed to pin my hands behind my head, longed to hear me tell him no. *You'll be my fat whore*, he said. *You'll fight me off, but you'll love every minute of it.*

While jarring, this was far from the last time it happened. Over the years, more and more men would disclose their desire to assault me. When I told one to stop, in my mid-twenties, he was taken aback. *I thought you were liberated. You should be grateful.* I was queer, which overwhelmingly meant I should be sexually flexible, available to be posed in any scene or position needed for men's gratification. I was also fat, which meant I'd be grateful for what I got. Even if it was violent. Even if I didn't consent.

For my thin friends, these rape fantasies were more of a rarity, the provenance of a particularly depraved kind of man. For me, it was so commonplace as to be routine. But more troubling than that were the reactions from thin people I didn't know as well. A family friend and self-proclaimed feminist, upon hearing about this onslaught of fantasies, congratulated me. *Isn't it great to be wanted?* And, more troublingly, *There's a lid for every pot.* As if I had been disheartened about the selection of men who would take me. As if their violence was a sign of hope.

One friend asked why I hadn't told anyone sooner. I was surprised by her question when the answer felt so evident. Like many women before me, when I share stories of harassment, catcalling, unwelcome advances, and violence, I am met with pushback. Unlike other women, that resistance comes as a question: *Who would want to rape you?*

There's a common misconception that fat bodies cannot be desired. This could not be further from the truth. Fat people date, marry, hook up, get lonely, and get laid just like anyone else. Yet still, we are regularly depicted on screens and pages, by media and loved ones, as undesirable and undesired. Fat Amy, Rebel Wilson's character in *Pitch Perfect*, is depicted in a hot tub full of men competing for her attention. Within the context of the film, this is played as a joke: How could so many muscular men want someone so fat? In *Norbit*, Eddie Murphy donned a fat suit to play a sexually voracious and demanding fat Black woman who constantly nagged her thin partner into unwanted, repulsive sex. Even the sympathetic portrayal of a sexualized fat woman in the Farrelly brothers' *Shallow Hal*, Hal's love interest is only attractive because her suitor is blinded to her body and only able to see her as an impossibly thin Gwyneth Paltrow.

Those depictions both rely on and reify long-standing beliefs that fat people are isolated, unloved, desperate, voracious. So, when we are harassed, catcalled, and assaulted, those moments are supercharged with entitlement and violence. *This was supposed to be easy. You were supposed to want me more than I want you.* And when we don't, they lash out.

It took me years to disclose my own experiences. Because, like any woman, I knew that stepping forward would mean standard denials, scrutiny, dismissals. But for all our talk about sexual assault being an act of power, not desire, as a fat woman I knew that those statements always came with caveats, asterisks, footnotes. I knew that my body was reliably withheld, an obvious exception to the rule. After all, we'd be grateful for whatever we got. *Who would want to rape us?*

This desirability myth—the deep-seated, ubiquitous cultural belief that fat people are categorically undesirable—means that our assault and harassment is unthinkable to most. But fat people experience sexual violence, and some are even targeted because of the likelihood we won't speak out. And *who would want to rape you?* is more than an anecdotal experience or a cultural meme. Academics at Brigham Young University found that fat survivors of rape were dramatically less likely to be believed than thinner victims.[15] In *Tipping the Scales of Justice: Fighting Weight-Based Discrimination*, Sondra Solovay tells the story of one fat woman who was harassed by a physician after surviving rape and another who sought a pregnancy test. "'My doctor said I couldn't get pregnant, I was fat, who would want to make me pregnant?' She was pregnant."[16] The desirability myth ensures that fat survivors will stay silent—and if they don't, they still won't be believed.

All this leaves fat people, especially fat women, vulnerable to sexual violence that is so ubiquitous it can be openly discussed and even systematized. In 2018 Cornell University's Zeta Beta Tau chapter was put on probation for a "pig roast" contest, to see which pledges could bed the largest number of fat women. "The rules were simple: Would-be brothers allegedly earned points for having sex with overweight women. If there was a tie at the end, the victory went to whoever had slept with the heaviest woman. New members were told not to inform the women about the contest, according to a university report."[17] Like many other fraternities, the brothers and pledges of Zeta Beta Tau participated in the long tradition of "hogging" and "pig roasts" designed to humiliate fat women by bedding them on a dare.

Researchers Ariane Prohaska and Jeannine Gailey, in studying men who participated in hogging, identified the related phenomenon of "rodeos," in which a group of men pull names from a hat to see who will be tasked with bedding a fat woman. When the sexual encounter occurs, it is watched, photographed, or videotaped by the other men, who may then reveal themselves in order to humiliate a naked and vulnerable fat woman who dared to trust a man with her body and desire. Prohaska and Gailey identified two primary motivations for hogging, pig roasts, and rodeos: Men view fat women as "easy targets" for sexual encounters, which gives men status in their peer groups, and men use hogging as an "excuse" for either their insecurities about their ability to date "thin" women, their drunkenness, or their attraction to fat women.[18]

That is, for men who participate in hogging, pig roasts, and rodeos, fat women are either a prop with which to build their own masculine credibility or a human shield to protect themselves from their own insecurities. When mixed with the bleach of toxic masculinity, the ammonia of the desirability myth sets fat women on a path to pervasive sexual harassment and assault, with no end or respite in sight.

Still, fat survivors face a staggering hill to climb. Despite the advent of the MeToo movement, fat survivors are largely shut out, still believed to be both undesirable and untrustworthy, unreliable narrators of our own painful experiences.

Our national conversation about sexual assault and harassment was— and is—a crucial flashpoint. Notably, it has been largely led by Hollywood actresses, the Jessica Albas, Salma Hayeks, and Rose McGowans known for their beauty. But in order to flourish, our national conversation will have to hold space for women whose leadership we struggle to respect, whose bodies we struggle to embrace. Even those who, in our heart of hearts, we still expect to be *grateful.*

We are in the midst of the largest-scale explicitly feminist conversation our culture has had in my lifetime, and we are in the throes of major changes around sexual violence and harassment. But today, the average American woman wears a size 16. And those plus-size women—the lion's share of a nation—have yet to be heard.

There are stories I proudly tell about my feminist lineage. My grandmother giving my mother a copy of *The Feminine Mystique* for her fifteenth birthday, in 1963. My grandfather trying to pull me out of high school to attend the Seattle protests of the World Trade Organization, explaining to me in detail the impacts of globalization on women half a world away. My mother, in the mid-90s, sharing that when she needed to command a room at work, she'd channel Hillary Clinton. My niece at the Los Angeles Women's March, flanked by both grandmothers and her mom. Her sign read *I can be president.*

There are stories that shaped my own feminism. The diversity training we underwent at my high school, when I saw the viciousness with which my wealthier white classmates rebuffed any discussion of racism at our school, jumping immediately to *I never owned any slaves.* Seeing a trans guy at school go to the boys' bathroom every day, only to be bullied and beaten. Walking through record stores with friends of color, wondering why mall security seemed to follow us everywhere.

I grew up with feminism, proudly lifted it high, felt its ragged edges, looked unflinchingly into its troubled past, pushed it to grow into a brighter future. Feminism was discussed often and openly at home. But as a fat kid, and a queer kid, despite my deep allegiance with the movement that had brought me into being, there were facets of feminism that never felt right.

My body, my choice was a rallying cry for pro-choice action, but it was often misappropriated by thinner feminists to foist diets upon fatter feminists, like me. And it never fully translated for trans women, who were told their bodies *weren't* theirs, their choices invalid and their identities unwelcome.

But the one I came to struggle with the most was an old classic: *rape isn't about sex, it's about power.*

I had long railed against sexual violence and the culture that allowed assailants—predominantly men—to assault survivors—predominantly women. I had long felt the cold, slapping rain of that culture sting my face, had long decried it with the indignation of the uninitiated. But it wasn't until my late twenties that I felt its gale force winds carry me away.

I was twenty-nine when I decided to move out of my apartment. The rent had been hiked for the fifth straight year in a row, and I found a house that I was wildly in love with, almost certainly available. My landlord required sixty days' notice, so I gave it. Ten days in, my new house fell through. In a rapidly gentrifying city, for a young organizer, most rental rates were wildly out of reach. After searching desperately for days, I finally decided to make a plea with the property manager. He had always seemed friendly, all warm smiles and goofy jokes. Besides, I was only fourteen days in to giving notice. With forty-six days left, they couldn't have rented it yet, could they?

I stopped by the office on my way home from work. I picked up a package and spoke with him for a few minutes. I felt the friction in his voice when he mentioned his ex-wife.

"Break ups, huh?" I offered weakly.

"Not break ups, *ex-wives*," he corrected. "You know how they can get."

I didn't, but I knew what he meant. I felt myself tense at this familiar undercurrent of hostility toward women. I imagined him telling his friends *she's totally crazy—like, psycho* about any woman who left him. A flash of what happens when men like that think you've betrayed them. I had a sudden urge to leave, quickly and casually. I reminded myself of our many warm interactions, dissuaded myself from that instinct to leave. The moment passed. The conversation moved on.

After a lull, I explained to him that my housing fell through. The situation was overwhelming—Where would I go? Where could I live?—and I heard my voice shake as I asked him, *Have you already... Is there any chance... Has the unit been rented yet?*

He told me it had, that a couple was moving in and needed it as soon as possible. *We were actually going to see if you needed to leave sooner.* I shook my head, feeling the sharp heat of impending tears.

He read my face, comforted me. "It's a rough situation. You're really feeling it, huh?" I nodded.

He had brought a crushing problem to me. Now he would bring its solution. He would, he said, be willing to talk to the renters, see if they could wait a week for the next available unit. He thought a woman across the hall was getting ready to leave.

I was overwhelmed, submerged in a wave of gratitude and relief.

"Would you?" I exhaled an ocean.

"For you? Of course." He smiled. He would call them first thing in the morning.

My thanks spilled out of me, like an overflowing glass. I could not thank him enough, I told him. I was so grateful and used every superlative I could muster.

What happened next is blurry, lost in a haze of adrenaline. What I remember is that he asked me to go to dinner with him that night, asked me if I wanted to come back to his place to listen to records and see what happened. What I remember is being compared favorably to his ex-wife. *You're so sweet*—not like her, of course. What I remember is declining as though defusing a bomb, careful to cut the right wire, careful not to move too quickly or make too much noise, body taut and breathing measured. What I remember is the way his face turned, the warmth that drained from his voice. *The couple would probably say no. It's probably not worth the trouble. You shouldn't bank on staying here.*

What I remember is lying in bed all evening, in silence, acutely aware that the man downstairs had the key to my apartment but still unable to move. What I remember is thinking of who I could call and anticipating the deep, sharp sadness that would come when they inevitably tried to talk me out of what had happened.

Weeks later, I called a friend who was an attorney. The friend was shocked, indignant, angry. They advised hiring a lawyer to write to the property management company, tell them what had happened with their employee, and let them know I was prepared to take action.

But I wasn't. I thought of the warmth in his face beforehand, his stories about his child. I thought about having to tell my coworkers why I was taking a day off work to go to court. I thought about telling my family and friends, envisioning each of their reactions, one by one. And I thought about the reactions from the lawyer, the company, the court. *Who would want her? Shouldn't she be grateful for the attention?*

And despite everything, I was. My body had always disqualified me from desire. It had always been posited as something for partners to look past so they could *see the real me*. It was a moat, and it made me a fortress that would never be attacked. I had been told for years, explicitly and implicitly, that I was simply too ugly to assault or harass. In that moment, despite everything, I felt afraid and I felt strangely validated. I had been so thoroughly shattered by the relentlessness of fat hate and the desirability myth that I felt, for once, that someone had seen me as beautiful enough to want.

I was confused. I was hurt. I was terrified of my own home, of leaving a forwarding address, of telling him where to find me. I was a tangle of thorny fears and instincts, perplexing and shameful reactions to a situation I was sure I should have prevented.

And yes, I was grateful. After all, *who would want me?*

Rape isn't about sex; it's about power.

This slogan, it struck me weeks after this experience, was the provenance of straight-size feminists. I hadn't been raped, certainly, but I had been coerced and threatened. It felt luxurious, insisting that sexual assault and harassment was only about power and never about desire. But as a fat woman, in that moment, it had felt so multifaceted. His actions and threats were enabled by power, of course, but they were more multidimensional than that.

What drew him to me was that I appeared to be an easy mark, and I was. What drew him to me was that I wouldn't be believed, so I wouldn't say anything—and I didn't. What drew him to me was the endless stream of sayings about fat women, the symphony of sexualized whispers that prepared him for this crescendo of a moment. *Better blow jobs* and *they'll do whatever you want* and *try so hard* and *so grateful in bed* all softened the ground for what came next. He knew that I was queer and that I had dated straight men, which meant that anything he wanted was something I could enjoy or feign enjoying. What drew him to me was the certainty that I would be sexually pliable both in partners and acts, a living doll who would never resist. What drew him to me was that my body made me too untrustworthy to be believed, so I would never speak up.

It was about sex *and* it was about power. It was also about desirability, beauty, privilege, and manipulation. From our disparate positions, both of us were well acquainted with a machine that silences fat survivors even before we speak. That machine is fueled by every joke, every comment, every deeply held belief that fat people cannot be wanted by anyone who isn't settling or somehow pathological in their desire. It is oiled by every media caricature of fat people as desperate, lonely, sexually voracious, driven crazy by unfulfilled desire.

And that machine is protected by the well-intentioned friends and family members who cannot quite bring themselves to grapple with the harsh reality, depth, and pervasiveness of fat hate. It is protected by a vicious instinct that can arise within even our closest loved ones: a predatory instinct that blames its prey for its own demise.

This machine is fueled, too, by my beloved feminist peers. Often, feminist discourse stays focused on sexual harassment and assault that don't reflect the fullness of fat women's experiences—nor do they reliably reflect the experiences of trans women, immigrant women, older women, poor women. There is a violence that comes with catcalling and sexual violence targeted at people who are culturally and sexually defined by their lack of desirability. Fatness has long been used as an attack on feminist movements. During the US movement for white women's suffrage, those opposed to women's civic engagement frequently depicted suffragettes as fat, unattractive, shrill, and demanding. In 1910, one humor magazine took aim at these fat, demanding, unreasonable women, portraying one such suffragette with a mean expression, an indisputably fat body, tight and "unbecoming" clothing, and unattractive, unfeminine men's oxford shoes. She holds a wooden spoon in one hand and a rolling pin in the other, implicitly threatening to hit the reader. Amy Erdman Farrell's *Fat Shame* analyzes this salient, early attack on fat bodies as both a site of and motivation for women's dissent. "The caption reads, 'Speaker of the House.' What a joke to suggest that women need more rights! Look what the desire for public citizenship has done to this woman, the cover says: it has turned her into a primitive, coarse beast, too ugly, too big, too fat to be a woman."[19] By contrast, Farrell describes a pro-suffrage poster that shows a young, thin, conventionally beautiful suffragist leading a march of young men behind her, "transfixed, it seems, by her beauty. The desire for suffrage, for the rights of public citizenship, has made this young woman all the more beautiful, all the more attractive to the gentlemen in her midst."[20] As with any political attack, we lose when we take the bait, and this first wave of suffragettes had taken the bait. In so doing, they ushered in over a century of feminism that insisted feminists could—and sometimes must—be sexually desirable to straight men. Despite their stalwart opposition to the sexual objectification of women, predominantly white feminist movements have long distanced themselves from these politicized stereotypes of feminists as

domineering, unsexed, unattractive, and fat. In so doing, whether intention-
ally or not, feminist movements have acquiesced to the sexual economy asserted by their opponents: fat women are both undesirable and unlikeable,
and therefore not useful to the movement. As such, the perceived alignment
of feminists with fat women became a political liability.

While that approach has slightly softened over time, contemporary feminism rarely addresses the unique needs and barriers faced by fat women.
Mainstream feminist conversations remain focused on misogyny that targets
women that are thinner, whiter, wealthier, and more traditionally feminine
than most of us. Popular campaigns like New York's Stop Telling Women to
Smile posters depict thin women with straight faces, a deadpan response to
a ubiquitous command of thinner women. Not only are fat faces notably absent from those campaigns, but the specific harassment faced by fat women
is missing too. These campaigns remain important and instructive, but they
are also incomplete, leaving out the millions of American women who wear
plus or extended plus sizes.

No, those prominent feminist campaigns and conversations don't make
room for catcalling as an expression of repulsion or rejection, or the complex
morass of emotions and dynamics that comes when men want someone who
is defined by their undesirability. They grapple with what it means to be
considered sexually accessible as a thin woman who is sexually liberated and
active but leave out fat women whose sexual disposability is assumed because
of the impossibility of finding her attractive.

Making room for fat women's experiences in feminist spaces is straightforward. It requires simply adjusting our understandings of sexual violence
to exist beyond the framework of desirability (even though we already insist
that it *is about power, not about sex*). But for all of us, thin and fat alike, expanding our framework would require acknowledging an axis of experience
that we tend to think of as both organic and earned. Even among the most
socially conscious of us, fatness is considered to be a moral failing and well
within our control. As such, thin bodies have earned their reverence and
fat bodies have earned their natural consequences: public shaming, denial
of healthcare, and a grisly side of sexual violence. Fat people have chosen
to neglect our bodies, the thinking goes, so we are not owed any deeper
thought or sympathy.

In order to acknowledge fatcalling and sexual violence targeting fat
women, thin feminists would have to acknowledge that bodies like mine

should not be publicly shamed. Thin feminists would need to return to the radical root that insists that no survivor of sexual violence deserved what befell them. *None of us are asking for it*—certainly not for daring to live in the only bodies we have.

But somehow, for many feminists, that feels too close to home. Acknowledging the pain of fat women would mean acknowledging their own complicity, often unthinking and unintentional. It would mean implicating their own bodies and sacrificing the privileges they feel certain they've earned. If we used the full force of feminist movements to argue against the validity of the privileges that come with living in a thin body, those privileges might fall away.

Making space for an emerging constituency in any movement is a straightforward, albeit difficult, task. Its ingredients are simple: *listening, believing, adjusting,* and *collaborating.* But sharing power has never been easy, and, like acknowledging other axes of oppression, making room for fat women within feminism will require some discomfort of the thinner women around who it has been historically centered. It will require their willingness to entertain the idea that their bodies are not accomplishments and that fat bodies are not failures. It will call upon the willingness to believe that they themselves *might become fat someday* and might still need feminism then. And it will rely upon those feminists' willingness to sit with the discomfiting knowledge that, despite the relentless, whipping winds of misogyny all around them, their bodies have still afforded them some shelter that others don't have.

To those feminists, my question is this: Can you love fat people enough to sacrifice your comfort?

CHAPTER 6

SUCH A PRETTY FACE

Risk taking had never been a strong suit of mine, but at twenty-one, I'd discovered a deep drive to get away, to build a new life. In that new life, I told myself, I'd be a writer. I'd write dangerous new plays and explore whatever ideas suited me. I'd read the works of Valerie Solanas and Angela Davis and as many iconoclastic revolutionaries as I could manage. I'd apply to the jobs I most wanted and to the graduate-level courses I longed to take. I'd say yes to any new opportunities that came my way. I would, I told myself, become a risk taker.

And I did. I started writing plays, submitting them to festivals, seeing my own work staged by actors I liked, and being critiqued and complimented by writers I admired. I said yes to parties and weekend trips around New England. I took graduate seminars with professors and students I looked up to. My brain buzzed and popped like neon with the charge of new ideas and a bolder self. I was uncovering the contours of who I could be when I wrangled my fear, and I loved the shape I was taking.

The deepest risk-taking challenge was dating. I hadn't really seen anyone since my first girlfriend in high school, nor had I made sense of the relationship or the breakup. Despite seeing a therapist regularly, I kept quiet on the subject of relationships. Even after several years, it still felt too tender to divulge, even in complete confidence to a paid professional. I told myself I simply hadn't hung in there. I wasn't a convincing enough cool girl. If I tried harder, suppressed the hurt feelings I was certain were unearned and unjustified, I knew I could do better if a second chance at love presented itself. I had to hope for some hypnotized partner to fall in love with my *inner beauty*.

That's when I met my first love.

He went to art school, and early in our courtship he invited me to a student show of his photography. Haunting photographs hung on the walls, a ghostly kind of self-portrait of his changing body. He had started testosterone shortly before we met, and the double-exposed photos seemed to show his body as a specter as the hormones took root.

We lived two states away from one another and on the weekends would meet in the middle in Boston, spending long days together. He wrote me letters nearly every day, and I responded like clockwork. His love letters landed like a blow, knocking the wind out of me. I wrote back on thick paper, sometimes sprayed with perfume. He put the letters up around his bedroom mirror. *You say such nice things about me. I figure if I keep looking at them, I'll start to believe it.*

Over time our Boston rendezvous turned into weekends at his apartment. We would lay together in his tiny bed and daydream of my postgraduation move to Boston. I started researching jobs and he started looking for apartments.

But every time I imagined our future, I couldn't imagine myself. This beautiful life belonged to someone else, and he deserved someone better. Someone easier, prettier, cooler, and of course, someone thinner.

I had never seen a fat woman in love—not in life, not in the media. I had never seen fat women who dated. I had never seen fat women who asserted themselves, whose partners respected them. Because this was uncharted territory, I assumed it was also unexplored. My risk-taking resolution ebbed from my broad, soft body. How could he love me if it meant loving *this?*

Despite having what was described as a "very pretty face," I was constantly reminded that my body was impossible to want. We were dating at the height of popularity of sites like *Hot or Not* and TV shows like *The Swan.* Everywhere I looked, bodies were openly critiqued and ranked, and mine steadily landed near the bottom of the scale—2, 3, 4. His thinness alone earned him a much higher standing. In the cruel calculus of dating and relationships, our numbers didn't match.

But it wasn't just him. I had learned that I was undesirable to almost everyone. Desire for a body like mine meant my partners were irrational, stupid, or resigned to settling for less than they wanted. In the years since my first breakup I had struggled to accept interest where I found it. No matter how a potential partner looked, no matter how enthusiastic they were,

I couldn't trust their attraction. I shrank away from their touch, recoiling from their hands like hot iron, believing their interest to be impossible or pathological. Any intimacy required vulnerability, and vulnerability inevitably led back to humiliation.

This is among the greatest triumphs of anti-fatness: it stops us before we start. Its greatest victory isn't diet industry sales or lives postponed *just until I lose a few more pounds*. It's the belief that our bodies make us so worthless that we aren't deserving of love, or even touch.

Over the coming weeks, as these little fissures opened into wounds, I dressed them by retelling myself the story of our relationship. It had always been impossible, too beautiful and tender to be true. Maybe he had taken pity on me, doing a charitable deed by showing affection to a pitiable fat girl. I told myself he didn't want to be with me. I told myself he was too gentle to do what he knew needed to be done and dump me. I told myself the best thing I could do for him was leave. So I did.

I didn't know how to be loved. I couldn't see it happening. So I broke both of our hearts.

Later in my twenties, after briefly dating a friend of a friend, I decided to return to dating apps. I was on Bumble for less than a day when I matched with someone. I sent him a message—just a waving-hand emoji, to see how he'd respond. This was the informal first step of my screening process. He didn't make it to the second.

I said hello. He said: *I love my women fat. Big girl usually means a big mouth too. Even a nice handjob is better when there's a chubby hand doing the work lol. Usually bigger girls are better at pleasing their men though.*

Welcome to dating apps.

Like any woman, I'd come to expect explicit photos, unwanted advances and, when I dared decline, epithets hurled too easily. But I also faced messages like these, tinged with entitlement to my fat body—a body that they expected was theirs for the taking simply because of the size of it. In their eyes, I wasn't a new land to conquer, held no promise of the thrill of the hunt presented by thinner women. No, I would go willingly, grateful for their conquest.

But more than that, this message mirrored so many experiences I'd had before. It echoed fraternity brothers' "hogging" competitions to bed fat women, their "pig roasts" to see who could sleep with the fattest woman, the endless barrage fat jokes on TV. It echoed the man in a bar who asked me for my number, face kind and expectant, before retreating to his friends to report back on their dare: he'd gotten the fattest girl's number. It echoed the formerly-fat date who'd complimented me on my confidence, told me he "used to be like that, until I realized I wanted anyone to fuck me ever," then asked me back to his place. It echoed the concerns from family and friends, dangling the promise of a loving, healthy relationship at a smaller weight: *I just want you to find someone.* Then, on top of all that, messages like these. Messages that received my body like tissue: plentiful, accessible, disposable, trash.

Fat people aren't the only ones who live with the repercussions of anti-fatness in our relationships. Those messages also land hard with people who date us, love us, marry us, sleep with us. They get trapped too. After all, in our cultural scripts, a fat partner is a failure at best, a shameful, pathological fetish at worst. Desiring fat people is something deviant to be hidden, to find shame in, to closet.

But the data and research around fat sexuality paint a wholly different picture. In *A Billion Wicked Thoughts*, Ogi Ogas and Sai Gaddam analyzed history's largest data bank on pornography viewers. They found that regardless of gender and sexual orientation, porn searches for fat bodies significantly outpaced searches for thin bodies. In fact, fat porn was the sixteenth most popular category, outranking categories like "anal sex" (#18), "group sex" (#24), "fellatio" (#28), and "skinny" (#30).[1] "For every search for a 'skinny' girl, there are almost three searches for a 'fat' girl."[2] Gay men's searches, too, revealed far more searches for "bears" (burly or fat men) than "twinks" (young, thin men).[3] On his attraction to fat women, one man told Ogas and Gaddam, "Bigger girls will have more fun and will work twice as hard to meet the standards of the skinny girls most people find attractive."[4] But despite being surrounded by women of all sizes, viewers opted instead to drive their desire into safe, siloed, and one-sided experiences, away from the prying eyes of the world around them.

While Ogas and Gaddam's research speaks only to sexual desire (not romantic attraction or aspirations), it certainly indicates that our cultural scripts around size and desire—that is, that thin people are inherently desirable and fat people are categorically undesirable—are rooted more in perception than research. The findings in *A Billion Wicked Thoughts* show us that, at the very least, attraction to fat people of all genders isn't a niche occupied solely by those who celebrate their desire. Rather, it points to the idea that fat bodies may be among the most widely desired, but that desire may be repressed—possibly thanks to pervasive stigma.

The now-defunct *Village Voice* illuminated some of the challenges faced by self-proclaimed "fat admirers" in a 2011 cover story. In "Guys Who Like Fat Chicks," reporter Camille Dodero shares the stories of several straight thin men who are predominantly attracted to fat women—and the social sanctions that threaten their masculinity and their social relationships. As one man put it, he was afraid to say he didn't notice a thin, conventionally attractive woman in school for fear of being met with "What are you, some sort of *fag?*" But even as he began dating, those fears were realized. "A rumor spread that he was gay, which he didn't bother to refute. Liking a fat girl was so much more of a preposterous scenario that he worried the truth would 'make it snowball even more.'"[5] Another man outlined similarly harsh social repercussions for expressing his attraction to fat women. "If someone starts talking about guys who like fat women or girls who like fat men, the first reaction is, 'Ewww.' [. . .] The second is, 'What the fuck is wrong with you?' The third is, 'That is so unhealthy, and you're killing the person you want to be with.' It all leads up to: 'We don't want to talk to you. Get the fuck away.'"[6]

Many men who are attracted to fat women find ways to express that desire while sheltering themselves from judgment and stigma. For many, that means seeking out pornography. Other straight-size men have secret sexual relationships with fat women, too afraid or disgusted to elevate those encounters to full-fledged relationships. In "Secret Relationships with Fat Women," Virgie Tovar recounted the patterns of one such relationship of her own. "Everything was intimate and magical when we were alone, and then all of a sudden it would stop being that. I would go from being a charmingly eccentric bohemian to being a monstrously crass bother."[7]

Tovar isn't alone. Formal research hasn't been published related to the phenomenon of secret fat relationships, but many fat people are familiar with its contours. When I asked fat Twitter users about their experiences with secret sexual and romantic relationships, the responses poured in:

"I let it happen because I thought it was the best I could do. He ended up being abusive and I still thought it was better than being alone. I tried to diet and lose weight in the hopes that maybe he would treat me better."

"Pretty much anyone I have ever been with has tried to keep me secret.
I peaced out when I realized what was happening."

"….yes….I married him. I dumped his ass and he realized the error of his
ways. He was 17 so it can be forgiven. We are in our 30s now and he's
happy im on his arm. Fat or not."

"Yes. :'(I was so DEEPLY insecure and I thought him to be
conventionally attractive – 'out of my league' – so I tolerated his shame
about fucking me for over a year. Literally a year of my life given to
someone who only took me on one public date."

"Very few people knew we were dating. He refused to hold my hand in
public. Went on for 6 months until he told me I HAD to lose weight, even
so far as say he would monitor my weight loss. I dumped him the next
day. The things he said and did still affect me today."

"It took two years to get the confidence to leave. And it was nearly
7 years before I met anyone else – I regretted leaving so many times
because it had been shit but it was something."

These fat people found themselves bound to relationships that were
lackluster at best, abusive at worst. They too had learned that their bodies
made them impossible to want and that any relationship at all was a windfall
to cling to at all costs.

When attraction to fat people is discussed, fetishism is never far behind.
Fetishism isn't in itself necessarily pathological; fetishes can be as simple as
consensual kinks, particularly intense attractions, or simple preferences. But
when fetishism is brought up with respect to fat attraction, it gathers like a
storm cloud.

To be clear, there are attractions to fatness that take such specific forms
that they are undeniably fetishistic. Feeders, for example, long to feed their
"feedee" fat partners, deriving pleasure from watching their fat partner eat
and, in some cases, from watching them gain more and more weight. Squash
fetishes, on the other hand, indicate a desire to be sat on or pinned beneath
their partner's fat body.[8]

Some fat people happily engage with these fetishes and find fulfillment (or paid work) in their role. Some do not. But many fat people have felt fetishism thrust upon them without their consent.

Fat fetishism has deep roots for many fat people, especially fat women. For some, size, desire, shame, and sex are a rat's nest, hopelessly tangled together. People who internalize anti-fat stereotypes—including the pervasive cultural belief that fat people are categorically unattractive or unlovable—are more likely to binge eat,[9] as are survivors of sexual assault.[10] Fat acceptance spaces frequently include heartbreaking stories of people whose relationships were kept secret by their partners. Worse still, some tell stories about working up the courage to share their experiences of sexual assault only to be categorically disbelieved. Given the pervasiveness of their experiences, is it any wonder that some fat people come to experience anyone else's desire for them as predatory?

Of course, not all fat people have lived these sex and relationship horror stories. But many of us have become so acculturated to them that we come to describe the vast majority of fat attraction as *fat fetishism*. When fat sex and dating are discussed, there's rarely room for simple attraction. But thin people are frequently attracted to other thin people without garnering suspicion of *fetishism*. They may find themselves drawn to brown-haired people, muscle-bound bodies, or tall partners. They can speak freely of the physical characteristics they like best: chiseled jawlines, long hair, slim legs. In the world of thin people, these are *types*, a physical attraction so universal that it is neutral.

Everyone, we are told, has a *type*. But if a thin person is reliably attracted to fat people, that type curdles and becomes something less trustworthy: a *fetish*. Fat people are so categorically undesirable, we're told, that any attraction to us must speak to a darker urge or some unchecked appetite.

There's no question that fat sexuality can be riddled with power imbalances and predatory behavior. But why is a healthy, natural attraction to fat bodies so difficult for us collectively to believe? Why do we so readily accept that thin bodies are universally desired and lovable, while so certainly rejecting the same prospect for fat bodies? Is there room to love the look of fat bodies without dropping into the sinister territory implied by a *fat fetish?* Can fat bodies be desired without becoming pathological?

For years, my body took center stage in my dating life. Dates constantly commented on my size, a knee-jerk reaction to their discomfort with their own desire. Over time, I came to experience *any* attraction as untrustworthy, as if danger lurked nearby. In retrospect, I worried for my bodily safety, as if only violence could develop an appetite for a body as soft as mine. And I worried that I would become a sexual curio, more novel than loved.

In a world so insistent that fat attraction is impossible, fat folks can end up experiencing *all* attraction as fetishism. And the culture around us reinforces that at every turn. The few fat love stories we see are fat people dating other fat people, usually in shared weight loss or food addiction programs, as with *Mike & Molly* or *This Is Us*. Fat people aren't just surrounded by pathology; our bodies are seen as manifestations of it.

We assume most—if not all—fat attraction is pathological. Even some of us with a deep commitment to body positivity and fat acceptance speak in hushed tones about *fat fetishism* and the shame of realizing we're dating a *chaser*, a *feeder*, or a *fat admirer.*

But when we do that, we imply that only thin people are worthy of genuine attraction—that, like health, happiness, and success, love can only be earned by thinness. Our inability to distinguish predatory sexual appetites from everyday desire ends up reinforcing the false idea that thin people lead fuller lives, deserve more, are more loved and more desirable.

Some workdays, after a difficult meeting, I would find my way to the nearby nail salon, carving out an hour from an interminably long day to gather myself, find a color, and renew my strength for what lie ahead. This was one of those days.

The TV was always mercifully on, its volume low and closed captioning scrolling by. As the evening news began, I let my eyes glaze over a story about a local pageant crowning high school Rose Festival Queens before suddenly being snapped back to attention. The news anchor's mute mouth was moving and the closed captioning scrolls running haltingly by with the words *obesity epidemic* appearing again and again. The news anchor was telling viewers about the dangers of bodies like mine, the plague we had loosed on the world around us. As she spoke, her words were captioned beneath an endless b-roll of fat bodies. They were presented as monstrosities, faceless ghouls, specters of a terrifying kind of fatness looming over the innocent thin.

I had seen footage like this countless times before: fat people filmed from the neck down, reduced to the swells and rolls of our bodies, their tides made spectacle. It's a trope that academic and activist Dr. Charlotte Cooper calls "headless fatties." "As Headless Fatties, the body becomes symbolic: we are there but we have no voice, not even a mouth in a head, no brain, no thoughts or opinions. Instead we are reduced and dehumanised as symbols of cultural fear: the body, the belly, the arse, food."[11] The footage always comes from public spaces, shot without heads or faces present, presumably shot without the consent so few fat people would give. Instead, their bodies are filmed surreptitiously, in secret, to be ogled by network news viewers for years to come.

As this particular story unfolded, I recognized the trappings of familiar settings. The herringbone brickwork of Pioneer Courthouse Square, just ten blocks from my office. The gracious and verdant trees at Waterfront Park, where I walked when I needed to decompress. Unlike the endless b-roll from far away, this footage was local. These are places I went. And these bodies looked like mine.

My breathing quickened, eyes scanning the screen for worn black Chelsea boots. I looked for a low-slung belly in dark wash jeans. I searched for a motorcycle jacket, blackberry fingernails, the ends of long, honey blonde hair.

While the rest of the customers relaxed into their services, I was on high alert. I was looking for myself.

That news footage was the most recent in a long line of media portrayals of fat people, but it was far from the first. For my whole, short life, bodies like mine had been presented on camera with disdain, disgust, lurid curiosity. Bodies like mine had been used to elicit laughter, revulsion, pity, and inspiration. Whether on the evening news or a late-night infomercial, in a family drama, or a rollicking comedy, bodies like mine were rarely full people. We were set pieces, props to elicit a series of reactions from the more real, thinner people on screen. We weren't people—we were just bodies. Disgusting bodies, funny bodies, pitiable bodies, fearful bodies, and sometimes magical bodies, defiant in the confidence we were never supposed to have. But never whole people. We were only rarely afforded our own plotlines, often relegated to being sassy best friends or miserable and pitiable unrequited lovers. When we were afforded real character development, it was always woefully limited, and the lion's share of plotlines orbited around our size: either in triumphant weight-loss narratives or wretched, pathetic tragedies. But whatever our narrative, it reliably provided a template for thinner people's understandings of what it meant to live in bodies like ours.

Scripted television and movies frequently present fat bodies as punch-lines. Melissa McCarthy and Rebel Wilson have made careers out of their strong comedic acting skill set, yes, and also out of scripts that overwhelmingly call for slapstick humiliation. In *Pitch Perfect 2*, the opening scene makes a joke of Rebel Wilson's character, Fat Amy, who sings from acrobatic silks while her costume rips, revealing her genitals. *Tammy*'s trailer features its star, Melissa McCarthy, trying and failing to hurl herself over a fast food restaurant's counter, then trying to rob the store by making her hand into the shape of a gun, building a plot around its low-income, fat main character's absurdity. *Avengers: Endgame*, a smash hit grossing over $2.6 billion worldwide, finds each of the Avengers dealing with an earth-shattering grief and survivor's guilt differently.[12] Thor's grief has manifested itself in alcoholism and weight gain, both of which are played on for laughs.

Dramas and reality TV often position fat bodies as pitiable or inspirational, two sides of the same flat coin. Near the turn of the millennium, FOX and ABC premiered two shows focused on weight loss and plastic surgery makeovers. *The Swan* (like its early 2000s contemporary *Extreme Makeover*) offered women the lives they dreamed of by giving them the bodies they'd dreamed of through drastic dieting, extreme exercise, and extensive plastic surgery.

Each episode began with an opening video detailing the contestant's dreary, hopeless life. Often, personal stories included deep traumas—miscarriages, divorce, family abandonment—combined with deep distress over the state of their bodies. Contestants daydreamed aloud about how their lives would be different if they were thinner, their ears pinned back, breasts augmented, fat sucked from their waists and thighs. They yearned for bodies that exemplified a narrow, thin, and inescapably white standard of beauty, often lightening their hair and straightening their noses.

Sylvia, a twenty-seven-year-old Latinx woman from Chicago, shared her story of trauma, bullying, and abandonment, explaining that her shameful weight came from the foods popular in her community. The camera followed her as she bought elotes from a street vendor, and as she did she listed the dish's ingredients: corn, butter, cheese, mayonnaise. The panel of all-white judges looks on, laughing heartily as one white judge clutches at her heart.[13] The footage is painful to watch: white professionals and network TV judges laughing too readily at Latinx foods and traditions, as they simultaneously work to "help" a working-class woman of color. After watching a few short minutes of Sylvia's story, the judges explain what they plan to do to her. A therapist diagnoses her trust issues, apparently based on the video presented. A plastic surgeon describes her face as having a "bland bone structure," before outlining his plan: cheek implants, chin implants, a brow lift, nose straightening, ear pinning, and "a lot of liposuction. Hopefully," he says, "that will inspire her to get on the program with Debbie," a personal trainer. Sylvia will be restricted to 1,200 calories per day using Nutrisystem, a diet that's been the subject of repeated lawsuits for allegedly causing gallbladder disease. For three months, she will work out for two hours each day, work with a therapist on camera, restrict her food intake, and undergo an intense battery of cosmetic surgeries and dental procedures. During that time, like all contestants, Sylvia was deprived of mirrors and, like some dystopian science fiction, her "work ethic" was monitored.

Sylvia's episode ended like every episode of *The Swan*: with her grand reveal. She entered a baroque mansion through its double front doors to a dozen applauding attendees of her coming-out party, predominantly made up of the surgeons and dentists who treated her. Her hair was newly blonde, styled into extravagant barrel curls, face slick with heavy makeup. Her body was newly slender, clothed in a strapless satin pageant gown with showy, glittery jewelry. She revealed that her boyfriend proposed to her and that she accepted. In the world of *The Swan*, this meant that her new body was already paying off. The final step of Sylvia's journey meant seeing her new reflection. Sylvia approached dramatically draped velvet curtains where, when they were drawn, she would face her reflection for the first time in months. The camera circled her face and body, searching for signs of tension as the show's taut score built toward its climax. The willowy blonde host in a plunging, bejeweled evening gown asked Sylvia if she was ready, then drew the curtains. Sylvia, like so many before her, laughed and then wept, gasping her thanks to the panel of surgeons and trainers who transformed her. But despite her best efforts, Sylvia was not selected to compete in the season finale's pageant.

Sylvia's appearance, like nearly every woman's on *The Swan*, offers its viewers a clear and simple arc. Women's lives are miserable because their bodies are hideous. Changing their bodies will open up the lives they've dreamed of—and, in the world of the show, it does. These newly glamorous "ugly ducklings" are welcomed into a more real world: one with happy marriages, obedient children, better jobs, and fuller lives. The Sylvia who ate elotes with her family was to be pitied. The Sylvia who restricted was to be celebrated as an inspiration for us all.

The Swan and *Extreme Makeover* created a template used for years to come. Most recently, *Revenge Body with Khloe Kardashian* has refined *The Swan*'s formula. Rather than focusing on a broad fairytale life promised by a thinner body, *Revenge Body* narrowed its focus: get revenge by getting thin. It's introduction, voiced by Kardashian, lays out the show's premise:

> I'm Khloe Kardashian. Growing up, people called me the fat, funny sister. Until one day, I started working out, eating right, and putting myself first. And you know what? I've never felt better. Now I'm helping others transform by hooking them up with my favorite Hollywood trainers and glam experts to turn their lives around and shut down the shamers. Because a great body is the *best* revenge.

In the world of *Revenge Body*, the way to "shut down the shamers" isn't to hold them accountable for their actions, to work through challenges in your relationship, or to heal from the emotional damage of shame—it's to get thin. In Kardashian's show, bodies are currency. Thin bodies are opulent, the representation of the old adage *living well is the best revenge*. Fat bodies cannot be *living well*—they are signs of shame, of failure, of succumbing to abuse. Only thinness can deliver wretched fat people from complicated relationships, heartbreak, and abuse.

One episode follows a queer couple, Sam and Nicole. Sam, a smaller fat person, exasperatedly tells the camera about her two-and-a-half-year relationship with Nicole, a larger fat and masculine-presenting person. We first meet Nicole as Sam walks in on her at a bar, hunched over a table full of burgers and wilted fried foods, asking for a side of ranch dressing. The table is covered with food—plates of deep-fried hot wings, onion rings shining with grease, thin hamburger patties with soft buns. The camera offers close-up shots of Nicole licking glistening fat from her fingers, offering viewers a kind of softcore pornography of disgust. Sam begs Nicole to stop eating the food on the table. "This is the reason why I'm..." Sam begins, searching for a word before backing up. "Covered up," she finishes finally, deflated.

In confessional footage, Sam laments the state not of her partner's conduct but of her body, wondering aloud how she's "supposed to find the other person attractive if . . ." before trailing off. She explains that she and Nicole haven't had sex in eight months and that she blames Nicole. "I do hold a lot of resentment toward her, because I know I would not have let myself get like this had it not been for our relationship." In *Revenge Body*, failing relationships aren't matters of communication, validation, or emotional support—changing bodies are to blame. And thinner partners, like Sam, are free to resent fatter partners, like Nicole, for failing to provide a body to which she is "supposed" to be attracted. Emotional support and healthy relationship practices don't matter—only bodies matter. At the end of the episode, after time apart and significant weight loss, Sam and Nicole have not substantively worked through the emotional issues in their relationship. Sam has not excised her resentment for Nicole; Nicole has not moved through her resistance to Sam's body mandates. But both are thinner. In a final scene in the grand setting of an empty Dodger Stadium, Nicole proposes to Sam, and Sam accepts, proving that, in the show's parlance, a *revenge body* can mend a weakened relationship.

Revenge Body, like *The Swan* before it, offers an etiology of fat bodies. During Sam and Nicole's episode, a personal trainer snaps at them, "The way you both got here? It's because you both sat on your asses and didn't eat well," he says, eyes sharp with irritation verging on anger. This is not the thesis of the show—*Revenge Body* does not argue this point—it takes it as a simple fact and claims a kind of bravery in its "tough love" for Sam and Nicole, blaming them on national television for what it sees as objectively failed bodies. Where *The Swan* elicited pity for its contestants "unacceptable" bodies, *Revenge Body* called for anger. *Remember that you are meant to hate this body. Remember that it is to blame for your failings, your shortcomings, your imperfect relationship. Remember that the only way to love this body is to be free of it.*

Other reality programs seem most focused on stoking their audiences' disgust and fear at the sight of fat bodies. TLC's *My 600 Pound Life* seems to consider itself an objective and tender documentary, all the while treating very fat people as freakshows, displaying their bodies and medical struggles to fuel audiences' disgust, revulsion, and sense of superiority. Viewers are invited into the power dynamic and narrative of a freakshow—a place where audience members' bodies, bodies that otherwise feel woefully inadequate, become suddenly superior by comparison. *At least I'm not that fat.* In 2016, BBC Three's *Obesity: The Post Mortem* purported to reveal "the dangers of fat to the human body" by televising a postmortem examination on a fat woman whose body was donated to science.[14] This unquestionably cruel premise made a cautionary tale out of a person who died, opening her naked and dismembered body up to open mockery and judgment from a nation of viewers at the one time she couldn't object or even consent—posthumously.

In 2005, on *The Tyra Banks Show*, the supermodel wore a fat suit to "experience what it's like to be obese."[15] Banks put on prosthetics, ill-fitting and drab clothing, a wig, outdated glasses, a hidden camera, and a fat suit to make her appear to be my size—roughly 350 pounds. "I started walking down the street and within 10 seconds, a trio of people looked at me, snickered, looked me right in my eye and started pointing and laughing in my face [. . .] and I had no idea it was that blatant."[16] While the intended message of Banks's show wasn't a harmful one, its execution left much to be desired. Real fat women were invited onto the show to share their experiences—not as supermodels who could remove their fat at the end of a day, but as living, breathing fat people who lived with open harassment regularly. Still, Banks's day of suffering took center stage, leaving the model in tears, to be consoled by the women who lived in the body she'd worn as a costume for just one day. Even when fat stories are told in nonfiction programming, thinness commands the spotlight.

In 2014, a dating website, Simple Pickup, replicated Banks's experiment, this time on a series of dates set up online. The introduction announces that "the number one fear for women dating online is that they're going to meet a serial killer. The number one fear for men? That the woman they meet is going to be fat."[17] This isn't a social experiment so much as a ruse, one not depicting the real-life experiences of a fat woman dating but rather pranking thin and muscular men with a high-drama bait-and-switch. The camera shows a woman's profile, featuring photographs of her thin, bikini-clad body, followed by a time-lapse application of a fat suit to an otherwise slight woman. She rubs her prosthetic belly while blowing kisses to the camera. Her laugh comes easily—this is a lark. As the dates progress, she baits the men. "You look *just* like your picture. It's crazy." "I can't say the same," responds one date. "You look so different from your picture," says another. "Maybe it's— I've been trying on this new lipstick, what do you think?" she answers coquettishly. Her behavior bears no resemblance to the straight fat women I know, often battle-scarred by their date's awkward and judgmental comments, with elaborate trap lines and disclosures to preempt further harm. The video comes across less as a "social experiment," as its tag line claims, and more as an extended practical fat joke.[18] The video went viral, and as of 2019, it has garnered more than thirty-three million views. "Kudos to the guy who stayed!" gushed *Cosmopolitan*.[19]

Some programs go even further, encouraging condescension toward and bullying of fat people as a favor to us, as a way to motivate our weight loss. (Note: all available research indicates that fat shaming leads to weight *gain*, not weight loss, and worse health outcomes—as do shaming and bullying for any reason.) Perhaps the most iconic example of this is *The Biggest Loser*, a primetime reality show that made a long-running hit out of exploiting fat people's emotional pain. The show followed a cohort of fat people competing with one another to see who could lose the most weight—all in front of a national audience. Contestants' calories were severely restricted and lengthy, extreme exercise routines became the crown jewel of the show. Its stars weren't the contestants but trainers Bob Harper and Jillian Michaels, who openly berated contestants who asked for breaks, often resorting to name calling and personal judgments. The show ran for seventeen seasons, from 2004 to 2016. A national study followed contestants for years after the show and found, among other things, that the show's tactics had left their metabolisms permanently damaged in what one doctor with the National Institutes of Health called "frightening and amazing."[20]

Despite this damning evidence regarding the show's approach, in 2019, USA Network announced that *The Biggest Loser* would return to the air the following year. "We're reimagining *The Biggest Loser* for today's audiences, providing a new, holistic 360-degree look at wellness, while retaining the franchise competition format and legendary jaw-dropping moments," said a statement from network president Chris McCumber, adding that USA was "excited to add another big, buzzy show to our growing unscripted lineup."[21] Even in a culture that increasingly pays lip service to body positivity and "wellness" over dieting, fat shaming never seems to go out of style.

In the last few years, a new kind of fat representation has become re-popularized, much of it echoing Tracy Turnblad, the lead character in John Waters's iconic film-turned-musical *Hairspray* (1988). Tracy, first played by a young Ricki Lake, has quickly become an icon for many young fat women, especially fat white women, and it's no wonder why. So many portrayals of fat people make our bodies into morality tales, warnings of the dangers of assumed gluttony or imagined sloth. Our bodies are consistently depicted as *befores*, forever yearning to become *afters*. But *Hairspray* bucks that trend. Tracy Turnblad's character development doesn't hinge on weight loss, remorse for "letting herself go," or guilt for her size. She is not a tool to stoke audiences' disgust, condescension, pity, or rage. She does not stand for anything, is not a symbol of capitalism run amok, or self-loathing, not a representation of bloated wealth or lazy poverty. Tracy simply stands for *herself*. And in recent years, more characters have begun to follow suit. Hulu's *Shrill*, Netflix's *Dumplin'*, and AMC's *Dietland* have all offered scripted versions of strong fat protagonists—all brought to life by fat writers who painstakingly work to eke out space simply to exist in the only bodies they've ever had. TLC's reality series *My Big Fat Fabulous Life* follows Whitney Way Thore, a fat dancer who isn't waiting for weight loss to live her best life. These programs—featuring fat characters, created by fat writers, played by fat actors—offer a rare glimpse into the lives of fat people *as we are*, not as thin people imagine us to be. Still, these characters remain painfully limited. All these shows center the stories of straight, cisgender, teenage, and adult white women in stubbornly heterosexual narratives. They focus on lead characters who are fat, but not *too* fat, and most center bodies with etiologies, explanations for bodies that deviate from the thinness audiences will expect. Yes, fat stories are rarely told by fat people—but when they are, they're told by and about those of us whose bodies are, aside from their fatness, already marked by privilege. The stories of fat white women are scarce; LGBTQ fat people, fat disabled people, and fat people of color are exponentially scarcer. Even when fat stories are produced, we're only offered one standard deviation from privilege.

Sometimes, the fat white women at the center of fat stories are party to the continued exclusion and erasure of women of color. When *Isn't It Romantic?* was released, Rebel Wilson, proudly trumpeted her role as its romantic lead. "I'm proud to be the first ever plus-size girl to be the star of a romantic comedy," said Wilson on *The Ellen DeGeneres Show*. But years earlier, Queen Latifah had starred in *The Last Holiday* and *Just Wright*. Just two years before Wilson's role, Mo'Nique had also starred in *Phat Girlz*. Upon being corrected by Black women on Twitter, Wilson began blocking those who sought to correct the record. She later stated that it "was never my intention to erase anyone else's achievements and I adore you Queen Latifah so, so much."[22] Still, her critics remained blocked and uncredited. Still, the lion's share of fat stories stubbornly center whiteness.

As much as some plucky, relatable fat characters have come into the mainstream, there's another side to confident fat leads. In reality shows and scripted programming, fat people are frequently used as props for building thinner people's confidence. In Greta Gerwig's critically acclaimed *Lady Bird*, the lead's best friend, Julie, plays a classic fat archetype—a best friend with no meaningful storyline or character arc of her own. When Julie learns she's been cast opposite Lady Bird's crush in their school play, she poignantly tells her self-absorbed best friend why it matters so much to her. "It's probably my only shot at that, you know?" Julie's most meaningful, personal scene finds her sitting alone on her couch on prom night, wearing a sweatshirt while she stares sadly at the television. Her night only begins when she gets a call from Lady Bird, the thinner character with a more real life.

Recent fat sitcom characters, confident though they may be, are still played for laughs—and their seemingly misplaced confidence becomes part of the joke. The show *30 Rock* saw its lead, Jenna Maroney, gain weight and make a punchline of herself, finding success and a new stream of cashflow from her new catchphrase "me want food!" *Parks & Recreation* featured Jerry Gergich, an exceptionally kind fat man with a kind and beautiful family. More a running joke than a character, despite his deep kindheartedness, Jerry is blamed by *everyone* for *everything*. His sweetness, deeply good heart, and thoughtful gestures don't matter; his body is still played for laughs, still inviting the blame for anything that goes wrong. Even confident fat characters have been reconfigured in thin folks' imaginations to be the butt of the joke. Our bodies are never just bodies; our stories, never our own.

Most media portrayals of fat people are designed to elicit a narrow band of reactions from thin viewers: Pity, which leads to inspiration. Anger, which fuels judgment. Disgust, which is believed to kickstart motivation, despite ample evidence to the contrary. Too often, these are the *only* reactions prompted for audiences when fat characters are on screen. And like the emotions they cue, the messages and tropes used in so much fat media representation are a similarly limited, well-tread territory that reduce fat characters to punchlines and punching bags.

Over the last thirty years, the majority of fat representation has pushed just a few reductive narratives that are tired, hackneyed, and as ubiquitous as ever. One of the most popular messages about fat bodies in film and television is that fat bodies are disgusting and funny. This is often promulgated through the use of fat suits, or "weight prosthetics," allowing disproportionately thin actors to portray fat characters as repulsive punchlines without ever engaging an actually fat person. These narratives overwhelmingly feature thin people dressing as fat people, often for the express purpose of mocking us and our bodies. The 1990s and early 2000s were replete with fat suit performances designed to elicit disgusted laughter, and they largely fall into one of three categories.

The first fat suit narrative shows a fat person's pitiable and limited life as a fat teenager, a gray and grainy "before" picture offered up as a tempting contrast to the technicolor "after" of the thin life that inevitably follows. Flashbacks to Monica Geller's youth on *Friends* found her fat and awkward. In *Just Friends*, Ryan Reynolds donned a fat suit to play Chris Brander, a formerly fat man whose "friend zoned" high school rejection led to major weight loss and an adulthood marked by endless sexual conquests. Fatness humanizes a thin person, makes sense of their adult insecurities and neuroses, and evens the playing field between the audience and an otherwise impossibly thin example of the beauty standard. Over the course of the story, we watch these recently thin protagonists come to accept that now that they're thin, they're deserving of the love and acceptance they've gained. (Stars, they're just like us!)

The second narrative offers fatness as evidence of or a consequence for bad behavior—a satisfying kind of *schadenfreude* offered as poetic justice for shallow and cruel characters whose terrible psyche is finally manifested in a body the story regards as objectively terrible. Ben Stiller's bullying character in *Dodgeball: A True Underdog Story* got his comeuppance in a final fat-suited scene, showing Stiller shirtless, surrounded by open bags of chips and popcorn, his naked belly covered in crumbs. In the books and films of J. K. Rowling's Harry Potter series, the fatness of Dudley Dursley and his father, Vernon, seem to be offered as evidence and manifestation of their stunted empathy and craven cruelty.

The third narrative is more overtly mean-spirited. In it, fat characters are played by thin actors for a mocking, cruel kind of comic relief. *The Klumps, Austin Powers*, and *Norbit* all used this approach: put thin actors in fat suits to play exaggerated, food-obsessed, physically repulsive, socially dense, and painfully unselfconscious people for laughs. Mike Myers's *Austin Powers* films featured a fat-suited Myers playing Fat Bastard, an angry, forever flatulent Scot known for constantly eating—eating human babies and little people, in particular. In *The Nutty Professor*, Eddie Murphy played an entire fat family, including Professor Sherman Klump, an accomplished scientist whose gluttony and clumsiness are reliably played for disgusted laughs. The trailer finds Professor Klump knocking a woman over on the dance floor, being called fat by his boss, and knocking over a table full of equipment to riotous laughter from a lecture hall full of students. At home, he dines with his family while his father angrily rails against weight loss. "I know what healthy is," he snaps, drowning a plate of meat and potatoes beneath cups of gravy.[23] Tyler Perry and Martin Lawrence caricatured fat Black women in their respective *Madea* and *Big Momma's House* franchises. The fat caricatures in these narratives are unquestionably cruel, designed exclusively to mock and shame fat people.

In all of these narratives, thin people write the script, thin people direct the movie, and thin people play fat people—and all center thinness as normal, good, and right by depicting fatness as a shameful, troubling, or comedic transgression. These are fat narratives created *entirely absent of any actual fat people*. All three present fatness not only as a changeable characteristic but as a prerequisite for a real, human, well-rounded life. Fat characters have not earned fat actors. Their stories are not worthy of fat writers.

Even more insidious than that is the quiet underpinning offered by fat suits. Fat suit narratives subtly assert that thin people know as much as (or more than) fat people do about what it's like to be fat, that fat bodies are only temporary, and that fat people who stay fat are simply shirking their responsibility to create a body that would earn them respect.

There is a cultural weight to fat suit narratives, and it pulls everyone down. These narratives are contrived by thin people for thin audiences, regularly taking a set of assertions for granted:

1. Becoming thin is a life accomplishment and the only way to start living a real, full, human life.
2. All fatness is a shameful moral failing.
3. Thinness is a naturally superior way of being.
4. Fat people who stay fat deserve to be mocked.

Fat suit narratives set up a painfully overt power dynamic, reinforced over and over and over again. But it's one that's so ubiquitous that we've come to passively accept it, using sheer exposure to quiet the objections of our conscience, which reminds us of what we already know: there is more than enough body shame to go around in the world.

Another predominant storyline is that fat love and sex—especially confident fat sexuality—are laughable. Fat sexuality becomes so unthinkable that the mere thought of it becomes a punchline. In *Pitch Perfect*, Rebel Wilson's character, Fat Amy, says she joins her college a capella group to get away from "all [her] ex-boyfriends," a line played for laughs. How could a fat girl have *multiple* ex-boyfriends and how could they possibly want her back? *Pitch Perfect 2* finds Rebel Wilson's character, Fat Amy, as a star soloist in a high-production performance at the Kennedy Center. She descends from the ceiling on acrobatic aerial silks and, as she swings from them, her costume rips at the crotch, revealing her bare buttocks. The camera seems to relish showing us the exaggerated disgust of the audience. One announcer shouts, "She's turning—brace yourselves!" while the other shrieks, "Not the front! Nobody wants to see the front!" before both revert to horror movie screams. Her fat body is depicted as being so comically undesirable that it unleashes terror in everyone who sees it.

The 2000 Tom Green comedy *Road Trip* also made a running joke of the categorical repulsiveness of fat women. In its trailer, we find out that Kyle (DJ Qualls) finds a love interest. Rhonda (Mia Amber Davis, a plus-size model) is Black and fat, her casting a lazy visual gag against Kyle's

pale, diminutive frame. Later, Kyle produces plus-size leopard-print pant-
ies to show his friends. "Did you kill a cheetah?" asks one incredulously,
before the camera savors each of the men's disgusted responses and mock-
retching. The simple fact of sleeping with a fat Black woman is a joke unto
itself. That punchline is compounded by Kyle's inability to meet the expectations of his straight, white, thin peers—presumably that he should pursue
a thin white woman.[24]

2007's *Norbit* makes fat sexual repulsion into a full-length movie. In it,
Eddie Murphy wears a fat suit to play Rasputia, a domineering fat Black
woman who bullies her thin partner, Norbit, into a relationship. In grade
school, Rasputia chases off Norbit's bullies before asking if he has a girlfriend. When he says no, she says, "You do now," and drags her unwilling
boyfriend away by the hand. The two stay together into adulthood, when
Rasputia grows into a shrill, sexually domineering and oblivious stereotype
of a fat Black woman. In the film's trailer, she tells a friend that she "can't
keep Norbit off" her, before the trailer shows Rasputia breaking their bed
repeatedly by launching herself onto her cowed, unwilling partner. As in
Pitch Perfect 2, Rasputia's body causes horror in everyone who sees it. At a
water park, the theme from *Jaws* plays ominously as she takes her seat at the
top of the waterslide, bystanders and children shrieking at the sight of her
bikini-clad body descending the slide. Like Saartjie Baartman, the South African woman put on display in nineteenth-century European freak shows for
her large buttocks and distinctly fat Black body, Rasputia's body is frequently
depicted as a monstrosity, played for both fear and disgust. The film is one
long fat joke, all hinging on the idea that this fat Black woman is categorically undesirable, that she has only found a partner through a comedic kind
of abuse, and that being desired by a fat Black woman is something to fear.[25]

Some films find fat attraction so categorically inconceivable that it requires head trauma or hypnotism. In the Farrelly brothers' *Shallow Hal*, Jack
Black's character needs to be hypnotized in order to find a fat woman attractive, paving the way for a feature-length fat joke. Amy Schumer starred in
I Feel Pretty, in which her character, Renee, sustained a head injury that left
her believing she was thin, gorgeous, and irresistible. Rebel Wilson's role in
Isn't It Romantic? followed suit. Wilson's character, Natalie, believes that a
man may be making a pass at her on the subway when, as it turns out, he only
wants to steal her purse. She runs away, running into a steel post and knocking herself out. When she comes to, she finds herself trapped in a romantic

comedy in which her leading man, played by Liam Hemsworth, falls in love with her at first sight.

While fat women are often portrayed as comically undesirable, fat men are often presented as unintelligent, oblivious, angry, or thwarted. American sitcoms frequently center around nuclear families, and those nuclear families regularly feature fat, hapless men married to thin, gracious women. Homer Simpson is an animated fat icon who is also famously unintelligent, incompetent, interpersonally oblivious, and negligent. His fat is such a stalwart feature of the show that, in one classic episode of *The Simpsons*, Homer purposefully gains weight so that he can seek disability-related accommodations to work from home. Following in Homer Simpson's footsteps is *Family Guy*'s Peter Griffin, also fat and unintelligent. Peter's size is frequently a plot point on the show. In one episode, his fat body causes him to develop his own gravitational pull powerful enough that household objects and small appliances fall into orbit around his body.[26] In another, he eats thirty hamburgers in one sitting, causing a stroke that leaves him paralyzed, limping, and with impaired speech. Peter Griffin and Homer Simpson are archetypes of fat, white, middle-class sitcom fathers whose size is openly ridiculed and who are too ignorant, gluttonous, and lazy to change their bodies.

When those fat sitcom dads are working class, however, they become angry and thwarted. Ralph Kramden, star of the classic 1950s sitcom *The Honeymooners*, is a modern root of this particular archetype. Kramden, played by Jackie Gleason, is a fat white working-class bus driver who frequently engages in get-rich-quick schemes. He threatens to abuse his wife, Alice, so frequently that his most famous catchphrase was uttered through gritted teeth, with one balled-up fist held in front of his face: "One of these days, Alice! Pow! Right in the kisser!" In the 1970s, *All in the Family*'s Archie Bunker became the fat white working-class sitcom father of note, both cantankerous and proudly regressive in his politics.

By the 1990s, many of TV's most notable angry fat dads were Black men. *Family Matters*' Carl Winslow was forever irritated by his nerdy neighbor Steve Urkel, frequently erupting in thwarted anger at the teen. On *The Fresh Prince of Bel-Air*, seemingly the entire personality of the family's patriarch, Uncle Phil, was comprised of mild irritation and major anger. The quick-tempered father figure is wealthy, Ivy League educated, and professionally accomplished as an attorney and a judge, but he still bears all the hallmarks of an archetypal working class thwarted, fat sitcom dad and a stereotypical angry Black man. Fat white fathers are afforded the opportunity to be unwise, negligent, and happily oblivious to the world around them. Fat Black fathers are marked by their short tempers and are forever thwarted by their own families.

Some fat characters are consumed by revenge, soured by their own failing bodies. Two of the 1990s' most iconic sitcom villains were fat people. On *Seinfeld*, Jerry's fat postal worker neighbor, Newman, constantly plotted to undermine him, earning him a spot on *TV Guide*'s "60 Nastiest Villains of All Time"[27] list and making him #16 on *Rolling Stone*'s "40 Greatest TV Villains of All Time" list.[28] Newman tattles on Jerry's bad behavior to Jerry's parents, causes a flea infestation in Jerry's apartment, and hides bags of lazily undelivered mail in Jerry's basement storage space. Like Ralph Kramden, Newman frequently launches shortsighted get-rich-quick schemes, such as driving empty cans and bottles to Michigan to redeem them for ten cents instead of New York's five-cent rate. As with many sitcom dads, Newman is neither thoughtful nor intelligent, but he is constantly scheming, either to accrue wealth or to take down the show's thinner title character.

The Drew Carey Show took the fat villain archetype one step further with Mimi Bobeck, a fat personal assistant who works with the show's title character. Mimi's clothing resembles that of a circus clown, all ruffled muumuus and shapeless caftans, and her sky-high blue eyeshadow appears to be modeled after famed drag queen Divine (herself the inspiration for *The Little Mermaid*'s Ursula, another iconic fat villain). Early in the show's run, Mimi is established as Drew's nemesis after he denies her a job because of her makeup. In subsequent episodes, Mimi torments Drew, gluing his hand to a pornographic magazine and later sending an unconscious and nonconsenting Drew to China. Mimi frequently insults Drew's weight, frequently calling him "Pig." Like Newman, Mimi's character is scheming and fixated on causing harm to the show's titular (and less fat) protagonist.

But thwarted, revenge-hungry fat villains are not solely the work of sitcoms. NBC's long-running police procedural drama, *Law & Order: Special Victims Unit*, has repeatedly featured plots centering fat villains who ultimately murder their tormentors. In the episode "Mean," Agnes Linsky is a working-class fat high school senior who is relentlessly bullied by a group of mean girls at her private school. The mean girls murder one of their friends, then accuse Agnes of being the perpetrator. After the group's arrest, Agnes hopes her bullying will end, but their final act is to take candid photographs of Agnes naked, changing in the school locker room, and circulate them to the rest of the class, unleashing a new wave of bullying from all sides. In the final scene, Agnes admits to murdering one of the bullies, tearfully telling detectives, "It was never going to stop."[29] In the episode "Fat," a Black man, Rudi Bixton, is beaten by two thin white teenagers simply for being fat. Rudi's fat younger siblings retaliate, assaulting his assailants as payback. When his assailants escape any legal accountability, Rudi fatally shoots them. When Rudi is convicted of murder, he is not present for the reading of the verdict, having been rushed to the hospital for an emergency amputation caused by his diabetes. One detective wonders aloud if a prison sentence is even necessary, since he assumes Bixton will soon die of the diseases brought on by his fatness.[30] Even when fat characters are endlessly tormented, defending our families and ourselves still makes villains of us.

Fat bodies are endlessly portrayed as the result of laziness, gluttony, and dysfunction. In *Mike & Molly*, the show's title characters meet in Overeaters Anonymous, its premise explaining why its leads have such abjectly failed fat bodies. In *This Is Us*, Chrissy Metz plays Kate Pearson, whose entire persona seems to revolve around her fatness, including her binge eating disorder. Kate's character has long been slated for a so-called "weight-loss journey," with NBC going so far as to famously mandate weight loss in Metz's contract as a requirement for her acceptance of the role.[31]

Even more infamously, the premise of Netflix's *Insatiable* hinged on its lead character's dramatic weight loss. Its lead character, Patty, is a fat high school student, relentlessly bullied for her weight. Patty is frequently depicted as slovenly and unable to stop binging on junk foods. Unable, that is, until she spends a summer with her jaw wired shut, returning in the fall as a thin and glamorous young woman with a thirst for revenge. Now, as a thinner—and more real—character, Patty can take her place as the show's lead, having shed her dysfunctional and pitiable fat body. In *Insatiable*, as in so much of film and television, fat bodies are always temporary, symptomatic of either pitiable dysfunction or sinful sloth and gluttony.

The theses about fat bodies presented in mainstream television and film are neither benign nor accidental. These well-worn tropes are extraordinarily reductive, and their impacts are far-reaching, both creating a social template for thin people's understandings and judgments of fat people, and simultaneously laying a narrow foundation for the kinds of people fat folks are allowed to be. Media representation of fat characters is tightly tied to a handful of wildly oversimplified stereotypes, perpetuating and magnifying them and flattening us in the process.

For some fat people, stories like these may ring true: they may be members of Overeaters Anonymous, like the title characters in *Mike and Molly*. They may have been ridiculed by thin lovers' friends, like Mia was in *Road Trip*. But even if they do ring true, fat people's lives are so much more than our bodies. Fat people have complex interior lives, complicated love lives, professional triumphs, and personal tragedies.

As it stands, the lion's share of fat stories are told by thin people whose limited imaginations reduce us to our aberrant bodies, but there are exceptions.

I first saw *Can You Ever Forgive Me?* alone. In it, Melissa McCarthy plays Lee Israel, an author whose work has lost interest, audience, and sales. She struggles to make ends meet, living on a shoestring in a cramped, messy apartment. Over the course of the film, she uses her writing talents to solve her financial problems—not through writing new books but through forging correspondences from Noel Coward, Dorothy Parker, and other literary luminaries. McCarthy plays Israel as she reportedly was: a prickly lesbian trying to eke out a living in a literary world that didn't want her work.

The film is a discomfiting symphony, all cacophonous accountability. Israel's ex, played by Anna Deavere Smith, offers insight into the demise of their relationship with the exhaustion of returning to well-trod territory. The FBI closes in on Israel as she continues to sell forged letters. She is held accountable for her behavior from her agent, her friend, her ex, and ultimately law enforcement. On every front, Israel is forced to face the consequences of a lifetime of bad behavior. Her character arc is a simple and internal one: Lee Israel realizes she's lived her life as an asshole, and that, as she presents her allocution in court, she has reaped what she has sown.

Lee Israel, both as she is played by McCarthy and as she lived, is no role model. She is neither a queer hero nor a fat icon, nor is she a triumphant underdog to be celebrated by her respective communities. But as the film drew to a close, I found myself weeping, a cathartic and guttural kind of cry. This was the representation I had needed for so long. Not a meticulously crafted Fabergé egg of a character, nor an impermeable fortress of a heroine. No, McCarthy's portrayal of Lee Israel was better than that. She had a privilege often reserved for thin men and exquisitely beautiful thin women. She was excruciatingly human, and she was deeply unlikable.

Can You Ever Forgive Me? doesn't present its lead in contrast to more real thin people. It does not force her through a weight-loss story arc to earn her redemption. It does not seek her redemption. Like Mary Louise Parker's character in *Weeds*, Julia Louis-Dreyfus in *Veep*, Hailee Steinfeld in *Edge of Seventeen*, Larry David in *Curb Your Enthusiasm*, and Woody Allen in nearly everything, McCarthy's Lee Israel was an asshole. As with those thinner counterparts, Israel's body is not chalked up to her character; it remains almost entirely uncommented upon. Her body is her body. Her character is her character. And her character is unsympathetic. *Can You Ever Forgive Me?* wasn't refreshing because its lead was a jerk; it was refreshing because she was a *person*.

In 2016, Taika Waititi directed *Hunt for the Wilderpeople*, starring Julian Dennison as Ricky Baker, a fat Māori boy whose preteen vandalism and hooliganism have made him the problem child of New Zealand's foster-care system. Baker is finally placed with his estranged aunt who, for the first time, shows the boy genuine love and care, embracing his quirks and working to make him happy. Shortly thereafter, his aunt passes away, leaving Ricky with his gruff uncle (Sam Neill) as the two voyage through the wilderness and grief together. Ricky Baker is flawed, having lived through so many traumas in his continuing childhood, but Waititi presents him as comedic and endearing, frustrated and vulnerable, tender and real. His body does not determine his story—his experiences and his character do.

"Can I show you something?"

A family member hands me her iPad, her face lit up with eager excitement. She holds it in front of both of us, sidling up to me, watching me closely for a happy or grateful reaction—something to reinforce her discovery. Instead, she watches my face fall.

On the screen are before and after pictures from surgeons' offices, advertisements for gastric bypass, and lap band surgeries. On the left side of the screen is a woman my size, slouching and exposed, in fitted workout clothing. Next to her is an image of that same woman, beaming and standing tall, half her previous size.

I am before. I am always before.

"I saw these pictures and I thought of you. Think of how much healthier you would be. The partners you could date. I know you love clothes—you could wear whatever you want!"

She pages through the pictures, watching my face for the happiness she's sure will come. The relief she imagines when I learn that there is a way out of the body that I have—all it will take is $23,000 to cut that body open, truss its organs, and leave it to shrink itself.

But in this moment, I have already been gutted.

I search the faces of the images of the "before" women. They stare ahead, blank, stony, knowing that the bodies they have—the ones they are not meant to have—will live on in this photograph.

When we reduce fat people to their bodies, to "before and after," or to bellies and rolls, we come to think of fat people as bodies without personhood. Fat bodies become symbols of disembodied disgust. As in a news report, at the very moment we are meant to be learning about fatness, the conversation is devoid not only of the voices of fat people but of our very faces.

These images—flattened, inhuman—reinforce so much troubling thinking about fat people. Whether background visuals on the news or before and after photos in advertisements, we are more symbol than human. We become effigies, archetypes, morality tales, punchlines, threats, epidemics, but never just people. We are captured, pressed between pages like butterflies, forever frozen to illustrate our anatomies. We do not speak. We do not move. We are only and forever bodies.

Fat people are afforded a voice or a face when our bodies change or when we express the grief, regret, guilt, and shame that thin people imagine must come from having bodies like ours. What they do not consider is the crumpling that happens when you see your body, every day, represented as a cautionary tale for someone else. If you are not careful, you may become a monstrosity like me, a before desperately awaiting an after. Because after, you can be heard. After, you are not required to renounce your own body in order to be accepted and embraced. You may share your experiences, hopes, dreams, plans, without weighing them down with caveats, dress sizes, inches, or pounds. After, you can have a face. After, you can smile. After, you can speak.

My body does not afford me those luxuries. My body is before.

But I don't choose to believe that.

I choose to believe that fat people can be genuinely attractive, truly loved, actually lovable, sincerely wanted.

I choose to believe that my fat friends and family members who are in love are loved fully, are fulfilled in those relationships, and that their partners are not somehow damaged for wanting them. I believe that my past loves with fat partners weren't some symptom of a sinister sickness for either of us, but something real and worthwhile.

I reject the notion that fat attraction is necessarily a fetish: something deviant, tawdry, vulgar, or dangerous. I choose to believe that my body is worthy of love—the electric warmth of real, full love. In many ways, it's not that simple. But in some ways, it is. I choose to believe that I am lovable, as is my body, just as both are today.

I believe that I deserve to be loved *in* my body, not in spite of it. My body is not an inconvenience, a shameful fact, or an unfortunate truth. Desiring my body is not a pathological act. And I'm not alone. Despite the never-ending headwinds, fat people around the world find and forge the relationships they want. There is no road map, so we become cartographers, charting some new land for ourselves. We live extraordinary lives, beloved by our families, partners, communities. Fat people fall wildly in love. Fat people get married. Fat people have phenomenal sex. Fat people are impossibly happy. Those fat people live in defiance of the expectations set forth for them. Their fat lives are glorious and beautiful things, vibrant and beyond the reach of what the rest of us have been trained to imagine. Let's imagine more.

FIRST, DO NO HARM

I was twenty-six years old the last time I saw a doctor.

I visited urgent care for an ear infection, a mildly embarrassing, infantile reaction to stress that my body had never seemed to move past. At work, we were at the height of a campaign, and I had yet to learn how to manage my stress more effectively. So I laid awake at night, restless and worried, until my body reacted. On this particular day it meant an ear canal so inflamed that it had nearly swollen shut.

I was accustomed to the routine: step on the scale and listen to a medical assistant wince and apologize for the fact of my weight. I usually sit on the chair next to the exam table, in case the table can't support my weight. Explain patiently to the doctor that despite being an adult, I still face this childlike condition. Joke about bubblegum-flavored chewable amoxicillin. Leave with a prescription for ear drops and ten days' worth of antibiotics. And, that's typically how it goes.

I had developed a skill set—a charm offensive as a preemptive strike against the assumptions that come along with a body like mine. Usually, it worked; nurses and doctors loosened up, lightened up their lectures, eased up on expressing their deep judgments and issuing mandates. But today, the charm offensive was useless. The doctor was a severe man without much humor to him. My jokes fell flat, my smiles went unreturned. With him, my warmth was somehow a liability. So I reverted to an all-business approach, mirroring his own. The appointment continued, cold and direct, without event. I thought I may have escaped the *de rigueur* lectures, the condescension, the heavy judgment that so often followed from healthcare providers. I was wrong.

As the doctor handed me prescriptions for ear drops and antibiotics, I asked about any after care I should take on. He sighed, eyes stern and brow furrowed in disapproval.

"You should lose weight," he said plainly. "Immediately."

My shoulders dropped, muscles going slack in the face of an exchange I'd had so many times before.

"My ears didn't get fat," I snapped back, without thinking, surprised at the force of my own irritation.

"You asked," he snapped. He glared for a moment, heaved another sigh, then left, his door slam thwarted by the muted, slow work of the door's quiet hinge. We were both frustrated, and neither of us got what we were looking for.

That sneaking wave of anger didn't emerge fully formed from whole cloth that day. It had been a long time coming. This was far from the first time a healthcare provider had prescribed weight loss for what I was certain was an unrelated condition. Every symptom I described, every malady that led me to seek treatment, had all been attributed to my size. If I weren't fat, I'd been told, I wouldn't have gotten strep throat, ear infections, a Charlie horse, or a common cold. I sat through countless appointments with doctors walking me through the BMI chart, pointing to my BMI of 50 and explaining to me that I was considered super morbidly obese. My body was a death sentence, and the only way to save my life, they insisted, was to get me to a "healthy weight" of less than one-third my size.

I had dieted and exercised, lost weight in major spurts (if only to regain it later), and the lowest weight I had ever managed was 275. Under the unforgiving rubric of the BMI, this was a failure of my character. I simply lacked the tenacity, the work ethic, the determination to become thin enough to save myself. My life was on the line, I was told, and I would only have myself to blame if I couldn't manage the impossible.

Not every healthcare provider lectured so sternly, but their anti-fatness showed up regardless.

I was visiting family in California when my hearing cut out. It was disorienting and alarming, losing one of my senses so abruptly. The world sounded muffled, like it was tucked away behind a closed door, distant and unreachable. A sharp pain somewhere between my ear and my skull served as a piercing reminder of the loss of my hearing. Alarmed and sympathetic, my mother drove me to the nearest urgent care that takes my insurance.

The nurse who greeted me was kind and warm. We talked freely as she took my vital signs, though our conversation was complicated by my failing hearing. She took my blood pressure, then looked at the cuff with a crooked frown. She took my blood pressure again, then made the same face. She excused herself to get another cuff—larger, this time.

I felt my heart beating in my throat. *What if something's wrong? What if my ears are just a symptom of something more sinister, more alarming? What if this is the death they've so long said was coming for me?*

"What's the matter?" I asked, trying to temper the frightened shake of my voice.

"I'm just not getting a good read," she said, adjusting the cuff once again.

"Is everything okay?" I asked, more afraid than before.

"It's coming back great," she said, the good news belied by her befuddled tone. "But that can't be right. Obese patients don't have good blood pressure."

She had learned that being fat meant being sick, and invariably, that sickness would lead to death. Just looking at me, she became certain that I must be in poor health. And her certainty was so great that it overrode the data in front of her. My sickness was inevitable, so good health was unfathomable.

I entrusted her with my health, and she couldn't see it.

Even outside the doctor's office itself, bias seemed to follow me everywhere. In the waiting room of the mental health department at my local Kaiser Permanente, I waited for an appointment to treat my panic disorder. Another patient leaned over to tell me *a woman your size shouldn't wear belts.* I wondered what treatment she was seeking.

Between appointments with healthcare providers, I found myself researching the experiences of fat patients and the most biased policies of providers. Somehow, that surreptitious research both quelled and fueled my growing dread and anxiety about my next visit. Shortly after my spat with the urgent care doctor, I stumbled upon a story from the South Florida *Sun Sentinel.* The reporter surveyed local obstetrics-gynecology practices and found that 14 percent had set a weight limit on their patients. "Fifteen obstetrics-gynecology practices out of 105 polled by the *Sun Sentinel* said they have set weight cutoffs for new patients starting at 200 pounds or based on measures of obesity—and turn down women who are heavier."[1] Three years later Helen Carter, a primary care physician in Massachusetts, publicly announced that she would no longer accept patients over 200 pounds.[2]

Every interaction around my healthcare became a minefield. Every conversation about my health left me nursing a wound that wasn't allowed to close long enough to heal. This was *Groundhog Day*, and I was stuck repeating the same doctor's appointment until—until what? Until I learned to act differently? Until I stopped hoping? Until I somehow became thin? Or until I gave up on my healthcare altogether?

Notably, my experiences are not unique—and they're far from the worst of their kind. Across the country, fat people are routinely denied medically necessary tests and care, regularly shamed by physicians, and assumed to be in ill health regardless of their bloodwork, heart rate, or blood pressure.

In 2016 Sarah Bramblette shared her story with the *New York Times*. Bramblette lives with lipedema, a condition impacting an estimated 11 percent of women, according to the National Institutes of Health.[3] Lipedema often stems from hereditary and endocrinological issues, though the causes of the condition are not confirmed, leaving women with significant deposits of fat in their legs.[4]

Like many women with lipedema, Bramblette was fat. And like many fat people, her doctor prescribed a very low-calorie diet—1,200 calories a day, the minimum amount that wouldn't trigger a starvation response, causing her body to cling to its fat. Bramblette wanted to know how much she weighed, so that she would know if her prescribed diet was working. But the doctor's scale only went up to 350 pounds—well below what Bramblette needed. She asked her doctor how she could be weighed. "The doctor had no answer. So Ms. Bramblette, 39, who lived in Ohio at the time, resorted to a solution that made her burn with shame. She drove to a nearby junkyard that had a scale that could weigh her."[5]

As a fat woman, Sarah Bramblette's experience terrifies me, not as some nightmarish dystopian future but as an ever-present, current possibility. The casual and thoughtless humiliation of fat people in medical settings takes place both intentionally—through shaming, mocking, berating, and "tough love"—and unintentionally when offices lack the exam tables, stirrups, gurneys, and scales that will hold us; the blood pressure cuffs that will fit around our arms;[6] or the crucial CT and MRI scanners that can accommodate our bodies.[7] Drug dosages, too, are based on appropriate amounts for thinner people. Testing is rarely performed on fat people, and drugs are often less effective on us, leading to underdosing of everything from antibiotics to chemotherapy.[8] Famously, Plan B—the emergency contraceptive—loses its effectiveness in those whose BMIs are in the overweight range, to say nothing of those of us who are categorized as "obese" or "extremely obese." That is, if a fat person needs emergency contraception and uses Plan B, they are significantly more likely to end up with an unplanned pregnancy. Despite this known vulnerability, as of this writing, no public research has been made available about the effectiveness of emergency contraception for fat people.[9]

Another patient, who asked to remain anonymous, shared her story with the *New York Times*. She walked through her home every day without incident. But, suddenly, that same short walk to her kitchen left her breathless and terrified for her health.

> Frightened, she went to a local urgent care center, where the doctor said she had a lot of weight pressing on her lungs. The only thing wrong with her, the doctor said, was that she was fat.
>
> "I started to cry," said the woman, who asked not to be named to protect her privacy. "I said: 'I don't have a sudden weight pressing on my lungs. I'm really scared. I'm not able to breathe.'"
>
> "That's the problem with obesity," she said the doctor told her. "Have you ever considered going on a diet?"
>
> It turned out that the woman had several small blood clots in her lungs, a life-threatening condition.[10]

In 2019, Rebecca Hiles made headlines with her story of medical neglect. As a teenager, Hiles had developed walking pneumonia that stayed with her for years. When she began to cough up blood, doctors prescribed an inhaler, and in subsequent visits, doctors insisted she should "just lose weight." Later, Hiles's coughing led to bladder leaks and vomiting. "When blood tests kept coming back normal, her doctors would say, 'We don't know what to tell you—it's clearly just weight related.'" It took six years to find a doctor who would refer her to a pulmonologist. Shortly thereafter, a CT scan revealed a malignant tumor, leading to near-immediate surgery. Hiles lost her left lung, "the bottom half of which was a black, rotting piece of dead tissue."[11] She soon learned that an earlier diagnosis at one of her countless doctor's appointments and emergency room visits could have saved her lung, and that a later diagnosis could have cost her her life. Hiles wrote on her blog:

> When my surgeon told me a diagnosis five years prior could've saved my lung, I remember a feeling of complete and utter rage. Because I remembered the five years I spent looking for some kind of reason why I was always coughing, always sick. Most of all, I remembered being consistently told that the reason I was sick was because I was fat.[12]

Hiles's experience illuminates the ways in which many healthcare providers rely on understanding their patients through what health policy and women's studies scholar Anna Kirkland calls "actuarial personhood," in which groups of people—such as fat people—are defined solely or primarily by the risk they are seen to pose.[13] According to Kirkland, actuarial personhood features "the collapse of traits of the person as a bodily individual with other features of her environment, family health history, and so on, such that the relevant description of her includes many details beyond her character and control."[14] In Hiles's case, doctors saw her first as fat, complete with those "many details" they assumed must describe her. Only years later did she find a provider who saw her as someone whose health needs might be as complex or dire as a thin person's. When it comes to fat patients, our bodies have been labeled an epidemic, our very presence somehow a threat to the health of those around us. For years Rebecca Hiles's doctors could only see the risk they projected onto her by virtue of her body, ascribing her symptoms to her size rather than her cancer.

Fat transgender people bear dual stigmas in medical settings. Those seeking surgery are frequently required by their doctors to lose significant amounts of weight prior to surgery. In most states, health insurance plans are free to exclude transition-related care, such as hormones and surgery, despite covering the same procedures in cisgender people (hormone replacement therapy, mastectomies, oophorectomies, and so forth). As of 2015, one in four trans people had been denied hormone therapy in the past year alone, and a staggering 55 percent had been denied coverage for surgery.[15] In TLC's *Too Fat to Transition*, fat transgender people are followed as they try to lose the amount of weight prescribed by their surgeons in order to receive the healthcare that may save them from bullying, discrimination, suicide, and murder.[16]

For thin people, these stories of fat patients simply trying to access basic healthcare may be sobering. But for fat people, they may elicit a combination of deep terror and sad familiarity. In 2016, 45 percent of women of all sizes said that they delayed doctors' appointments until they lost weight.[17] A study published in the *Journal of the American Academy of Nurse Practitioners* showed that the degree of avoidance increased with fatter women. "Weight-related reasons for delaying/avoiding healthcare included having 'gained weight since last healthcare visit,' not wanting to 'get weighed on the provider's scale'" (or, as in the case of Sarah Bramblette, not having a scale that would hold them), "and knowing they would be told to 'lose weight.'"[18] In a cruel twist, a study called "The Ironic Effects of Weight Stigma" revealed that weight stigma *increases* the likelihood of eating caloric foods like candy and chips. The study subjects who perceived themselves as fat—regardless of their actual weight— were more likely to eat those foods than those who didn't perceive themselves as fat.[19] Another study, published in 2018 in the journal *Body Image*, found that the fatter a woman was, the more likely she was to internalize anti-fat stigma, to harbor guilt and shame about her own body, and to avoid health-care.[20] A 2013 study found that fat people who internalized anti-fat stigma had lower self-esteem, higher levels of depression and anxiety, and worsened overall health.[21] Research has also linked internalized weight bias to predia-betes and "a conglomerate of cardiovascular disease risk factors that strongly increases the risk for diabetes, heart disease, and stroke."[22] That is, what we think of as health risks associated with being fat may in fact be health risks of experiencing discrimination and internalizing stigma.

But this internalized stigma doesn't simply emerge cut from whole cloth. It is woven into nearly every aspect of society in the United States. The Rudd Center for Food Policy and Obesity at Yale University and Harvard University's implicit bias research both indicate that anti-fat stigma is on the rise in the United States, and healthcare providers are no exception to that trend.[23] Like the rest of us, doctors, nurses, and healthcare providers of all stripes have internalized deeply flawed, harmful stereotypes and judgments about fat people. But unlike the rest of us, healthcare providers are in posi-tions of immense power. We count on them to define what the symptoms in our bodies mean. We count on them to tell us how to prolong our lives and stave off early death. And we count on them to interpret our bodies clearly for us, trusting them implicitly with our very lives. But for fat people, as stories like Rebecca Hiles's show, healthcare providers' interpretation is clouded by their judgment with staggering regularity. And despite health-care providers' extensive training on the mechanics of our bodies, the train-ing is modeled on the realities of thin bodies and rarely teaches providers to confront their own bias. In some cases, it may even enhance their bias.

Over the last two decades, a growing body of research has indicated a frightening trend of anti-fatness among healthcare providers. In 2001 the *International Journal of Obesity* published a study that found those anti-fat judgments caused material differences in the outcomes of care received by fatter patients. In office visits with fat patients, the study found that many physicians wrote notes "suggesting a belief that those who are overweight must also be unhappy and unstable," including comments like "this woman has a very unhappy life," "suffering underlying depression," and "most likely a drug addict."[24] Of the 122 primary care physicians who participated in the study, 10 percent suggested anti-depressants for their fat patients. Fat patients also received shorter visits. The average office visit for a thin pa-tient with a migraine headache is 31 minutes. For a patient with an BMI considered as "obese," that time drops to twenty-two minutes. "Certainly if physicians give additional tests (whether weight-related or not) to heavier patients, they may be giving compromised care—they are doing more tests in a much shorter period of time. [. . .] The pattern of responses seems to reflect that physicians feel more negativity toward heavier patients."[25] The fatter the patient, the more likely the doctor will describe the office visit as "a waste of their time" and the patients as "more annoying." If a physician saw more fat patients, they said, they "would like their jobs less."

A 2003 study published in *Obesity Research* confirmed that "primary care physicians view obesity as largely a behavioral problem and share our broader society's negative stereotypes about the personal attributes of obese per-sons."[26] Of the 620 physicians who participated in the study, more than half described fat patients as "awkward, unattractive, ugly, and noncompliant." Over one-third called fat patients "weak-willed, sloppy or lazy."[27] Among health professionals specializing in the study and treatment of obesity, re-search findings are similarly bleak. In a 2012 study, researchers used the Implicit Attitudes Test to measure weight bias in 389 researchers, students, and clinicians. Participants overwhelmingly believed that fat people were "lazy, stupid, and worthless."[28] As the study's authors note:

> These findings are noteworthy given that the sample was comprised of professionals who treat and study obesity, a group that understands that obesity is caused by genetic and environmental factors and is not simply a function of individual behavior. Hence, the stigma of obesity is so strong that even those most knowledgeable about the condition infer that obese people have blameworthy behavioral characteristics that contribute to their problem (i.e., being lazy). Furthermore, these biases extend to core characteristics of intelligence and personal worth.[29]

Even the experts to which fat people are expected to entrust our health and our very lives exhibit not only implicit bias but explicit personal judgment of the patients they study and treat. More troubling, younger participants showed greater bias against fat people, particularly around perceived worthlessness, lack of goodness, and lack of intelligence, seemingly indicating that the problem of anti-fat bias may persist well into the future.

And those attitudes aren't just internal—they significantly impact the care fat patients receive. Another study, published in the journal *Obesity*, found that primary care physicians "demonstrated less emotional rapport with overweight and obese patients."[30] In 2009, the *Journal of Clinical Nursing* published a study finding that anti-fat attitudes extended to nurses, too, and that professional nurses were more likely to harbor anti-fat bias than nursing students. "The majority of participants perceived that obese people liked food, overate, and were shapeless, slow, and unattractive. Additionally, over one half of participants believed that obese adults should be put on a diet while in hospital."[31] Yet another study of more than three hundred autopsies showed that "obese patients were 1.65 times more likely than others to have significant undiagnosed medical conditions [. . .] indicating misdiagnosis or inadequate access to healthcare."[32] Even providers who specialized in eating disorders exhibited significant anti-fat attitudes.[33]

Medical students exhibit striking rates of anti-fat bias, too, according to the journal *Obesity*. Seventy-four percent of medical students surveyed for the study exhibited some form of anti-fat attitudes, including dislike, blame, and fear. Sixteen percent agreed with the statement "I really don't like fat people much," 13.5 percent reported that they "have a hard time taking fat people seriously," and 36.6 percent—over one-third of medical students— held the belief that "fat people tend to be fat pretty much through their own fault."[34] Research shows that anti-fat bias may be contagious, catching from doctors to the medical students they instruct. In one of their studies, Mayo Clinic researcher Sean Phelan asked students if they had witnessed medi- cal school faculty making jokes, making derogatory statements, or taking discriminatory action against fat patients. On average, students' explicit bias *increased* during the course of medical school, often influenced by faculty's openly anti-fat attitudes and actions.[35] "We found that having experienced these things was a predictor of weight bias getting worse over the course of medical school. It speaks to a hidden curriculum," said Phelan.[36]

At every phase of their careers, healthcare providers of all stripes exhibit staggering levels of both overt and implicit bias against fat patients—and the fatter you are, the bigger the price you pay. These damning findings, con- firmed time and time again, suggest that fat patients don't just *feel* uncared for when we seek medical care—there's a good chance we *are* uncared for.

The bias of healthcare providers hasn't gone wholly unchallenged within their field. Despite this powerful current of anti-fat bias, some providers are swimming upstream, creating and using radically different frameworks for addressing fat folks' health needs.

Perhaps the most widely known of these is Health at Every Size, a frame- work popularized by Dr. Lindo Bacon. Health at Every Size (sometimes shortened to HAES) focuses on moving away from exercise and dieting as a punishing, endless march toward a tenuous beauty standard most of us will never attain. Instead, Dr. Bacon's approach focuses on mindful, intuitive eating, honoring our bodies' hunger and fullness cues, and exercise from a place of joy and fun. That is, rather than constantly self-flagellating for our failure to become a vision of perfect thinness, and rather than focusing on *looking like* a healthy person (what does health look like, anyway?), Health at Every Size prioritizes *taking on the behaviors* that contribute to greater over- all health—regardless of the number on the scale.

Dr. Bacon isn't alone, either. A growing number of "anti-diet dietitians" are changing the conversation among registered dietitians. Michelle Allison, Christy Harrison, Vincci Tsui, Anna Sweeney, Dana Sturtevant, Rebecca Scritchfield, and others are focused on shifting our cultural conversations about nutrition, diet, and our bodies. Like Dr. Bacon, many of these dietitians are working to center acceptance of our bodies, rather than rejection.

A growing number of doctors, dietitians, nurses, and other healthcare providers are questioning our cultural dogmas around weight and health, finding new and more forgiving paths to nurturing our own mental and physical well-being. But there's still so much more to do. While fatness has been widely and readily blamed for all manner of ills in healthcare spaces, little has been explored about the relationship between weight stigma and health. Despite prioritizing the social determinants of health— economic stability, food security, the built environments that surround us, access to culturally competent healthcare, and discrimination, among others—many healthcare providers and researchers still remain oddly silent on the topic of weight stigma. When research is conducted on the overwhelmingly negative impacts of anti-fatness, it seems to change little in healthcare provision itself. Even the anti-obesity research to which many healthcare providers are exposed is far from impartial and is funded and publicized by diet companies or pharmaceutical companies with weight-loss drugs to sell.[37] Not only are healthcare providers underinformed about the impact of their bias on patients' health and well-being, they are also *selectively informed* by moneyed interests keen on promoting their products.

The evidence that we do have about the impacts of weight stigma is troubling at best. One study showed that when participants experienced anti-fatness, "their eating increases, their self-regulation decreases, and their cortisol (an obesogenic hormone) levels are higher relative to controls, particularly among those who are or perceive themselves to be overweight."[38] Another found that experiencing anti-fatness led to avoidance of exercise.[39] Most damning of all, a study engaging 13,692 older adults found that "people who reported experiencing weight discrimination had a 60% increased risk of dying, independent of BMI."[40] Anti-fat bias, not fatness itself, may be fat people's greatest health risk.

But when it comes to turning the tide of medical bias against fat patients, research shows there's hope in a number of tactics, some of which are surprisingly simple. In 2011 researchers found that just one lecture on weight stigma and weight controllability significantly reduced psychology students' anti-fat bias. (Notably, following the lecture, students were also less likely to describe fat people as unattractive.)[41] A similar study in 2013 found effective bias intervention with a video that was just seventeen minutes long.[42] A 2012 study found that healthcare professionals who watched short films designed to reduce anti-fat bias did indeed curb their explicit bias, though their implicit attitudes remained intact.[43]

A meta-analysis of weight bias interventions found that, while none fully eradicated anti-fat bias, many led to a "small to moderate" shift in attitudes.[44] But given the relentless stigma so many fat patients face at the hands of their healthcare providers, even a small change could make a major impact. All we have to do is *try*.

At thirty-four years old—eight years after my last visit to the doctor's office—I made another appointment. The night before the appointment, I laid awake in a sleep mask, eyes open in forced darkness. A tidal wave of memories crashed over me, and I was submerged: The nurse who took my blood pressure four times, frowning, because she couldn't believe it was healthy. The doctor who prescribed weight loss as aftercare for an ear infection. The doctor who refused to touch me and, therefore, refused to treat me. The flush of my face when I say, *Yes, I eat vegetables* and *I cook my meals at home*. The familiar look of skepticism that follows, often paired with a long sigh. *Look, I can't help you if you're not going to tell me the truth*. The doctor after doctor who denied even simple tests or exams for nearly every health condition until I lost weight. The prescription for anxiety and depression: lose weight. The treatment for a persistent, mysterious hormonal imbalance: lose weight. The intervention for endless bleeding: lose weight. The frustration at being told I wasn't worth caring for until I was thin. Basic healthcare was a carrot, and these visits were the stick. Unlike so many before me, horses broken and tamed by constant punishment, I felt certain I'd never get what I needed so desperately, dangling just inches from my hungry mouth.

On the afternoon of my appointment, I was ragged, frayed from lack of sleep. I walked into the doctor's office, voice shaking and legs weak with anticipation. The medical assistant called me behind the glass, into the depths of the office. She was kind and outgoing, chatty and engaging, and I was grateful for the distraction. She measured my height: five feet, ten inches. She measured my weight: I looked away.

In the exam room, she took my blood pressure only once and, thankfully, noted my vitals without comment. She removed two vials of my blood, thick and blackish red. I was struck with the surreal vertigo of seeing my body outside itself. She asked if I was sexually active and about the gender of my partners. I told her I was and that my partners over the years had been multiple genders. Her face shattered into a smile.

"Hey girl!" she beamed, holding up an ID tag marked with a strip of rainbow tape. I laughed, surprised by the force and volume of my own voice, a little loosing of so much tension. When she left the room, I felt my heart's contractions in my chest, but the tight, pulsing anxiety that gripped my head had faded. Oceans of blood still rushed behind this dam of my body.

When the doctor entered, he met my eyes, smiled warmly, and got down to business.

"Smoke?"

"No."

"Never?"

"One cigarette in high school. I was like a cartoon of an after school special. Those weren't my real friends," I joked. He smiled kindly, the way you do when you're humoring someone, stopping just short of pitying them.

"Drink?"

"One or two."

"A day?"

"A week. I've never been much of a drinker."

"Recreational drugs?"

"No, never."

"Cannabis?"

"No." He nodded, smiling as he noted it on my chart. "I know," I added ruefully. "I'm boring."

"There's another word for that," he said. "Healthy." The word hit me hard. Despite years of organic eating and focusing on nutrition, no one had ever called me healthy.

He asked more questions and finished taking my medical history. I answered his questions honestly and asked for the tests I thought I needed. He never objected, never contradicted, never rolled his eyes or heaved a sigh. He listened, and as I watched expressions flicker across his kind and pensive face, it struck me that he might even have believed me.

"There's one more thing we should talk about." I felt my voice shake as I said it. "It's just about my history with doctors." He looked up from the chart, still calm, but more alert.

"I feel like I know what you're going to say," he said, nodding. "Go on."

I told him that I'd only been to emergency care for the better part of a decade, and I knew it wasn't helpful. I told him that I stopped seeing doctors because they stopped seeing me. So many wouldn't touch me, wouldn't examine me, wouldn't ask questions, wouldn't refer to specialists, or write prescriptions. Everything, I told him, led back to the weight loss that years of dieting and disordered eating never delivered.

I told him I was happy to talk about behaviors, and I meant it. I would talk about practices and food, and I wasn't seeking medication or kid gloves. But the answer to nearly every health problem I had faced had come without investigation, without curiosity, without seeing anything but the size of me. I told him that my body cast a long and wide shadow and that every doctor seemed focused on its silhouette, not the body from which that shadow stretched. If every prescription was to suddenly stop having the body I had always had, I said, that wasn't going to happen. After all, twenty years of constant, punishing effort hadn't changed the shape of my skin.

I told him about everything I'd done to manage the health that was so readily ignored by providers. I tracked food and vitamins in a daily diary; used a nutrition tracker to calculate vitamins, minerals, macronutrients, and amino acids; kept a calendar of exercise to ensure I was regularly moving; maintained mental healthcare and kept going to the dentist; prepped meals at home from local produce from farmers' markets and CSAs. I told him about hiring a personal trainer, and about trying every diet I could for a decade.

As I spoke, the rushing waters built beneath the skin that was so thick for so long. Those waters, that blood, were turbulent with the force of experiences that had gone unheard and unregistered for years and years. I heard my voice crack when I told him that I had tried everything I could since my teenage years. In that time, my body did not change. Neither did my healthcare.

"It sounds like your health matters a lot to you," he offered, his eyes meeting mine.

And suddenly, I wept. Mine was a wailing and irrepressible grief, called up only by this simple act of recognition. All the years of effort, all the machinations to avoid humiliation and erasure, and someone had finally noticed. Later that day, I realized that despite years of trying, no one had ever told me that I cared about my health. And I did. I do.

"I'm sorry," I told him. "I don't know why I'm crying."

But we both knew. The dam had burst.

In the coming days, I waited for test results, nervous as anyone would be. But my heart beat steadied. The blood calmed in my veins. The waters found their cadence, flowing easy and fast over the wreckage of the dam.

I didn't know what came next, but I knew that at least I'd be heard.

CHAPTER 8

THE WORLD TO COME

There is a world beyond this one.

In that world, diversity in size and shape are understood to be part of the natural variance of human bodies, from very fat people to very thin ones. So, too, are fluctuations in weight. We do not wring our hands or punish ourselves for one, five, ten pounds' change in weight. Sudden, dramatic weight loss or gain is cause for concern only because of what underlying conditions they may point to, not because weight itself is stigmatized. Bathroom scales are now largely specialized, a piece of medical equipment used temporarily or infrequently for endocrine disorders or heart conditions linked to sudden and significant changes in weight. The BMI, too, has become a relic, a kind of crude measurement understood to be a harmful, reverse-engineered calculation to defend a cruel and widespread bias. It has been tossed on the junk heap of historical pseudoscience, alongside hysteria and phrenology.

In that world, each of us is judged based on our actions, not our bodies. We do not draw conclusions about others' character based on the way they look, what they eat, how they move, or how they live their lives differently than ours. Bodies are not believed to be meritocracies and thinness is not understood to be a crowning achievement. Like hair color and height, our size is a simple and uninteresting fact about each of us in that world. It is not something over which to be fixated or troubled, and it is widely understood to be a staggeringly boring topic of conversation. Diet talk is a thing of the past, understood to be a troubling and harmful trigger for people with eating disorders and fat people alike, replaced instead by grounded, emotional reflections on the ways our bodies change like the seasons. The weight-loss industry is widely written off as a scam, some perplexing, sepia-toned relic of a time gone by.

Healthcare is accessible regardless of size, shape, or ability. Doctors, nurses, and healthcare providers of all kinds examine fat patients with the same level of attentiveness and curiosity as thin patients. Health insurance is free and available to all of us, and insurers don't require weight loss before covering medically necessary treatments. Health outcome gaps are closing between fat and thin people, and doctors are trained in providing competent care to fat patients, patients of color, immigrant patients, trans and nonbinary patients, and intersex patients. Eating disorders are understood as a public health concern and an issue of racial, gender, and economic justice.

The bullying of fat children and adults is no longer regarded as a simple fact but as a troubling trend that needs to be quashed. In schools, teachers and parents respond to the bullying of fat kids by holding bullies accountable for their actions rather than mandating that children transform their bodies in order to preserve their safety and dignity. In intimate partner relationships, researchers seek to end the abuse of fat partners as a key aspect of combatting domestic and sexual violence. Workplaces no longer tolerate diet talk or casual bullying of fat colleagues and subordinates. Most of us, regardless of size, pride ourselves on interrupting the harassment and discrimination targeting fat people.

In that world, there is a vibrant movement for body justice that understands the pressures each of us face to maintain the sovereignty of our bodies that are uniquely informed by both our identities (internal, not always visible) and the way our bodies present (external, based on others' perception). This movement understands that ending police violence is an issue of body justice, particularly for Black, Latinx, and indigenous people. It understands that accessibility and disability justice are central to body justice, and that failing to make the movement accessible means *failing to make the movement*. It understands that accessibility for people with chronic illnesses and invisible disabilities are as important as more visible gestures of accessibility, such as wheelchair ramps and ASL interpretation. It understands that, in many ways, anti-fatness relies on the logic of ableism and that bias and bigotry will manipulate and utilize the logic that's available to them, so liberating *any* of our bodies will require liberating *all* of our bodies. That movement works to end compulsory genital surgeries and hormonal treatments for people born intersex and to preserve consenting access to similar treatments for people who are transgender. The movement understands that increasing access to childcare, prenatal care, adoption, and abortion are all crucial and essential body justice issues for people with uteruses, as is protection from forced sterilization. The movement knows that migration is a core human right and that the sovereignty of our bodies should not and cannot collapse in the face of artificial and imagined borders. It understands, too, that justice hinges on self-determination and that there can be no body sovereignty without tribal sovereignty.

Unlike its diluted predecessor, body positivity, the movement for body justice understands that each system of oppression needs to be understood on its own terms, and as part of an interdependent web of oppressions that impacts all of us. This movement knows that we cannot attain and preserve body sovereignty by broad platitudes and whitewashing the differences between our experiences. Instead, it is honest about power and privilege, and it is thoughtful and diligent in dismantling the systems of oppression that keep our bodies out of our own control. It is a hub of community-led movements, not a substitute for them, and it does diligent work to provide the most effective, desired, and meaningful support it can to marginalized communities. Its organizing is tender and relational, making space for holding the traumas caused by our oppression, for building a broad and brave vision for a more liberated world, and for driving toward it with anger and joy.

In this world, the dual abilities to be seen and heard are understood to be our birthrights. Fat people are not expected to earn media representation through the penitence of thinness or the mirage of health. Movies and TV shows regularly include the stories of disabled people, people of color, immigrants, trans people, intersex people, and yes, fat people. Those stories are informed by their identities, but characters' humanity is rarely overshadowed by the systems of oppression that impact them. Human experiences deserving of empathy are no longer restricted to a single size or body type.

Clothing access has changed too. Manufacturers have followed plus-size brands, and nearly every retailer sells nearly every article of clothing in sizes 00 to 40—at minimum. Every size is available in store, not just online, and fit models are used to show how clothing fits differently on different sizes and builds. Adaptive clothing is widely available from clothing retailers, too, meeting the needs of disabled people, nursing parents, seniors, and people with sensory integration issues, among others.

In that world, you can see me. My body does not make me your built-in ego boost or reassurance (*at least I'm not* that *fat*), your uncomfortable denial (*sweetie, no, you're not fat!*), your cautionary tale, or the outlet for so much body-based anger and angst. My body is the vessel that brings me to you, yes, and it is also an important part of who I am. It informs my experience in important ways and, in that world, you understand and respect that experience. You only claim it as your own if it *is*, and if our experiences are shared. We see each other, tenderly hold the young shoots where our experiences grow apart, and work to build a world as gentle as our friendship.

In that world, I can see you, and I can *trust* you. Let me trust you.

We have reached for that world before, but found our attempts swallowed up by the privilege we failed to acknowledge and the very industries we tried to escape.

The body positivity movement, which gained prominence in the 2010s, is an attempt at creating a new way of understanding our bodies, but it always stopped short of full-throated inclusion for all of us—especially those of us who are very fat. At the outset of its popularization, body positivity felt broad, welcoming, all-encompassing. It held the promise of a home for all of us. Very fat people—like me—wouldn't have to worry about bullying in the guise of concern. Trans people could rest assured that their healthcare would be championed wholeheartedly, their gender expressions embraced openly, surgery offered without BMI-based restrictions. People of color could believe that their bodies would be represented lovingly, placed carefully in the context of their families, communities, histories, and identities. People with disabilities could trust that any space calling itself body positive would strive for full accessibility and wouldn't build its credibility on the false foundation of ability or the cruel betrayal of health.

When it first rose to popularity, body positivity appeared to me as a shining city on a hill. Its majestic grid stretched out before me, each neighborhood planned with precision and care. Its map was beautiful and specific, offering modest homes for those of us who'd been shut out for so long. Finally, we could release the exhaustion of educating everyone on our bodies, of convincing them that the blood in our veins was worth their respect. Finally, we could find respite, knowing that a movement would strive to understand our bodies. Finally, we could be free. If our bodies were not celebrated, they would at least be left in our own care.

Like so many fat people, I did not come to body positivity for self-esteem. I did not come to body positivity because I wanted to feel beautiful or loved—those things had always lay beyond the reach of our cultural imagination for people with bodies like mine. I came to body positivity because I cared about being human. As a fat person, my humanity was—and is—too readily erased, eclipsed by either beauty or health. I came to body positivity because it held the promise of something radical—the possibility that I, as a very fat person, could be seen and understood for who I am. Not because I am happy or healthy, thin, or beautiful, but because I am *human*.

But that was before the skyrocketing popularity of body positivity. It was before their slouched stomachs with one small fat roll were called *brave*. This was before fat shaming was defined in the popular imagination by the inaccurate judgment of thin women as fat: straight-size women who embodied the beauty standard like pop stars Jessica Simpson and Kelly Clarkson, or Donald Trump scapegoat and Miss Universe winner Alicia Machado. Before fat shaming came to mean *hurting thin women's feelings by incorrectly calling them fat*. It was before Dove defined *real beauty* as multiracial and multi-height, but still free of transgender people, still free of people with disabilities, still free of rolling fat or puckered skin. Before fashion magazines and retailers agreed to stop airbrushing their photographs but kept the same impossibly thin models. It was before marketing campaigns quietly wrote the rest of us out of body positivity and before so many thin people's body positivity came with caveats: *As long as you're happy and healthy. As long as you're not, you know,* obese. *As long as you're not glorifying obesity.* It was before body positivity became pride in thin, fair, feminine, able bodies. It was before that grand vision of a shining city on a hill became a mirage.

Over time, body positivity has made its constituency clear. It has widened the warm and fickle embrace of beauty standards ever so slightly. Now it showers its affections not only on beautiful, able-bodied, fair-skinned women under a size 4 but on beautiful, able-bodied, fair-skinned women under a size 12. Body positivity has widened the circle of acceptable bodies, yes, but it still leaves so many of us by the wayside. Its rallying cry, *love your body*, presumes that our greatest challenges are internal, a poisoned kind of thought about our own bodies. It cannot adapt to those of us who love our bodies, but whose bodies are rejected by those around us, used as grounds for ejecting us from employment, healthcare, and other areas of life.

Overwhelmingly, the popularization of body positivity has reinforced the exclusion that fat people experience everywhere else. It doesn't make thin people less afraid of saying "fat" or being fat. While body positivity held the promise of advocating for all of us, it refused to name our bodies. It could not push for meaningful distinctions between thin bodies and fat bodies, nor the social realities that come with each. When we are not pushed to see our bodies as they are seen by those around us, we cannot have real conversations about the distinct challenges our bodies carry with them, much less how to remedy those challenges. When we are not pushed to see our bodies as they are, we are all left to our default perception—the deep, enduring belief that each of us is unforgivably fat. Diet culture hinges on all of us seeking to become thin, thinner, thinnest, engaged in an endless quest to shrink ourselves at all costs. When we are left to our own devices, we retreat to focusing on the problem of our own mindsets rather than the problem of our internalized biases, the harms we (often unintentionally) cause to those around us, and the ways in which others' bodies invite different experiences than our own. We universalize our own experience, assuming that *believing we are too fat* is the same as *being treated with the discrimination that too readily plagues undeniably fat people.*

Thin people especially struggle to say "fat," the hypothetical that has hurt them so deeply. But as an undeniably fat person, the word isn't hurtful to me. It cannot be, because I do not have the luxury of escaping it. Instead, I am beholden to someone else's discomfort with a word that has never accurately described them. Even as a very fat person, when I enter body positive spaces, I cannot be trusted to describe myself as fat, and I cannot expect support when the truth of my body is hurled at me as an insult. I cannot be responsible for naming my own skin. Body positivity quarantines the words used to describe bodies like mine and, in the process, shuts out those bodies themselves. We need the courage to say the word "fat" and the wherewithal to see all of our bodies accurately. Without it, we cannot name our bodies, nor can we truly embrace and understand all of us who have sought out this movement that felt so essential.

This newly popularized body positivity drowns out so many of us, reducing problems of social exclusion to issues of self-esteem and body image. It focuses on normalizing the moments in which thin bodies appear fat, rather than tackling the more intransigent and troubling systems of privilege and oppression that marginalize those of us who *are* fat. It disproportionately centers the experiences of cis women who are thin, white, Western, abled, straight. And in so doing, it writes out those of us more than one standard deviation from the mean—we can be people of color, or we can have a disability, or we can be transgender, or we can be fat, but we cannot dare be more than one.

There is certainly room to reclaim body positivity for more of us. Undeniably, work can be done to create stronger representation for the rest of us. Someone can make that space. But I am, *you know, obese,* so it isn't mine to take up. Instead, I want to build this grand and risky world: a world defined not by platitudes and self-esteem but by access, vulnerability, justice, candor, and courage. And to move past the barriers of the body positivity movement, we'll need all of that and more.

To build this world, straight-size people will need to learn to think of their own experiences and internal struggles in precise terms, no longer universalizing insecurity or bad body image the way they so long have. They will need to engage in conversations about oppression and discrimination, even when those aren't the primary markers of their experiences, acknowledging the critical difference between their internal hurt and fat people's systemic oppression. The work of straight-size people will need to be courageous, vulnerable, and uncomfortable. It will require them to get painfully honest with themselves, acknowledging that they have been trained to judge and marginalize fat people and, whether they intend to or not, they are often active participants in perpetuating and expanding anti-fatness. They will need to interrogate and jettison all the ways, big and small, that they've come to marginalize fat people, from posting triumphant before and after weight-loss photos to reassuring themselves that they're *not that fat* when they see a body like mine. And they will need to come to a place of deep understanding and belief that their body—their very own—is not necessarily an accomplishment, not a reward, not a reflection of a laudable work ethic or intense tenacity, but of a series of factors that are largely out of their own control.

Straight-size people will need to acknowledge that their raised consciousness is only useful to fat liberation and body sovereignty insofar as it leads to meaningful, risky, and sustained action. In a world built for straight-size people, for the first time, they will need to risk their comfort for those of us who don't have that privilege. They'll need to intervene in anti-fatness wherever it occurs, and wherever they can, from calling out fat jokes to intervening in anti-fat street harassment, from boycotting the diet industry to leading other thin people through their own learning about anti-fatness. Straight-size people will need to advocate for changes in policy, lobbying for federal bills to regulate airline seat size, advocating for local policies to ban anti-fat discrimination, and ending the "biggest loser" competitions that hurt and harm so many of their coworkers, including fat people and people with eating disorders. Straight-size people will need to trust fat people enough to believe us, and they'll need to believe us enough to advocate with us.

Fat people will need to honor that trust with risk. We'll need to muster the fortitude: to do things we're told we can't, to wear things we're told we shouldn't. We'll need to risk advocating for ourselves, even when it's risky (it's always risky). We'll need to give up the quiet safety of anonymity and instead step into courageous vulnerability, giving voice to the painful experiences we've been so long trained to withhold—the ones we've been shown, time and time again, that so many straight-size people will dismiss or defend but never just *hear*. Building a movement for fat justice will require our leadership, which will mean taking the dual risks of public advocacy and of meaningful accountability to one another, across lines of identity and experience. We'll need to take on the painstaking work of building a movement that is both tender and radical, caring and visionary.

But the first step for all of us will be to let go of the magical thinking of thinness. Stop believing that a thinner body will bring us better relationships, dream jobs, obedient children, beautiful homes. Stop waiting to do the things we love until we've lost ten, twenty, fifty, one hundred pounds. Come to truly believe what we already know, and what so much data tells us: the vast majority of us don't lose significant amounts of weight and the few who do don't maintain weight loss in the long term. Nearly twenty years of dieting has shown me that I will never be thin. I believe to my core that I will also never wear straight sizes. I also believe that my life is worth living, worth embracing, worth loving, and celebrating. And it's worth all of that now—not two hundred pounds from now.

Building that world will require cultural and legal change too. After all, we live in a world in which fat people face staggering disparities in employment, healthcare, accessibility, and then insists those disparities are our own fault for failing to achieve and maintain thin bodies. Even when faced with data and personal experiences that illustrate the troubling depths of anti-fatness, we are too often told that these systemic problems are a result of our individual decisions. If we were just thin, we wouldn't experience all of this. In the bizarre logic of anti-fatness, fat people are to blame for our bodies, our experiences of marginalization, and even our own abuse.

We need a world that insists upon safety and dignity for *all of us*—not because we are beautiful, healthy, blameless, exceptional, or beyond reproach, but because we are *human beings*. And for fat people—especially very fat people—that world can feel so very far away when our days are reliably marked by open disdain, perfectly legal discrimination, and sometimes even violence. The marginalization and public abuse of very fat people is so commonplace that it has become accepted, but that doesn't make it acceptable. As it stands, the law is silent on many issues facing fat people—and where it's not silent, it often upholds our oppression and discrimination. Here are some things we can do to stem the tide of systemic, institutional harms facing fat people.

END THE LEGAL, WIDESPREAD PRACTICE OF WEIGHT DISCRIMINATION

In forty-eight of the fifty US states, it is perfectly legal to deny someone housing, employment, a table at a restaurant, or a room in a hotel *just because they're fat*.[1] State and federal judges have repeatedly upheld the right of employers to discriminate on the basis of size. At the most basic level, banning anti-fat discrimination and ensuring equal pay will be essential to helping fat people survive and thrive. We'll need to ban workplace weigh-ins for cocktail waitresses and flight attendants, to end pay bonuses for weight loss, and to stop workplace weight-loss competitions. We can work to establish meaningful laws and impact litigation to end weight-based discrimination.

REALIZE THE PROMISE OF HEALTHCARE FOR FAT PEOPLE

Fat people deserve responsive, competent healthcare and access to the same diagnostic tests and treatments that thin people get. As it stands, hospitals are not required to have equipment on hand that accommodates fatter people, from exam tables to MRI machines. Doctors are free to set weight limits on the patients they're willing to see, and some do. The FDA doesn't require testing of drugs on fatter people, which means that crucial drugs like emergency contraception have significantly reduced effectiveness on people who weigh more than 165 pounds.[2] Transgender people faced weight-based barriers to accessing lifesaving medical care, including gender affirming surgeries. We can end these unnecessary restrictions and barriers by passing a fat patients' bill of rights. We can require that healthcare providers undergo weight bias training as part of their existing schooling and continuing education requirements, and insert into training curriculums more information about the social determinants of health and the toll that discrimination and shaming can take on any marginalized patient—including fat patients. We can insist that the medical field catch up to its own research and acknowledge that fatness isn't a failure of personal responsibility but the result of a complex set of factors that may include our environments, our genes, our existing physical and mental health diagnoses, and the shame and marginalization we experience. And we can demand healthcare that works for all of us—not just those of us who are healthy or who look thin.

INCREASE ACCESS TO PUBLIC SPACES

We can ensure that public spaces, from restaurants to airplanes, state buildings to new housing, are accessible for fat people and disabled people. We can make sure that our spaces have chairs without restrictive armrests, tables and booths that aren't bolted down, and that we have seating with weight limits of five hundred pounds or more. We can advocate for federal bills that seek to regulate minimum airplane seat size and ensure that disabled people and fat people can fly safely, with our dignity intact, and without worrying that regressive policies won't leave us stranded far from home, without refunds or recourse. We can win airline seating that's safe and comfortable for all of us, regardless of weight, height, ability, or age. And we can grow in the direction of universal design, building environments that work for families and individuals, fat people and thin people, abled and disabled people alike.

END ANTI-FAT VIOLENCE

There is a casual violence that too often comes with living in a fat body, and that violence warps and multiplies for fat people of color. Anti-fatness and racism conspire to scapegoat and harm fat people of color, as in the case of Amber Phillips, a fat Black airline passenger whose seatmate, a thin white woman, called the cops on her.[3] Fat people—especially fat women—have written time and time again about the dangers of fatcalling, a kind of street harassment that uniquely targets fat people and often includes threats of physical and sexual violence. Like thin people, fat people are frequently the targets of sexual harassment and assault, and the violence that faces us is often supercharged with a sense of entitlement to our bodies and the belief that we should be grateful for any sexualized attention at all. While sexual violence regularly targets fat people, we are significantly less likely to be believed or taken seriously than our thinner counterparts.[4] Fat people are far from the only ones who experience sexual violence, but anti-fat bias means that our experiences are less likely to be believed, investigated, prosecuted, or pursued at all. Developing public education campaigns, points of intervention, and meaningful consequences to combat fatcalling and the racist, anti-fat violence that targets fat people of color will be essential to protecting fat people's physical safety. Increasing training of first responders to support survivors of sexual assault will also be essential to combatting the dramatically under-addressed epidemic of sexual violence facing fat people.

END THE APPROVAL OF WEIGHT-LOSS DRUGS WITH DANGEROUS—EVEN FATAL—SIDE EFFECTS

Diet drugs and supplements aren't just the products of junk science—they put lives at risk. People of all sizes who take diet pills have experienced major health complications and, in many cases, death. While diet drugs and supplements impact people of all sizes, fat people are under a unique, constant, and unyielding pressure to lose significant amounts of weight immediately. Standing up for fat people will require us to increase federal regulation of products claiming to aid in weight loss. It will require us to build in checks for the sensationalist, false claims of people like Dr. Oz,[5] and to counter those baseless assertions with the real-life harms of diet culture.[6] It will require us to hold a simple line: diet pill manufacturers (such as Hydroxycut, Alli, Fen-Phen) and diet food purveyors (such as Nutrisystem, Jenny Craig, Weight Watchers) may only make claims that are based on repeated clinical trials conducted by independent, third-party researchers—not bankrolled by corporations invested in making sensational claims.

STAND UP FOR FAT KIDS

In most states, size is not a protected class, which means that states with anti-bullying laws often don't extend those protections to fat children and teens. We have to recognize that fat hate starts young, that its trauma can last a lifetime, and that early intervention will be essential to raising a generation of more compassionate people. We'll need to end the strikingly common practice of state-mandated BMI report cards. And we'll need to develop campaigns for children's public health that don't blame them for their own circumstance.[7] Vulnerable, oft-targeted fat kids aren't responsible for the bullying they experience—bullies are.

The policy, cultural, and institutional change goals listed here are only a beginning, but they will take decades of concerted research, organizing, advocacy, and movement building to accomplish. Their outcomes will be modest: Offer bullied fat children the support and protection we offer to thinner targets of bullying. Create basic pathways for legal recourse for employees who are fired solely because of the way they look. And regulate diet drugs the way we regulate anything else. For thin people, these aims may seem too low. But for fat people, they may save our dignity, our self-determination, and our very lives.

Building this brave new world will require major shifts of each of us. It cannot end with plumbing our own internal depths, rooting out our internalized anti-fat bias, but that is where it will need to begin. We will need to retrain ourselves to understand a new, compassionate set of principles that can guide our actions:

> That our bodies are just *bodies*, not synecdoche for our character, not a badge of work ethic—just *bodies*. That our bodies are *our own*, not subject to street harassment, mandates to change, or unwelcome "advice" no matter how well-intended. That health is multifaceted, made up of a wide range of factors, from our mental health to our dis/ability, our blood pressure to our t-cell count; it cannot be reduced to a single measure, much less a number on a bathroom scale. That health is not a simple or monolithic reward for the penitent but largely an outgrowth of our existing privileges: having access to health insurance, receiving competent care from providers, and being born into able bodies. That illness and disability are not punishments for failing to stay vigilant but are variances in humans that have always existed. That diabetes and heart disease aren't an opportunity for thinner people to gloat but

health conditions that deserve competent treatment and compassionate care.

That fatness is not a failure and, subsequently, that thinness is not an
accomplishment. The size of our bodies is largely beyond our own
control, and even in the few occasions when it isn't, thinness *cannot* be a
prerequisite for basic respect, dignity, provision of services, or meeting
basic needs like getting a job or finding food.

That anti-fatness isn't the exception; it's the rule. Anti-fat bias is not
the work of a few bad apples or a marginal group that decides to harm
fat people. Anti-fat bias is a cultural force that simultaneously shapes
and is expressed through our most commanding institutions: government, healthcare, education, and media. Anti-fatness isn't just something each of us bears—it's something we *become*. It takes over us, a
virus that infects the way we see ourselves and those around us. It slips
into our bloodstreams with ease, latches onto us, seeps into the way we
see our friends, our family, strangers on the street. It warps our vision
and our relationships. Anti-fatness is not the result of an active choice
to wield it, like some biological weapon. No, anti-fatness is a passive
default. We are all its carriers. We breathe it in every day.

There are no prerequisites for human dignity. For that reason, there can
be no caveats in body justice or fat justice.

Retraining ourselves to guide our actions with these basic principles is
deceptively simple but will be difficult. Building a new world always is.

So let's get to work.

ACKNOWLEDGMENTS

There are so many wonderful people who have made this book possible, both directly and indirectly.

My agent, Beth Vesel, approached me about writing this book before I even imagined it possible. Her guidance and support have been invaluable throughout.

Joanna Green, my phenomenal editor at Beacon, provided crucial guidance, posed thought-provoking questions, and helped to shape this book at every step along the way. I am so incredibly fortunate to have worked with her.

Caleb Luna, Dan Lynn, Kivan Bay, Angus Maguire, Alejandro Juarez, and Gina Susanna all read early versions of this manuscript, and each provided deeply helpful feedback.

Fat community kept me grounded and connected throughout the process of writing this book about the thornier parts of our shared experiences. David McElhatton, Sophia Carter-Kahn, Sofie Hagen, Jes Baker, JerVae Dionne, Rebecca Eisenberg, Samantha Peterson, Da'Shaun Harrison, Ushshi Rahman, Nicolette Mason, Jesse Dangerously, Shilo George, Sarah Hollowell, Kristin Chirico, Rachel Kacenjar, Shannon Purser, Rebecca Alexander, and Meghan Tonjes have all been wonderful supports.

My writing wouldn't have reached nearly the audience it has without the early support of wonderful, generous people: Dr. Roxane Gay, Dr. Lindo Bacon, Jameela Jamil and IWeigh, Mickey Boardman at *Paper*, Matt McGorry, Michael Hobbes at *Huffington Post*, Melissa Fabello, Stephanie Georgopulos at *Medium*, Sally Tamarkin at *SELF*, and Jeanie Finlay of Glimmer Films, among many others.

My friends and family put up with a lot during the writing of this book. Particular thanks to my parents, my brother, my niece and nephew, and my wonderful sister-in-law for her steady guidance throughout. Thanks, too, to Lisa, Kim, Tara, Rossi, Hill-Hart, Allyson, Olivia; to Alejandro for continually pushing me to deeper, more compassionate ways of thinking about bodies and oppression; and to Angus for telling me to start sharing my writing to begin with.

And, of course, I wouldn't have the language for any of this without a vibrant, tenacious, decades-long movement for fat liberation. My endless gratitude to Marilyn Wann, Sonya Renee Taylor, Lesley Kinzel, Marianne Kirby, Ragen Chastain, Kate Harding, Dr. Charlotte Cooper, Dr. Cat Pausé, Evette Dionne, Paul Campos, Sondra Solovay, Shoog McDaniel, Dr. Sabrina Strings, and Stacy Bias, and to organizations such as the National Association to Advance Fat Acceptance (NAAFA), the Association for Size Diversity and Health (ASDAH), NOLOSE (dedicated to ending the oppression of fat people and creating vibrant fat queer culture), the Fat Underground, the New Haven Fat Liberation Front, and countless more fat activists, scholars, organizations, and community leaders.

NOTES

INTRODUCTION

1. "The Body Positive—About Us," Body Positive, https://www.thebodypositive.org/about#About-Us, accessed February 7, 2020.

2. "The Body Positive—About Us."

3. The Body Positive, "The Be Body Positive Model: Core Competencies," Google Drive, https://drive.google.com/file/d/oB8YMMhy3aiHmUENUUlJBMGFTSjA/view, accessed February 7, 2020.

4. Carey Goldberg, "Study: Bias Drops Dramatically for Sexual Orientation and Race—but Not Weight," *CommonHealth*, WBUR, January 11, 2019, https://www.wbur.org/commonhealth/2019/01/11/implicit-bias-gay-black-weight.

5. Leigh Weingus, "Body Neutrality Is a Movement That Doesn't Focus on Your Appearance," *Huffington Post*, August 15, 2018, https://www.huffpost.com/entry/what-is-body-neutrality_n_5b61d8f9e4bode86f49d31b4?guccounter=1.

6. "Body Sovereignty," Simon Fraser Public Interest Research Group, https://sfpirg.ca/infohub/body-sovereignty, accessed February 7, 2020.

7. The Fat Lip Podcast, "Ash on Instagram: 'Okay, I Always Get Asked about This . . . ,'" Instagram, https://www.instagram.com/p/BtUApeGAvVA, accessed March 30, 2020.

8. *Macmillan Dictionary*, "fatphobia (n.)," https://www.macmillandictionary.com/us/dictionary/american/fatphobia, accessed February 7, 2020.

9. Robert Crawford, "Healthism and the Medicalization of Everyday Life," *International Journal of Health Services* 10, no. 3 (1980): 365–88, https://doi.org/10.2190/3h2h-3xjn-3kay-g9ny.

10. Fall Ferguson, "The HAES® Files: Speculations on Healthism & Privilege," *Health at Every Size®* (blog), *Association for Size Diversity and Health*, December 9, 2013, https://healthateverysizeblog.org/2013/11/19/the-haes-files-speculations-on-healthism-privilege.

11. Hilary George-Parkin, "68% Of American Women Wear a Size 14 or Above," *Racked*, June 5, 2018, https://www.racked.com/2018/6/5/17380662/size-numbers-average-woman-plus-market.

12. George-Parkin, "68% Of American Women."

13. Online Etymology Dictionary, "obesity (n.)," https://www.etymonline.com/word/obesity, accessed February 7, 2020.

14. Christy Harrison, "What Is Diet Culture?" *Christy Harrison* (blog), August 10, 2018, https://christyharrison.com/blog/what-is-diet-culture.

CHAPTER 1: INTO THIN AIR

1. Craig M. Hales, Margaret D. Carroll, Cheryl D. Fryar, and Cynthia L. Ogden, "Prevalence of Obesity Among Adults and Youth: United States, 2015–2016," (NHS Data Brief, October 2017), https://www.cdc.gov/nchs/data/databriefs/db288.pdf.

2. "'Incredible Shrinking Airline Seat': US Court Says Seat Size a Safety Issue," *Guardian*, July 29, 2017, https://www.theguardian.com/business/2017/jul/29/incredible -shrinking-airline-seat-us-court-says-seat-size-a-safety-issue.

3. "Air Passengers Get Bigger, Airline Seats Get Smaller," *USA Today*, March 8, 2018, https://www.usatoday.com/story/opinion/2018/03/07/air-passengers-get-bigger -airline-seats-get-smaller-editorials-debates/397083002.

4. Scott McCartney, "You're Not Getting Bigger, the Airplane Bathroom Is Getting Smaller," *Wall Street Journal*, August 29, 2018, https://www.wsj.com/articles/youre-not -getting-bigger-the-airplane-bathroom-is-getting-smaller-1535553108.

5. Leslie Josephs, "House Passes Bill to Require Minimum Standards for Airplane Seat Size and Legroom," CNBC, September 27, 2018, https://www.cnbc.com/2018/09 /27/airplane-seat-sizes-would-be-regulated-in-faa-law.html.

6. Robert D. Hershey, "Alfred E. Kahn Dies at 93; Prime Mover of Airline Deregulation," *New York Times*, December 28, 2010, https://www.nytimes.com/2010/12/29 /business/29kahn.html.

7. Susan S. Lang, "Economist Alfred Kahn, 'Father of Airline Deregulation' and Former Presidential Adviser, Dies at 93," *Cornell Chronicle*, Cornell University, December 27, 2010, http://news.cornell.edu/stories/2010/12/ alfred-kahn-father-airline-deregulation-dies-93.

8. Edward A. Smeloff, "Utility Deregulation and Global Warming: The Coming Collision," *Natural Resources and Environment* 12, no. 4 (n.d.): 280–85, https://www.jstor .org/stable/40923749?seq=1#page_scan_tab_contents.

9. "A Brief History of the FAA," Federal Aviation Administration, US Department of Transportation, January 4, 2017, https://www.faa.gov/about/history/brief_history.

10. Erin Corbett, "Congress Is Addressing Cramped Airplane Seats This Week, an Irritating Issue on Both Sides of the Aisle," *Fortune*, September 24, 2018, https://fortune .com/2018/09/23/congress-airplane-seat-legroom-law-bill-faa.

11. Lori Aratani, "Can You Fit in This Bathroom? Passengers Are Growing but Airplane Bathrooms Are Shrinking," *Washington Post*, November 17, 2018, https://www .washingtonpost.com/graphics/2018/local/airplane-bathrooms/?noredirect=on.

12. Kari Paul, "Court Orders FAA to Address 'The Case of the Incredible Shrinking Airline Seat'—This Is How Much They've Actually Shrunk," *MarketWatch*, Dow Jones & Company, August 1, 2017, https://www.marketwatch.com/story/ american-airlines-to-shrink-legroom-for-these-coach-passengers-2017-05-03.

13. Kari Paul, "FAA Declines to Put a Stop to the 'Incredible Shrinking Airline Seat,'" *MarketWatch*, Dow Jones & Company, July 10, 2018, https://www.marketwatch .com/story/faa-declines-to-put-a-stop-to-the-incredible-shrinking-airline-seat-2018 -07-09.

14. Corbett, "Congress Is Addressing Cramped Airplane Seats."

15. US Congress, House, SEAT Act of 2017, HR 1467, 115th Cong., introduced in House March 19, 2017, https://www.congress.gov/bill/115th-congress/house-bill/1467/text?r=196.

16. "Customer of Size," Southwest Airlines, https://www.southwest.com/html/customer-service/extra-seat/?clk=GFOOTER-CUSTOMER-COS, accessed October 24, 2019.

17. "Customer of Size Seating Guidelines," Alaska Airlines, https://www.alaskaair.com/content/travel-info/policies/seating-customers-of-size, accessed October 24, 2019.

18. "Can I purchase an extra seat for myself or something I'm transporting?," Spirit Airlines, https://customersupport.spirit.com/hc/en-us/articles/202098626-Can-I-purchase-an-extra-seat-for-myself-or-something-I-m-transporting, accessed October 24, 2019.

19. Embry Roberts, "Plus-Size Woman Bravely Confronts in-Flight Body Shamer—See the Video," TODAY.com, July 3, 2017, https://www.today.com/style/plus-size-model-natalie-hage-confronts-body-shamer-plane-t113429.

20. David Moye, "385-Pound Man Kicked Off United Flight for Row Mate's Comfort," *HuffPost*, April 5, 2016, https://www.huffpost.com/entry/man-kicked-off-united-flight-weight_n_57042023e4b0b90ac270750a.

21. Dareh Gregorian, "EXCLUSIVE: Airlines Settle $6M Lawsuit in Death of Bronx Woman Who Was 'Too Fat' to Fly Home to the U.S." *New York Daily News*, January 9, 2019, https://www.nydailynews.com/news/national/exclusive-airlines-settle-6m-lawsuit-death-bronx-woman-fat-fly-home-article-1.1931576.

22. "Nicole Arbour's AWKWARD Interview on *The View*," What's Trending, September 17, 2015, 2:25, video, https://www.youtube.com/watch?v=IjlVPzGXTP0.

23. "Nicole Arbour on *The View*," Ronnie, September 16, 2015, 6:43, video, https://www.youtube.com/watch?v=yMhsSb2BvnQ.

24. "Should Obese People Have to Buy Two Seats on a Plane?" The Young Turks, December 4, 2009, 5:21, video, https://www.youtube.com/watch?v=z74EqQfWMUA.

25. Goldberg, "Study: Bias Drops Dramatically for Sexual Orientation and Race—but Not Weight."

26. Hanae Armitage, "Low-Fat or Low-Carb? It's a Draw, Study Finds," *Stanford Medicine News Center*, Stanford University, accessed October 24, 2019, https://med.stanford.edu/news/all-news/2018/02/low-fat-or-low-carb-its-a-draw-study-finds.html.

27. Craig M. Hales et al., "Prevalence of Obesity Among Adults and Youth."

28. Fairygodboss, "The Grim Reality of Being a Female Jobseeker," https://res.cloudinary.com/fairygodboss/raw/upload/v1518462741/production/The_Grim_Reality_of_Being_A_Female_Job_Seeker.pdf, accessed October 23, 2019.

29. Ronald Alsop, "Fat People Earn Less and Have a Harder Time Finding Work," BBC News, December 1, 2016, https://www.bbc.com/worklife/article/20161130-fat-people-earn-less-and-have-a-harder-time-finding-work.

30. Shana Lebowitz, "Science Says People Determine Your Competence, Intelligence, and Salary Based on Your Weight," *Business Insider*, September 9, 2015. https://www.businessinsider.com/science-overweight-people-less-successful-2015-9.

31. Alsop, "Fat People Earn Less and Have a Harder Time Finding Work."

32. Suzanne McGee, "For Women, Being 13 Pounds Overweight Means Losing $9,000 a Year in Salary," *Guardian*, October 30, 2014, https://www.theguardian.com/money/us-money-blog/2014/oct/30/women-pay-get-thin-study.

33. Lisa Quast, "Why Being Thin Can Actually Translate into a Bigger Paycheck for Women," *Forbes*, August 21, 2012, https://www.forbes.com/sites/lisaquast/2011/06/06/can-being-thin-actually-translate-into-a-bigger-paycheck-for-women/#1a59c0267b03.

34. Megan Orciari, "Body Weight and Gender Influence Judgment in the Courtroom," *YaleNews*, Yale University, January 8, 2013, https://news.yale.edu/2013/01/08/body-weight-and-gender-influence-judgment-courtroom.

35. Matthew Rozsa, "Judge: Overweight Teen Victim May Have Been 'Flattered' by Sexual Assault," *Salon*, October 27, 2017, https://www.salon.com/2017/10/27/judge-overweight-teen-victim-may-have-been-flattered-by-sexual-assault.

36. Zak Cheney-Rice, "NYPD Union Lawyers Claim Eric Garner Would've Died Anyway Because He Was Obese," *Intelligencer*, June 14, 2019, http://nymag.com/intelligencer/2019/06/eric-garner-death-inevitable-says-lawyer.html.

37. Cheney-Rice, "NYPD Union Lawyers Claim Eric Garner Would've Died Anyway Because He Was Obese."

38. Areva Martin, "Weight Discrimination Is Legal in 49 States," *Time*, August 16, 2017, https://time.com/4883176/weight-discrimination-workplace-laws; Sarah Kim, "Washington State Supreme Court Rules That Obesity Is a Disability," *Forbes Magazine*, July 19, 2019, https://www.forbes.com/sites/sarahkim/2019/07/18/washington-state-supreme-courts-obesity-disability/#1e5a504cd274.

39. Josh Sanburn, "Too Big to Cocktail? Judge Upholds Weight Discrimination in the Workplace," *Time*, July 26, 2013, http://nation.time.com/2013/07/26/too-big-to-cocktail-judge-upholds-weight-discrimination-in-the-workplace.

40. MarketResearch.com. "U.S. Weight Loss Market Worth $66 Billion," PR Newswire, June 26, 2018, https://www.prnewswire.com/news-releases/us-weight-loss-market-worth-66-billion-300573968.html; Charlotte Markey, "5 Lies from the Diet Industry," *Psychology Today*, January 21, 2015, https://www.psychologytoday.com/us/blog/smart-people-don-t-diet/201501/5-lies-the-diet-industry.

41. "The Biggest Loser: Fall 2011–2012 Ratings," Canceled Renewed TV Shows, TV Series Finale, February 8, 2012, https://tvseriesfinale.com/tv-show/the-biggest-loser-ratings-2011-2012.

42. *Woman's World*, December 31, 2018.

43. "Poverty," Healthy People 2020, U.S. Department of Health and Human Services, https://www.healthypeople.gov/2020/topics-objectives/topic/social-determinants-health/interventions-resources/poverty, accessed October 24, 2019.

44. "Overweight & Obesity Statistics," National Institute of Diabetes and Digestive and Kidney Diseases, U.S. Department of Health and Human Services, August 1, 2017, https://www.niddk.nih.gov/health-information/health-statistics/overweight-obesity.

CHAPTER 2: BECOMING AN EPIDEMIC

1. *The Dr. Oz Show*, "Is It Child Abuse to Have a Fat Child?," aired May 24, 2011, in broadcast syndication, Sony Pictures Television.

2. Locke Hughes, "The 6 Best Weight-Loss Camps for Lasting Results," *Women's Health*, June 11, 2019, https://www.womenshealthmag.com/weight-loss/a19975513/weight-loss-camps.

3. Warren E. Leary, "Major U.S. Report on the Diet Urges Reduction in Fat Intake," *New York Times*, July 28, 1988, sec. A.

4. Leary, "Major U.S. Report on the Diet Urges Reduction in Fat Intake."

5. Paul F. Campos, *The Obesity Myth: Why America's Obsession with Weight Is Hazardous to Your Health* (New York: Gotham Books, 2004), 3.

6. Leary, "Major U.S. Report on the Diet Urges Reduction in Fat Intake."

7. *Agriculture Improvement Act of 2018*, Public Law 115–334, 115th Cong. (2018), https://www.congress.gov/bill/115th-congress/house-bill/2/text.

8. "Farming's Sustainable Future," *Knowable Magazine*, https://www.knowable magazine.org/page/farmings-sustainable-future, accessed October 22, 2019.

9. Campos, *The Obesity Myth*, 3.

10. "Let's Move! America's Move to Raise a Healthier Generation of Kids," National Archives and Records Administration, https://letsmove.obamawhitehouse.archives .gov/about, accessed October 22, 2019.

11. Fed Up, RADiUS-TWC, 2014, http://fedupmovie.com.

12. "Let's Move! America's Move to Raise a Healthier Generation of Kids."

13. Lesley Kinzel, "How Childhood-Obesity Fight Damages Self Esteem," *Newsweek*, May 26, 2010, https://www.newsweek.com/how-childhood-obesity-fight-damages -self-esteem-70289.

14. Kinzel, "How Childhood-Obesity Fight Damages Self Esteem."

15. Kate Dailey, "Georgia Obesity Campaign Sparks Fierce Online Reaction," BBC News, March 6, 2012, https://www.bbc.com/news/magazine-16939718.

16. Hannah R. Thompson and Kristine A. Madsen, "The Report Card on BMI Report Cards," *Current Obesity Reports* 6, no. 2 (November 2017): 163–67, https://doi.org /10.1007/s13679-017-0259-6.

17. SAGE, "Most Parents Don't Believe Their Child's BMI Report Card," *ScienceDaily*, February 14, 2018, https://www.sciencedaily.com/releases/2018/02/1802140 93647.htm.

18. Kevin A. Gee, "School-Based Body Mass Index Screening and Parental Notification in Late Adolescence: Evidence from Arkansas's Act 1220," *Journal of Adolescent Health*, June 23, 2015, https://www.sciencedirect.com/science/article/pii/S1054139X15002232.

19. Kristine A. Madsen, "School-Based Body Mass Index Screening and Parent Notification," *Archives of Pediatrics & Adolescent Medicine* 165, no. 11 (2011): 987, https://doi .org/10.1001/archpediatrics.2011.127.

20. J. P. Ikeda, P. B. Crawford, and G. Woodward-Lopez, "BMI Screening in Schools: Helpful or Harmful," *Health Education Research* 21, no. 6 (2006): 761–69, https://doi.org/10.1093/her/cyl144.

21. "Body Mass Index Report Cards: A Path to Weight Stigma," Center for Discovery, October 21, 2019, https://centerfordiscovery.com/blog/body-mass-index-report -cards.

22. Deborah Carr and Michael A. Friedman, "Is Obesity Stigmatizing? Body Weight, Perceived Discrimination, and Psychological Well-Being in the United States," *Journal of Health and Social Behavior* 46, no. 3 (2005): 244–59, https://doi.org/10.1177 /002214650504600303.

23. Rebecca M. Puhl and Kelly D. Brownell, "Confronting and Coping with Weight Stigma: An Investigation of Overweight and Obese Adults," *Obesity* 14, no. 10 (2012): 1802–15, https://doi.org/10.1038/oby.2006.208.

24. Alexis Conason, "The Ironic Effects of Weight Stigma," *Psychology Today*, March 14, 2014, https://www.psychologytoday.com/us/blog/eating-mindfully/201403/the -ironic-effects-weight-stigma.

25. Kathleen Lebesco, "Fat Panic and the New Morality," in *Against Health: How Health Became the New Morality*, ed. Jonathan Metzl and Anna Kirkland (New York: New York University Press, 2010), 73.

26. Sandra Aamodt, "Why You Can't Lose Weight on a Diet," *New York Times*, May 6, 2016, https://www.nytimes.com/2016/05/08/opinion/sunday/why-you-cant-lose -weight-on-a-diet.html.

27. "Jean Nidetch: Weight Loss Therapy," *Who Made America?*, PBS, https://www .pbs.org/wgbh/theymadeamerica/whomade/nidetch_hi.html, accessed October 22, 2019.

28. "Jean Nidetch: Weight Loss Therapy."

29. Sholnn Freeman, "Heinz Selling Its Weight Watchers Unit," *New York Times*, July 23, 1999, https://www.nytimes.com/1999/07/23/business/heinz-selling-its-weight -watchers-unit.html.

30. Danielle Wiener-Bronner, "Weight Watchers Announces Free Memberships for Teens," *CNN Business*, February 7, 2018, https://money.cnn.com/2018/02/07/news /companies/weight-watchers-free-memberships/index.html.

31. Sylvia R. Karasu, "Adolphe Quetelet and the Evolution of Body Mass Index (BMI)," *Psychology Today*, March 18, 2016, https://www.psychologytoday.com/us/blog/the-gravity -weight/201603/adolphe-quetelet-and-the-evolution-body-mass-index-bmi.

32. Jodi O'Brien, *Encyclopedia of Gender and Society* (Los Angeles: Sage, 2009).

33. Rachel P. Maines, *The Technology of Orgasm: Hysteria, the Vibrator, and Women's Sexual Satisfaction* (Baltimore: Johns Hopkins University Press, 2001).

34. Michael Castleman, "'Hysteria' and the Strange History of Vibrators," *Psychology Today*, March 1, 2013, https://www.psychologytoday.com/us/blog/all-about-sex/201303 /hysteria-and-the-strange-history-vibrators.

35. Sabrina Strings, *Fearing the Black Body: The Racial Origins of Fat Phobia* (New York: New York University Press, 2019).

36. Strings, *Fearing the Black Body*.

37. Strings, *Fearing the Black Body*.

38. Jessica Firger, "There's a Dangerous Racial Bias in the Body Mass Index," *Newsweek*, May 7, 2017, https://www.newsweek.com/2017/05/19/obesity-childhood-obesity -body-mass-index-bmi-weight-weight-gain-health-595625.html.

39. Endocrine Society, "Widely Used Body Fat Measurements Overestimate Fatness in African-Americans, Study Finds," *ScienceDaily*, June 22, 2009, https://www .sciencedaily.com/releases/2009/06/090611142407.htm.

40. Karasu, "Adolphe Quetelet and the Evolution of Body Mass Index (BMI)."

41. Karasu, "Adolphe Quetelet and the Evolution of Body Mass Index (BMI)."

42. "Who's Fat? New Definition Adopted," CNN, June 17, 1998, https://www.cnn .com/HEALTH/9806/17/weight.guidelines.

43. Kelly Fitzgerald, "Obesity Is Now a Disease, American Medical Association Decides," *Medical News Today*, August 17, 2013, https://www.medicalnewstoday.com/articles /262226.php.

44. Anna North, "Weigh Less, Pay Less: Whole Foods Offers Discount Based on BMI," *Jezebel*, January 25, 2010, https://jezebel.com/weigh-less-pay-less-whole-foods -offers-discount-based-5456561.

45. Amy Stillman, "Mexican Oil Company Offers BMI Bonus for Thin Workers," *TIME*, August 2, 2019, https://time.com/5642965/pemex-health-bonus-weight-loss -waistline.

46. "2015 Employer Health Benefits Survey – Section Twelve: Health Risk Assessment, Biometrics Screening and Wellness Programs," Henry J. Kaiser Family Foundation, September 14, 2016, https://www.kff.org/report-section/ehbs-2015-section-twelve-health-risk-assessment-biometrics-screening-and-wellness-programs.

47. Howard LeWine, "Diabetes Can Strike Hard Even When Weight Is Normal," *Harvard Health* (blog), Harvard Health Publishing, August 8, 2012, https://www.health.harvard.edu/blog/diabetes-can-strike-hard-even-when-weight-is-normal-201208085121.

48. Gina Kolata, "One Weight-Loss Approach Fits All? No, Not Even Close," *New York Times*, December 12, 2016, https://www.nytimes.com/2016/12/12/health/weight-loss-obesity.html.

49. Rebecca M. Puhl and Chelsea A. Heuer, "Obesity Stigma: Important Considerations for Public Health," *American Journal of Public Health* 100, no. 6 (2010): 1019–28, https://doi.org/10.2105/ajph.2009.159491; Goldberg, "Study: Bias Drops Dramatically for Sexual Orientation and Race—but Not Weight."

50. Mayo Clinic Staff, "Stress and High Blood Pressure: What's the Connection?," Mayo Clinic, Mayo Foundation for Medical Education and Research, January 9, 2019, https://www.mayoclinic.org/diseases-conditions/high-blood-pressure/in-depth/stress-and-high-blood-pressure/art-20044190.

51. Deepak Bhatt, "'Stress' Cardiomyopathy: A Different Kind of Heart Attack," *Harvard Health* (blog), Harvard Health Publishing, August 5, 2019, https://www.health.harvard.edu/blog/stress-cardiomyopathy-a-different-kind-of-heart-attack-201509038239.

52. "Mental Health," American Diabetes Association, https://www.diabetes.org/diabetes/mental-health, accessed October 22, 2019.

53. "Fatal Pulmonary Hypertension Associated with Short-Term Use of Fenfluramine and Phentermine," *New England Journal of Medicine* 337, no. 20 (1997): 1483–83, https://doi.org/10.1056/nejm199711133372023.

54. Gina Kolata, "After 'The Biggest Loser,' Their Bodies Fought to Regain Weight," *New York Times*, May 2, 2016, https://www.nytimes.com/2016/05/02/health/biggest-loser-weight-loss.html.

55. Gina Kolata, "Americans Blame Obesity on Willpower, Despite Evidence It's Genetic," *New York Times*, November 1, 2016, https://www.nytimes.com/2016/11/01/health/americans-obesity-willpower-genetics-study.html.

56. Campos, *The Obesity Myth*, 67–68.

57. Erin Fothergill, Juen Guo, Lilian Howard, Jennifer C. Kerns, Nicolas D. Knuth, Robert Brychta, Kong Y. Chen, et al., "Persistent Metabolic Adaptation 6 Years after 'The Biggest Loser' Competition," *Obesity* 24, no. 8 (2016): 1612–19, https://doi.org/10.1002/oby.21538.

58. Kolata, "After 'The Biggest Loser,' Their Bodies Fought to Regain Weight.'"

59. Harriet Brown, "Planning to Go on a Diet? One Word of Advice: Don't," *Slate*, March 24, 2015, https://slate.com/technology/2015/03/diets-do-not-work-the-thin-evidence-that-losing-weight-makes-you-healthier.html.

CHAPTER 3: WHAT THINNESS TAKES

1. "How You Can Get Tickets for Oprah's '2020 Vision' Tour with WW," *O, the Oprah Magazine*, January 9, 2020, https://www.oprahmag.com/life/a28899378/oprah-ww-tour. When I created this citation, the website's title autopopulated as "You Can Now Get a 3-Month WW Membership for Less, Courtesy of Oprah!"

2. Taffy Brodesser-Akner, "Losing It in the Anti-Dieting Age," *New York Times*, August 2, 2017, https://www.nytimes.com/2017/08/02/magazine/weight-watchers-oprah-losing-it-in-the-anti-dieting-age.html.

3. Angelica LaVito, "Oprah Winfrey's Stake in Weight Watchers Falls by $48 Million in Minutes after Shares Crater 30 Percent," CNBC, February 27, 2019, https://www.cnbc.com/2019/02/26/oprah-winfreys-stake-in-weight-watchers-falls-by-48-million-in-minutes.html.

4. LaVito, "Oprah Winfrey's Stake in Weight Watchers Falls."

5. Shannon Rosenberg, "Weight Watchers to Offer Free Memberships for Teens and People Are NOT Here for It," *BuzzFeed*, February 14, 2018, https://www.buzzfeed.com/shannonrosenberg/weight-watchers-free-membership-teenagers.

6. Rosenberg, "Weight Watchers to Offer Free Memberships for Teens."

7. Louise Foxcroft, "How We Fought Fat throughout History," BBC Timelines, BBC, December 10, 2015, https://web.archive.org/web/20190331172847/https://www.bbc.com/timelines/z9nfyrd.

8. Foxcroft, "How We Fought Fat throughout History."

9. Nicolas Rasmussen, "America's First Amphetamine Epidemic 1929–1971," *American Journal of Public Health* 98, no. 6 (2008): 974–85, https://doi.org/10.2105/ajph.2007.110593.

10. "Nutri-System Diet Led to Gallbladder Disease, Suits Say," *Los Angeles Times*, March 20, 1990, https://www.latimes.com/archives/la-xpm-1990-03-20-fi-827-story.html.

11. Luisa Yanez, "Nutri/System Settles Local Lawsuits," *Sun Sentinel* (Florida), October 5, 2018, https://www.sun-sentinel.com/news/fl-xpm-1991-11-07-9102150288-story.html.

12. Gina Kolata, *Rethinking Thin: The New Science of Weight Loss—and the Myths and Realities of Dieting* (New York: Farrar, Straus & Giroux, 2007), 23.

13. Kate Cohen, "Fen Phen Nation," PBS, November 13, 2003, https://www.pbs.org/wgbh/pages/frontline/shows/prescription/hazard/fenphen.html.

14. Cohen, "Fen Phen Nation."

15. Interview with Stuart Rich, MD, "Dangerous Prescription," *Frontline*, PBS, November 13, 2003, https://www.pbs.org/wgbh/pages/frontline/shows/prescription/interviews/rich.html.

16. Michael D. Lemonick, "The New Miracle Drug?," *Time*, September 23, 1996, http://content.time.com/time/magazine/article/0,9171,985187,00.html.

17. Cohen, "Fen Phen Nation."

18. Cohen, "Fen Phen Nation."

19. S. E. Swithers, S. B. Ogden, and T. L. Davidson, "Fat Substitutes Promote Weight Gain in Rats Consuming High-Fat Diets," *Behavioral Neuroscience* (2011).

20. Sondra Solovay, *Tipping the Scales of Justice: Fighting Weight-Based Discrimination* (Amherst, NY: Prometheus, 2000), 191.

21. Solovay, *Tipping the Scales of Justice*, 193.

22. A. J. Stunkard, "An Adoption Study of Human Obesity," *New England Journal of Medicine* 315, no. 2 (1986): 128–30, https://doi.org/10.1056/nejm198607103150211.

23. Solovay, *Tipping the Scales of Justice*, 193.

24. Kolata, "After 'The Biggest Loser,' Their Bodies Fought to Regain Weight."

25. Solovay, *Tipping the Scales of Justice*, 211.

26. Solovay, *Tipping the Scales of Justice*, 211.

27. Campos, *The Obesity Myth*, 33–34.

28. Hailey Middlebrook, "Yo-Yo Dieting Dangerous for Women's Hearts, Study Says," CNN, November 15, 2016, https://www.cnn.com/2016/11/15/health/yoyo -dieting-harms-hearts/index.html.

29. "Weight Cycling Is Associated with a Higher Risk of Death, Study Finds," *ScienceDaily*, November 29, 2018, https://www.sciencedaily.com/releases/2018/11 /181129153837.htm.

30. Center for Eating Disorders at Sheppard Pratt, "What Causes an Eating Disorder? Underlying Causes," https://web.archive.org/web/20190708154247/https://eating disorder.org/eating-disorder-information/underlying-causes, accessed April 6, 2020.

31. "Eating Disorder Statistics," National Association of Anorexia Nervosa and Associated Disorders, https://anad.org/education-and-awareness/about-eating-disorders /eating-disorders-statistics, accessed February 15, 2020.

32. "Eating Disorder Statistics."

33. "Eating Disorder Statistics."

34. Leslie A. Sim et al., "Eating Disorders in Adolescents with a History of Obesity," *Pediatrics* 132, no. 4 (2013): e1026–e1030, https://pediatrics.aappublications.org /content/132/4/e1026.

35. "Statistics & Facts," Global Wellness Institute, https://globalwellnessinstitute .org/press-room/statistics-and-facts, accessed February 14, 2020.

36. "Orthorexia," National Eating Disorders Association, December 13, 2019, https://www.nationaleatingdisorders.org/learn/by-eating-disorder/other/orthorexia.

37. "Eating Disorder Statistics."

38. "Dr. Oz Admits Products He Promotes Don't Pass 'Scientific Muster,'" *Huff-Post*, June 18, 2014, https://www.huffpost.com/entry/dr-oz-congress_n_5504209.

39. "Dr. Oz Admits Products He Promotes Don't Pass 'Scientific Muster.'"

40. Maggie Fox, "The 'Dr. Oz Effect': Senators Scold Mehmet Oz for Diet Scams," NBCNews.com, February 12, 2017, https://www.nbcnews.com/better/diet-fitness/dr-oz -effect-senators-scold-mehmet-oz-diet-scams-n133226.

41. Colin Campbell, "Watch Congress Make 'An Example Of' Dr. Oz," *Business Insider*, June 17, 2014, https://www.businessinsider.com/watch-congress-make-an-example -of-dr-oz-2014-6.

42. James Hamblin, "Senators Told Dr. Oz to Stop Claiming That Diet Pills Are Miracles," *Atlantic*, June 18, 2014, https://www.theatlantic.com/health/archive/2014/06 /magic-weight-loss-pills-may-not-exist/372958.

43. Hamblin, "Senators Told Dr. Oz to Stop Claiming That Diet Pills Are Miracles."

44. Jim Edwards, "How Hydroxycut Stays in Business Despite Deaths, Recalls and a Class-Action Suit," CBS News, June 3, 2011, https://www.cbsnews.com/news/how -hydroxycut-stays-in-business-despite-deaths-recalls-and-a-class-action-suit.

45. "The $72 Billion Weight Loss & Diet Control Market in the United States, 2019–2023—Why Meal Replacements Are Still Booming, but Not OTC Diet Pills," ResearchAndMarkets.com, Business Wire, February 25, 2019, https://www.businesswire .com/news/home/20190225005455/en/72-Billion-Weight-Loss-Diet-Control-Market.

46. "Global Weight Loss and Weight Management Market 2018 Analysis, Size, Share, Facts and Figures with Products Overview, Services and Forecast 2023," Reuters, January 16, 2018, https://web.archive.org/web/20190521150310/https://www.reuters .com/brandfeatures/venture-capital/article?id=25242.

47. Cristin D. Runfola et al., "Body Dissatisfaction in Women across the Lifespan: Results of the UNC-SELF and Gender and Body Image (GABI) Studies," *European Eating Disorders Review* 21, no. 1 (2012): 52–59, https://doi.org/10.1002/erv.2201.

48. "Some People Would Give Life or Limb Not to Be Fat," *YaleNews*, Yale University, September 9, 2011, https://news.yale.edu/2006/05/16/some-people-would-give-life-or-limb-not-be-fat.

CHAPTER 4: ON CONCERN AND CHOICE

1. Jillian Michaels (@JillianMichaels), "Why Are We Celebrating Her Body? Why Does It Matter? Why Aren't We Celebrating Her Music?," Twitter, January 8, 2020, https://twitter.com/AM2DM/status/1214966495912058881?ref_src=twsrc^tfw|twcamp tweetembed|twterm1214966495912058881&ref_url=https://www.yahoo.com/lifestyle /jillian-michaels-criticizes-lizzo-body-diabetes-223919002.html.

2. Heidi Stevens, "Column: Jillian Michaels' Concern for Lizzo's Health Is as Phony as It Is Misguided," *Chicago Tribune*, January 9, 2020, https://www.chicagotribune .com/columns/heidi-stevens/ct-heidi-stevens-lizzo-jillian-michaels-fat-shaming-0109 -20200109-uk5ht6q075c7bdkpd5vfuxvcka-story.html.

3. Ally (@nametags), "Just Gonna Leave This Here for You @JillianMichaels," Twitter, January 8, 2020, https://twitter.com/nametags/status/1214982591629185025?ref_src =twsrctfw|twcamptweetembed|twterm^1214982591629185025.

4. Suzy Byrne, "Jillian Michaels Stands by Controversial Comments about Lizzo's Weight: 'I Am a Health Expert!'" Yahoo!, January 9, 2020, https://www.yahoo.com /entertainment/jillian-michaels-stands-by-controversial-comments-about-lizzo -212046368.html.

5. James Fell, "'It's a Miracle No One Has Died Yet': The Biggest Loser Returns, Despite Critics' Warnings," *Guardian*, January 4, 2016, https://www.theguardian.com /tv-and-radio/2016/jan/04/the-biggest-loser-returns-despite-critics-warnings.

6. Rebecca M. Puhl et al., "Internalization of Weight Bias: Implications for Binge Eating and Emotional Well-Being," *Obesity* 15, no. 1 (2012): 19–23, https://onlinelibrary .wiley.com/doi/full/10.1038/oby.2007.521.

7. K. A. Matthews et al., "Unfair Treatment, Discrimination, and Ambulatory Blood Pressure in Black and White Adolescents," *Health Psychology* 24, no. 3 (2005): 258–65, http://dx.doi.org/10.1037/0278-6133.24.3.258.

8. Kelli E. Friedman et al., "Weight Stigmatization and Ideological Beliefs: Relation to Psychological Functioning in Obese Adults," *Obesity Research* 13, no. 5 (2005): 907–16, https://onlinelibrary.wiley.com/doi/full/10.1038/oby.2005.105.

9. Friedman et al., "Weight Stigmatization and Ideological Beliefs," 907–16.

10. Tracy L. Tylka et al., "The Weight-Inclusive versus Weight-Normative Approach to Health: Evaluating the Evidence for Prioritizing Well-Being over Weight Loss," *Journal of Obesity* (2014): 1–18, https://www.hindawi.com/journals/jobe/2014/983495.

11. Rebecca Puhl, Joerg Luedicke, and Jamie Lee Peterson, "Public Reactions to Obesity-Related Health Campaigns," *American Journal of Preventive Medicine* 45, no. 1 (July 2013): 36–48, https://doi.org/10.1016/j.amepre.2013.02.010.

12. Rebecca Puhl, Jamie Lee Peterson, and Joerg Luedicke, "Fighting Obesity or Obese Persons? Public Perceptions of Obesity-Related Health Messages." *International Journal of Obesity* 37, no. 6 (2012): 774–78, https://doi.org/10.1038/ijo.2012.156.

13. Robert Weiss, "Guilt = Good, Shame = Bad," *Psychology Today*, January 6, 2014, https://www.psychologytoday.com/us/blog/love-and-sex-in-the-digital-age/201401/guilt-good-shame-bad.

14. Michael G. Marmot, "Status Syndrome: A Challenge to Medicine," *JAMA* 295, no. 11 (2009): 1304–7, http://citeseerx.ist.psu.edu/viewdoc/download?doi=10.1.1.471.9269&rep=rep1&type=pdf.

15. Guy Branum, "Actually, Everyone Is Born Fat," Twitter, June 18, 2016, https://twitter.com/guybranum/status/744210423524659201.

16. "HIV Basics: Overview: Data & Trends: U.S. Statistics," HIV.gov., Centers for Disease Control and Prevention, September 25, 2019, https://www.hiv.gov/hiv-basics/overview/data-and-trends/statistics.

17. Lynda Cowell, "The Women Who Want to Be Obese," *Guardian*, March 18, 2010, https://www.theguardian.com/lifeandstyle/2010/mar/18/women-obese-donna-simpson-gainers.

18. Carrie Weisman, "The Men Who Like to Make Their Women Large and Getting Larger," *Salon*, March 27, 2017, https://www.salon.com/2017/03/26/the-men-who-like-to-keep-their-women-large.

19. Stuart Wolpert, "Dieting Does Not Work, UCLA Researchers Report," UCLA Newsroom, April 3, 2007, http://newsroom.ucla.edu/releases/Dieting-Does-Not-Work-UCLA-Researchers-7832.

20. Meg Selig, "Why Diets Don't Work … and What Does," *Psychology Today*, October 21, 2010, https://www.psychologytoday.com/us/blog/changepower/201010/why-diets-dont-work-and-what-does.

21. Wolpert, "Dieting Does Not Work."

22. Ben Tinker, "Why Exercise Won't Make You Lose Weight," CNN, January 5, 2019, https://www.cnn.com/2019/01/04/health/diet-exercise-weight-loss/index.html.

23. Julia Belluz and Christophe Haubursin, "The Science Is In: Exercise Won't Help You Lose Much Weight," *Vox*, updated January 2, 2019, https://www.vox.com/2018/1/3/16845438/exercise-weight-loss-myth-burn-calories.

24. Michael Hobbes, "Everything You Know About Obesity Is Wrong," *HuffPost*, September 19, 2018, https://highline.huffingtonpost.com/articles/en/everything-you-know-about-obesity-is-wrong.

25. Kolata, "After 'The Biggest Loser,' Their Bodies Fought to Regain Weight."

26. "Adult Obesity Facts," Centers for Disease Control and Prevention, https://www.cdc.gov/obesity/data/adult.html, accessed March 11, 2020.

27. Kolata, "One Weight-Loss Approach Fits All?"

28. Kolata, "One Weight-Loss Approach Fits All?"

29. Wendy Brown, *Regulating Aversion: Tolerance in the Age of Identity and Empire* (Princeton, NJ: Princeton University Press, 2006), 25.

30. Brown, *Regulating Aversion*.

CHAPTER 5: THE DESIRABILITY MYTH

1. Jennifer Earl, "2,000 Women Defend 'Dancing Fat Man' from Fat-Shaming Bullies," CBS News, March 6, 2015, https://www.cbsnews.com/news/internet-defends-dancing-man-from-body-shaming-bullies.

2. Lesley Kinzel, "True Tales of Street Harassment (and My Anger Issues)," *XOJane*, August 4, 2011.

3. Monica Potts, "Street Harassment Is Universal and Age-Old," *Vogue*, October 31, 2014, http://www.monicapotts.com/portfolio/2014/12/2/street-harassment-is-universal -and-age-old.

4. Hollaback, "Holla 101: A Street Harassment Curriculum," https://www .ihollaback.org/app/uploads/2017/01/Holla-101-Hollaback-School-Curriculum-ilovepdf -compressed.pdf, accessed March 13, 2018.

5. Harriet Brown, *Body of Truth: How Science, History and Culture Drive Our Obsession with Weight—and What We Can Do about It* (Cambridge, MA: Da Capo, 2016), 138.

6. Kinzel, "True Tales of Street Harassment."

7. Philippe Leonard Fradet, "Survey Says!: 5 Myths About Fat Men and Dating," *The Body Is Not An Apology*, September 30, 2017.

8. Fradet, "Survey Says!"

9. Katelyn Burns, "My Intersection with Being Trans and Fatphobia," *Medium*, January 17, 2016.

10. James Burford and Sam Orchard, "Chubby Boys with Strap-Ons: Queering Fat Transmasculine Embodiment," in *Queering Fat Embodiment*, ed. Cat Pausé, Jackie Wykes, and Samantha Murray (New York: Routledge, 2016), 61–73.

11. Pamela C. Regan, "Sexual Outcasts: The Perceived Impact of Body Weight and Gender on Sexuality," *Journal of Applied Social Psychology* 26, no. 20 (1996): 1803–15, https://doi.org/10.1111/j.1559-1816.1996.tb00099.x.

12. V. Jagstaidt et al., "Relationships between Sexuality and Obesity in Male Patients," *New Trends in Experimental & Clinical Psychiatry* 13, no. 2 (1997): 105–10.

13. Lily Herman, "People Are Body-Shaming the Woman Accusing Usher of Giving Her Herpes," *Allure*, August 9, 2017.

14. Monique Judge, "I, a Fat, Beautiful Black Woman, Get Lots of Sex. Why Does That Bother You?," *Root*, August 7, 2017, https://www.theroot.com/i-a-fat-beautiful -black-woman-get-lots-of-sex-why-d-1797621695.

15. Rachel Howe and Niwako Yamawaki, "Weight-Based Discrimination of Rape Victims," *Journal of Undergraduate Research* (2013), http://jur.byu.edu/?p=4406.

16. Solovay, *Tipping the Scales of Justice*, 220.

17. Cleve Wootson, "Cornell Fraternity on Probation after a 'Pig Roast' Contest to Have Sex with Overweight Women," *Washington Post*, February 7, 2018, https://www .washingtonpost.com/news/grade-point/wp/2018/02/07/cornell-frat-on-probation-after -a-pig-roast-contest-to-have-sex-with-overweight-women.

18. Ariane Prohaska and Jeannine Gailey, "Fat Women as 'Easy Targets,'" in *The Fat Studies Reader*, ed. Esther Rothblum and Sondra Solovay (New York: New York University Press, 2009), 158–66.

19. Amy Erdman Farrell, *Fat Shame: Stigma and the Fat Body in American Culture* (New York: New York University Press, 2011), 82.

20. Farrell, *Fat Shame*.

CHAPTER 6: SUCH A PRETTY FACE

1. Ogi Ogas and Sai Gaddam, *A Billion Wicked Thoughts: What the Internet Tells Us about Sexual Relationships* (New York: Dutton, 2011), 252–53.

2. Ogas and Gaddam, *A Billion Wicked Thoughts*, 33.

3. Ogas and Gaddam, *A Billion Wicked Thoughts*, 136.

4. Ogas and Gaddam, *A Billion Wicked Thoughts*, 33.

5. Camille Dodero, "Guys Who Like Fat Chicks," *Village Voice*, May 4, 2011, https://www.villagevoice.com/2011/05/04/guys-who-like-fat-chicks.

6. Dodero, "Guys Who Like Fat Chicks."

7. Virgie Tovar, "Take the Cake: Secret Relationships with Fat Women," *Ravishly*, March 2, 2017, https://ravishly.com/2017/03/02/take-cake-secret-relationships-fat-women.

8. Mark D. Griffiths, "The Fat Fetish, Explained," *Psychology Today*, June 30, 2015, https://www.psychologytoday.com/us/blog/in-excess/201506/the-fat-fetish-explained.

9. Puhl et al., "Internalization of Weight Bias," 19–23.

10. Olga Khazan, "Abused as Children, Obese as Adults," *Atlantic*, October 8, 2016, https://www.theatlantic.com/health/archive/2015/12/sexual-abuse-victims-obesity/420186.

11. Charlotte Cooper, "Headless Fatties," Dr. Charlotte Cooper, January 2007, http://charlottecooper.net/fat/fat-writing/headless-fatties-01-07.

12. "Avengers: Endgame," Box Office Mojo, https://www.boxofficemojo.com/release/rl3059975681, accessed February 12, 2020.

13. *The Swan*, in broadcast syndication, FOX, 2004.

14. *Obesity: The Postmortem*, dir. Melanie Archer, BBC Three, September 2016, https://www.bbc.co.uk/programmes/p046n462.

15. "Tyra Banks Dons Fat Suit to Understand Obesity." TODAY.com, NBC Universal, November 2, 2005, https://www.today.com/popculture/tyra-banks-dons-fat-suit-understand-obesity-wbna9900379.

16. "Tyra Banks Dons Fat Suit to Understand Obesity."

17. "Fat Suit Tinder Date (Social Experiment)," Kong Pham, September 24, 2014, 4:34, video, https://www.youtube.com/watch?v=2alnVIj1Jf8.

18. "Fat Suit Tinder Date (Social Experiment)."

19. Emma Barker, "The Horrifying Reality of How Overweight Women Are Treated on Dates," *Cosmopolitan*, October 9, 2017, https://www.cosmopolitan.com/sex-love/news/a31477/horrifying-reality-of-overweight-women-dating/?src=spr_TWITTER&spr_id=1440_92529044.

20. Kolata, "After 'The Biggest Loser,' Their Bodies Fought to Regain Weight."

21. Lynette Rice, "USA Network Is Bringing Back *The Biggest Loser*," Explore Entertainment, May 13, 2019, https://ew.com/tv/2019/05/13/usa-bringing-back-the-biggest-loser.

22. Paula Rogo, "Rebel Wilson Is Now Blocking Black Twitter after Being Called Out," *Essence*, November 5, 2018, https://www.essence.com/celebrity/rebel-wilson-blocking-black-twitter-monique-queen-latifah.

23. "The Nutty Professor Official Trailer #1—Eddie Murphy Movie (1996) HD," Movieclips Classic Trailers, January 9, 2012, 1:47, video, https://www.youtube.com/watch?v=03wJ-jzZqBw.

24. "Road Trip—Trailer," YouTube Movies, May 16, 2013, 2:19, video, https://www.youtube.com/watch?v=RXmANho-2Bg.

25. "Norbit (2007) Trailer #1," Movieclips Classic Trailers, May 9, 2018, 1:58, video, https://www.youtube.com/watch?v=-_xorfEce4U.

26. *Family Guy*, season 14, episode 17, "The Fat Guy Strangler," aired November 17, 2005, in broadcast syndication, FOX, 2005.

27. Bruce Bretts and Matt Roush, "Baddies to the Bone: The 60 Nastiest Villains of All Time," *TV Guide*, March 25, 2013, 14–15.

28. Sean T. Collins, "40 Greatest TV Villains of All Time," *Rolling Stone*, September 4, 2019, https://www.rollingstone.com/tv/tv-lists/40-greatest-tv-villains-of-all-time-26500 /kilgrave-jessica-jones-37084.

29. *Law & Order: Special Victims Unit*, season 5, episode 17, "Mean," aired February 24, 2004, in broadcast syndication, NBC, 2004.

30. *Law & Order: Special Victims Unit*, season 7, episode 20, "Fat," aired May 2, 2006, in broadcast syndication, NBC, 2006.

31. Faith Brar, "Chrissy Metz On How Self-Acceptance Helped Her Lose 100 Pounds," *Shape*, August 2, 2019, https://www.shape.com/celebrities/news/chrissy-metz -panic-attack-weight-loss-journey.

CHAPTER 7: FIRST, DO NO HARM

1. Bob LaMendola, "Some OB-GYNs in South Florida Turn Away Overweight Women," *Sun Sentinel*, October 9, 2018, https://www.sun-sentinel.com/health/fl-xpm -2011-05-16-fl-hk-no-obesity-doc-20110516-story.html.

2. Moira Lawler et al., "Doctor Turns Away Obese Patients," EverydayHealth.com, August 29, 2012, https://www.everydayhealth.com/weight/0829/doctor-turns-away -obese-patients.aspx.

3. "Lipedema," Genetic and Rare Diseases Information Center, US Department of Health and Human Services, October 5, 2016, https://rarediseases.info.nih.gov/diseases /10542/lipedema.

4. "Lipedema."

5. Gina Kolata, "Why Do Obese Patients Get Worse Care? Many Doctors Don't See Past the Fat," *New York Times*, September 25, 2016, https://www.nytimes.com/2016 /09/26/health/obese-patients-health-care.html.

6. Katie Zezima, "Increasing Obesity Requires New Ambulance Equipment," *New York Times*, April 8, 2008, https://www.nytimes.com/2008/04/08/health/08ambu.html.

7. Kolata, "Why Do Obese Patients Get Worse Care?"

8. "Fat Shaming in the Doctor's Office Can Be Mentally and Physically Harmful," American Psychological Association, August 3, 2017, https://www.apa.org/news/press /releases/2017/08/fat-shaming.

9. Princeton University Office of Population Research, "Emergency Contraception: EC for Obese Women," Princeton University, February 22, 2019, https://ec.princeton .edu/questions/ecobesity.html.

10. Kolata, "Why Do Obese Patients Get Worse Care?"

11. Maya Dusenbery, "Doctors Told Her She Was Just Fat. She Actually Had Cancer," *Cosmopolitan*, April 17, 2018, https://www.cosmopolitan.com/health-fitness /a19608429/medical-fatshaming.

12. Dusenbery, "Doctors Told Her She Was Just Fat."

13. Anna Kirkland, *Fat Rights: Dilemmas of Difference and Personhood* (New York: New York University Press, 2008), 102.

14. Kirkland, *Fat Rights*, 102.

15. S. E. James et al., *The Report of the 2015 U.S. Transgender Survey* (Washington, DC: National Center for Transgender Equality, 2016), https://www.transequality.org /sites/default/files/docs/USTS-Full-Report-FINAL.PDF.

16. *Too Fat to Transition*, in broadcast syndication, TLC, 2016.

17. "Women's Heart Health Hindered by Social Stigma About Weight," Medscape, April 3, 2016, https://www.medscape.com/viewarticle/861382.

18. Christine Aramburu Alegria Drury and Margaret Louis, "Exploring the Association between Body Weight, Stigma of Obesity, and Healthcare Avoidance," *Journal of the American Academy of Nurse Practitioners* 14, no. 12 (2002): 554–61, https://doi.org/10.1111 /j.1745-7599.2002.tb00089.x.

19. Alexis Conason, "The Ironic Effects of Weight Stigma," *Psychology Today*, March 14, 2014, https://www.psychologytoday.com/us/blog/eating-mindfully/201403/the -ironic-effects-weight-stigma.

20. Janell L. Mensinger et al., "Mechanisms Underlying Weight Status and Health-care Avoidance in Women: A Study of Weight Stigma, Body-Related Shame and Guilt, and Healthcare Stress," *Body Image* 25 (2018): 139–47, https://doi.org/10.1016/j.bodyim .2018.03.001.

21. Anja Hilbert et al., "Weight Bias Internalization, Core Self-Evaluation, and Health in Overweight and Obese Persons," *Obesity* 22, no. 1 (2013): 79–85, https://doi .org/10.1002/oby.20561.

22. Scott Kahan and Rebecca M. Puhl, "The Damaging Effects of Weight Bias Internalization," *Obesity* 25, no. 2 (2013): 280–81, https://doi.org/10.1002/oby.21772.

23. *Today Show*, "Heavy? Your Doc May Discriminate against You," TODAY.com, July 1, 2011, https://www.today.com/news/heavy-your-doc-may-discriminate-against -you-wbna43553032#.V69FcZMrLBI; Goldberg, "Study: Bias Drops Dramatically for Sexual Orientation and Race—but Not Weight."

24. M. R. Hebl and J. Xu, "Weighing the Care: Physicians Reactions to the Size of a Patient," *International Journal of Obesity* 25, no. 8 (2001): 1246–52, https://doi.org/10.1038 /sj.ijo.0801681.

25. Hebl and Xu, "Weighing the Care."

26. Gary D. Foster et al., "Primary Care Physicians' Attitudes about Obesity and Its Treatment," *Obesity Research* 11, no. 10 (2003): 1168–77, https://doi.org/10.1038/oby .2003.161.

27. Foster et al., "Primary Care Physicians' Attitudes about Obesity and Its Treatment."

28. Marlene B. Schwartz et al., "Weight Bias Among Health Professionals Specializing in Obesity," *Obesity Research* 11, no. 9 (2012): 1033–39, https://doi.org/10.1038/oby .2003.142.

29. Schwartz et al., "Weight Bias Among Health Professionals Specializing in Obesity."

30. Kimberly A. Gudzune et al., "Physicians Build Less Rapport with Obese Patients," *Obesity* 21, no. 10 (2013): 2146–52, https://doi.org/10.1002/oby.20384.

31. Man-Yuk Poon and Marie Tarrant, "Obesity: Attitudes of Undergraduate Student Nurses and Registered Nurses," *Journal of Clinical Nursing* 18, no. 16 (July 6, 2009): 2355–65. https://doi.org/10.1111/j.1365-2702.2008.02709.x.

32. "Fat Shaming in the Doctor's Office Can Be Mentally and Physically Harmful," American Psychological Association, August 3, 2017, https://www.apa.org/news/press /releases/2017/08/fat-shaming.

33. "Study Reveals Healthcare Staff's Negative Attitudes towards Obese Patients They Treat," *Nursing Standard* 28, no. 6 (2013): 15–16, https://doi.org/10.7748/ns2013 .10.28.6.15.s21.

34. Sean M. Phelan et al., "Implicit and Explicit Weight Bias in a National Sample of 4,732 Medical Students: The Medical Student CHANGES Study," *Obesity* 22, no. 4 (2014): 1201–8, https://doi.org/10.1002/oby.20687.

35. Sean M. Phelan et al., "The Mixed Impact of Medical School on Medical Students' Implicit and Explicit Weight Bias," *Medical Education* 49, no. 10 (2015): 983–92, https://doi.org/10.1111/medu.12770.

36. "Do Doctors Dislike Overweight Patients?" Office of Research & Development, US Department of Veterans Affairs, https://www.research.va.gov/currents/0815-2.cfm, accessed January 17, 2020.

37. Kirkland, *Fat Rights*, 111.

38. A. Janet Tomiyama et al., "How and Why Weight Stigma Drives the Obesity 'Epidemic' and Harms Health," *BMC Medicine* 16, no. 1 (2018), https://doi.org/10.1186/s12916-018-1116-5.

39. Tomiyama et al., "How and Why Weight Stigma Drives the Obesity 'Epidemic.'"

40. Tomiyama et al., "How and Why Weight Stigma Drives the Obesity 'Epidemic.'"

41. Phillippa C. Diedrichs and Fiona Kate Barlow, "How to Lose Weight Bias Fast! Evaluating a Brief Anti-Weight Bias Intervention," *British Journal of Health Psychology* 16, no. 4 (2011): 846–61, https://doi.org/10.1111/j.2044-8287.2011.02022.x.

42. Yasmin Poustchi et al., "Brief Intervention Effective in Reducing Weight Bias in Medical Students," *Family Medicine* 45, no. 5 (2013): 345–48, https://www.ncbi.nlm.nih.gov/pmc/articles/PMC3791507/?report=classic.

43. Judy Anne Swift et al., "Are Anti-Stigma Films a Useful Strategy for Reducing Weight Bias Among Trainee Healthcare Professionals? Results of a Pilot Randomized Control Trial," *Obesity Facts* 6, no. 1 (2013): 91–102, https://doi.org/10.1159/000348714.

44. Morgan Lee et al., "Malleability of Weight-Biased Attitudes and Beliefs: A Meta-Analysis of Weight Bias Reduction Interventions," *Body Image* 11, no. 3 (2014): 251–59, https://doi.org/10.1016/j.bodyim.2014.03.003.

CHAPTER 8: THE WORLD TO COME

1. Martin, "Weight Discrimination Is Legal in 49 States"; Rachel La Corte, "Washington Court: Obesity Covered by Antidiscrimination Law," *Seattle Times*, July 12, 2019, https://www.seattletimes.com/seattle-news/washington-court-obesity-covered-by-antidiscrimination-law.

2. Erin Hendriks and Linda Prine, "Reduced Effectiveness of Emergency Contraception in Women with Increased BMI," *American Family Physician*, August 15, 2014, https://www.aafp.org/afp/2014/0815/p209.html.

3. Chantal Da Silva, "An American Airlines Passenger Says Staff Called Police on Her for 'Flying While Fat and Black,'" *Newsweek*, April 30, 2018, https://www.newsweek.com/american-airlines-passenger-says-she-was-kicked-flight-flying-while-fat-and-905945.

4. Niwako Yamawaki et al., "The Effects of Obesity Myths on Perceptions of Sexual Assault Victims and Perpetrators' Credibility," *Journal of Interpersonal Violence* 33, no. 4 (2015): 662–85, https://doi.org/10.1177/0886260515613343.

5. Amber Phillips, "That Time Congress Railed against Dr. Oz for His 'Miracle' Diet Pills," *Washington Post*, September 15, 2016, https://www.washingtonpost.com/news/the-fix/wp/2016/09/15/that-time-congress-railed-on-dr-oz-for-his-miracle-diet-pills/?noredirect=on.

6. Stuart Wolpert, "Dieting Does Not Work, UCLA Researchers Report." UCLA, May 10, 2019, https://newsroom.ucla.edu/releases/Dieting-Does-Not-Work-UCLA -Researchers-7832.

7. Kathy Lohr, "Controversy Swirls around Harsh Anti-Obesity Ads," NPR, January 9, 2012, https://www.npr.org/2012/01/09/144799538/controversy-swirls-around -harsh-anti-obesity-ads.

INDEX

ableism, 10, 54, 155, 157. *See also* disability justice
abortion, 156
abuse, 29, 115, 116, 131, 155. *See also* anti-fat attitudes; fat shaming; physical violence against fat people; sexual violence
acceptance. *See* fat acceptance
accessibility of healthcare, 154–56, 162–63. *See also* medical bias and discrimination
acting, 43. *See also* media representations of fatness
activism. *See* fat activism
actuarial personhood, 144
adaptive clothing, 156
adoption, 156
African Americans, 25, 48–49, 78, 155. *See also* racism
Airline Deregulation Act (1978), 17–18
airline industry, 17–20, 161, 163. *See also* flying experiences of fat people
Alaska Airlines, 18–19
Alli (weight loss drug), 164
All in the Family (television show), 132
Allison, Michelle, 148
AM2DM (television show), 74
American identity and fat shaming, 53–54. *See also* fat shaming

American Journal of Preventative Medicine, 79
American Journal of Public Health, 83
American Medical Association, 50
amphetamine epidemic, 59, 60
anger, 16, 72–73, 123, 128, 132, 157. *See also* physical violence against fat people
anorexia nervosa, 50, 62, 63. *See also* eating disorders
anti-fat attitudes: by Arbour, 22, 23; author's personal experience with, 1–3, 13–17, 28–30, 71–73, 90–91, 136–37; on choice, 81–82, 86, 88–89, 104; concern and concern trolling, 73–81, 88–89; coping mechanisms against, 41, 43; defined, 10; effects on physical and mental health, 51–52, 78–79, 90–91, 125, 145, 149; fat justice against, 6–8, 29, 160–66; in feminist movements, 104, 108–10; historical overview of, 47–48; institutionalism of, 28; internalization of, 28, 40, 78, 79, 82, 117, 145; by medical care providers, 139–50; towards men, 97–99; public opinion polls on, 52–53, 66, 78; research studies on, 23–24, 25–26, 146–47; on sexuality, 97–99,

186